Praise for *The Babel M*

T0049927

'Quite simply, and quite ridiculo~~us~~, [this is one of] the most illuminating books I have ever read. I thought I was obsessive, but Keith Kahn-Harris is playing a very different sport. He really has discovered the whole world in an egg.'

Simon Garfield, author of *Just My Type*

'There is a delicious humour implicit in every page ... [the book] is filled with a sense of wonder, gazing at languages that neither the writer nor reader understands ... *The Babel Message* was such fun that I even went out and bought a Kinder Surprise Egg.'

Mark Forsyth, *The Spectator*

'Astonishingly rich ... Kahn-Harris writes clearly and entertainingly, with a gentle, self-deprecating humour. The book is also unexpectedly profound.'

Times Literary Supplement

'Keith Kahn-Harris is a genial, eloquent guide, with a serious message ... This is a book written with passion and humanity.'

Mark Glanville, *Jewish Chronicle*

'This is a wonderful book. A treasure trove of mind-expanding insights into language and humanity encased in a deliciously quirky, quixotic quest. I loved it. Warning: this will keep you reading.'

Ann Morgan, author of *Reading the World: Confessions of a Literary Explorer*

'I would warn everyone to read and keep this beautifully written book ... Keith explores the world of language – what it is, what it means and how we use it. Keith's precisely written prose celebrates the wonderful imprecision of language in all its glory.'

James Ward, founder of The Boring Conference
and author of *Adventures in Stationery: A Journey Through Your Pencil Case*

'*The Babel Message* is a gloriously inflected record of an obsession ... [It] manages to teach us a great deal about language – its protean energy and its slipperiness – but also makes us properly laugh (a rare Venn diagram, believe me). ... Kahn-Harris's fan-boy passion for the gorgeous surface of written language and his own skill in deploying it make the book a complete delight.'

John Mitchinson, author of *The QI Book of General Ignorance*

'In this unlikely story of a quixotic translation, Keith Kahn-Harris illuminates how language-learning can hone our minds, strengthen our empathy, and lead us all to justice. Read this book – and immerse yourself in the raw pleasure of linguistic diversity.'

Daniel Bögre Udell, Executive Director, Wikitongues

THE
BABEL
MESSAGE

THE
BABEL
MESSAGE

———

*A Love
Letter to
Language*

———

**KEITH
KAHN-
HARRIS**

ICON

This edition published in the UK in 2022
by Icon Books Ltd, Omnibus Business Centre,
39–41 North Road, London N7 9DP
info@iconbooks.com
www.iconbooks.com

Previously published in the UK in 2021 by Icon Books Ltd

Sold in the UK, Europe and Asia
by Faber & Faber Ltd, Bloomsbury House,
74–77 Great Russell Street,
London WC1B 3DA or their agents

Distributed in the UK, Europe and Asia
by Grantham Book Services,
Trent Road, Grantham NG31 7XQ

Distributed in Australia and New Zealand
by Allen & Unwin Pty Ltd, PO Box 8500,
83 Alexander Street, Crows Nest, NSW 2065

Distributed in South Africa
by Jonathan Ball, Office B4, The District,
41 Sir Lowry Road, Woodstock 7925

Distributed in India
by Penguin Books India, 7th Floor, Infinity Tower – C,
DLF Cyber City, Gurgaon 122002, Haryana

ISBN: 978-178578-895-6

Typeset in Noto Serif by Marie Doherty

Printed and bound in Great Britain
by Clays Ltd, Elcograf S.p.A.

Contents

Part 4: The Babel Message

ABOUT THE AUTHOR

Dr Keith Kahn-Harris is a sociologist and writer. He combines freelance writing with an academic teaching and research career. *The Babel Message* is his seventh book, but his first on the multilingual warning messages inside Kinder Surprise Eggs. His website is kahn-harris.org

*To my father, Paul Harris, who has taught
me absolutely nothing about language
but absolutely everything about pursuing
one's interests, come what may.*

WARNING, read and keep

In the Babel myth, God thwarts the builders of the Tower by creating a 'confusion of tongues'. In this book I will exult in this confusion. I will show you what a short message written by an Italian confectionery manufacturer looks like when translated into dozens of languages, most of which I cannot speak and many of which are in scripts I cannot even read.

And there may very well be mistakes.

The final chapter of my previous book began with a Hebrew epigraph.[1] Even though I speak and read the language, at some point in the preparation of the proofs the letters were reversed by the non-Hebrew-speaking typesetter. It's an easy mistake to make; Hebrew is written from right to left and including such a script in an English manuscript is asking for trouble. It was up to me to spot it though, and I didn't.

While I am going to do my darnedest to ensure that no language is presented back-to-front, I cannot guarantee that somewhere along the line, a letter might be dropped, an accent might be missed, or something else will go horribly wrong in my attempts to wrangle these unruly beasts in order to present them to you, the reader, for your delectation. Indeed, some readers did point out that there were a couple of mistakes in the hardback edition. While they have been corrected for this paperback edition, I am not complacent; there may be more.

No one knows all of language. Even aspects of one's own tongue can be confusing. We make do with what we have. In this book I have set out to celebrate the diversity of language using the tools I have available. Those tools included my training and experience as a sociologist, an uneven grounding in linguistics and a reasonable, but not fluent, knowledge of several languages. That's more than most, less than some. But reproducing the many languages in this book correctly would be a challenge for even the most impressive polyglot or the most experienced professional linguist.

Acceptance of the risk of mistakes is a precondition for using any language. It's certainly essential for anyone who aspires to revel in the diversity of languages. And it was also necessary for Ferrero, the company that produces the multi-lingual warning messages discussed in this book.

If language weren't risky, if we were not always in danger of being misinterpreted, where would be its pleasures and its value? The alternative – a single logical language, perfectly understood by everyone equally – would lead to a tyranny of dullness. As I will argue towards the end of this book, Babel may be confusing and chaotic, but it's also invigorating and exciting. What's more, if we can learn to enjoy the languages we do not understand, and take pleasure in the risks of mis-understanding, we might even be able to get along with each other better.

Some readers who speak a language presented in the book might contest the wording of a particular translation. If so, that's fine – translation cannot be an exact science – and I encourage readers to send me alternative translations via my website. Corrections of my mistakes are welcome. I am always up for correcting myself in public.

If wrangling languages is a challenge, wrangling human beings is even harder. Happily, in researching and writing this book, it has often been a pleasure. I still can't believe that I have managed to turn such a quixotic project into a book. So thanks to my agent Antony Topping for making the impossible

possible and to Duncan Heath and the team at Icon for taking such a leap of faith. My wife and children have shown extreme fortitude in coping with this latest meander in what has always been an idiosyncratic career. I will always treasure the conversations we have had around the dinner table about this project.

Thanks to the friends and contacts on social media who enjoyed the translations with me when I posted them and who 'got' the project from the outset. For years I've been writing about how social media brings out the worst in us. Sometimes though, it can be a place of joy and laughter. I am grateful to everyone who has reminded me of that.

Thanks to Yaron Matras, Nick Gendler and Deborah Kahn-Harris, who read drafts of the book, making many useful suggestions and pointing out some of the more embarrassing errors. The errors that they did not spot are my responsibility alone.

Most of all, my heartfelt thanks to the dozens of people and organisations who provided me with translations, connected me with other translators or gave me advice and suggestions. I am still stunned that so many people answered my pleas. In fact, I have received so many translations that I could not include all of them in this book (a constantly updated list can be found via my website). I've credited individual translations that appear in the book to their authors in the endnotes and, in addition, here is the full, glorious list:

Glenn Abastillas, Kamila Akhmedjanova, Rashad Ali, Nicholas Al-Jeloo, Merjen Arazova, Carmen Arlando, Glexi Arxokuna, Costas Avramidis, Gavin Bailey, Jenny Bailie, John Baird, Xavier Barker, Jesmar Luke T. Bautista, Brian Bourque, Clive Boutle, Daniel Boyarin, Shamma Boyarin,

Jackson Bradley, Ross Bradshaw, Jeffrey Brown, Dale Buttigieg, Malcolm Callus, Vivienne Capelouto, Felisa Castro Bitos, Andrea Cavaglia, Sally Caves, Kate Clark, Culture Vannin, Alinda Damsma, Khulgana Daz, Kelvin Dobson, Jenny De Guzman, Henri de Nassau, Tebôd de Rogna, Stephen DeGrace, Michel DeGraff, Maricar Dela Cruz, Meryam Dermati, Luke Doran, Bruno Estigarribia, Clive Forrester, Adam Frost, Louise Gathercole, Mark Geller, Richard Goldstein, Guernsey Language Commission, Ida Hadjivaynis, Tony Hak, Jan Havliš, Christoph Helbig, Aliaksandr Herasimenka, George Hewitt, Hnolt, Achim Grundgeiger, Thorsten Hindrichs, Elliott Hoey, James Hopkins, Dauvit Horsbroch, Colin Ireson, Sulev Iva, Marta Jenkala, Jasmin Johnson, Daniel Jonas, Lily Kahn, Kobi Kahn-Harris, Gabriel Kanter-Webber, Thomas Kim, L'Office du Jèrriais, Jorge Lambia, Teresa Labourdette, Loïc Landais, Joseph Langseth, Damian Le Bas, Tsheten Lhamo, 'Liberal Elite', Lia Rumatscha, London Euskera Irakaslea, Fernando López-Menchero, Kelly MacFarlane, Rahima Mahmut, Norah Makhubela, William Manley, Josephine Sitoy Maranga, Alena Marková, Jan Marquis, Yaron Matras, Puey McCleary, Richard E. McDorman, Yoseph Mengitsu, Gorka Mercero Altzugarai, Shido Morozof, Peter Miller, Krikor Moskofian, Carola Mostert, Naja Motzfeldt, Pierrick Moureaux, Anupama Mundollikkalam, Jo-Ann Myers, Nir Nadav, Julian Nyča, Liam Ó Cuinneagáin, Ofis Piblik ar Brezhoneg, Veturliði Óskarsson, Claude Passet, Megan Paul, John Payne, David Peterson, Siva Pillai, Sally Pond, Krishna Pradhan, Guy Puzey, John Quijada, Gary-Taylor Raebal, Hadzibulic Ridburg, Elvire Roberts, Wrenna Robson, Gerald Roche, Simon Roper, Richie Ruchpaul, Tom Ruddle, Arawi Ruiz, 'Dr St Ridley Santos', Stella Sai Chun, Mark Sanchez, Erich Schmidt, James Seymour, Neil

Shaw-Smith, Owen Shiers, Jonas Sibony, Param Singh, Dave Snell, Christine Stewart, Sebastian Suh, Jeremy Swist, Tamil Studies UK, Christian Thalmann, James Thomas, Fiorenzo Toso, Anna Treschel, Riitta Valijärvi, Oana Uta, Simon Varwell, Zareth Angela Vergara, Danelle Vermuelen, Lars Sigurdsson Vikør, Lina Vdovîi, Craig Volker, Imke von Helden, Shaul Wachsstock, Anne Waldek-Thill, Jeremy Wallach, Yair Wallach, Neil Walley, Jackson Walter, James Ward, Michael Wegier, Rebekka Weinstein, Patrick Wilcox, Joseph Windsor, Lidia Wojtczak, Abigail Wood, Kylie Wright, Ghil'ad Zuckermann.

A surprising obsession

Eggs are joyous things.

The egg represents life itself, the possibility of something wonderful emerging from within a hard yet brittle shell. The egg is celebration and hope. The contents are a source of mystery and wonder. Who can resist the lure of discovering what the egg contains?

Like the real eggs they resemble, there is something so *right* about Kinder Surprise Eggs. The outer foil is a riot of orange and white, festooned with multicoloured, bouncy letters. Unwrap it and you find the smooth, warm colour of its chocolate shell; slightly sticky yet delicately firm. The underside of the shell recalls white albumen and within it the yolk – a bright yellow capsule – tempts you with its secrets. Break it open and there is a further puzzle: what will the toy look like once assembled?

I hate to resort to the cliched term 'iconic' to describe Kinder Surprise Eggs, but they are certainly instantly familiar, loved by many (not just children) and drawing on the deepest levels of human symbolism. No wonder that every month, the number of Kinder Surprise Eggs sold worldwide would be enough to cover the surface of Tiananmen Square in Beijing.[1] And as with other classic brands – Heinz Tomato Ketchup for example – most of its competitors are fated to be seen as second-rate.

Iconic products such as Kinder Surprise Eggs are often taken for granted. They are just *there*, nestling on the shelves of a supermarket or (as in my local corner shop) on the counter next to the cash register. I don't remember a time when I didn't know that Kinder Surprise Eggs existed. When my children were younger, the Eggs were a handy go-to treat to keep them busy or distracted. I knew what they were and what to expect of them; they were reliable. I didn't pay much attention to them.

Yet at some point I found something within a Kinder Surprise Egg that forced me to sit up and pay attention; to stop taking them for granted and look at them with fresh eyes. One day, as I was assembling the toy for my son, I glanced at the small sheet of paper included within the capsule. I had seen it before, maybe I had even read it, but on this occasion I actually *saw* it. It drew me in, sparking an obsession that has lasted for years, long after my children entered adolescence and were no longer interested in the product.

The flimsy document found in Kinder Surprise Eggs – only 12cm by 5cm, covered on both sides with tiny text – has become, for me, a kind of treasure map. It has led me on an adventure that is still unfolding.

Why not join me on the journey? To do so, all you need to do is to buy a Kinder Surprise Egg. Before you eat the chocolate and have fun with the toy, take a close look at the slip of paper that remains.

What you are now holding in your hands will vary, depending on which country you bought the egg in (about which, more later). But in Europe, as well as in large swathes of Asia and the Middle East, this is what it will look like on the front and back:

IMPORTED BY: ИЗГОТОВИТЕЛЬ / ВИРОБНИК: FERRERO TRADING LUX S.A. ADDRESS / АДРЕС / АДРЕСА: 16, ROUTE DE TREVES L-2633 SENNINGERBERG - LUXEMBOURG. / FERRERO ARGENTINA S.A. LOS CARDALES, (2814) Pcia. DE BUENOS AIRES. / FERRERO DE MÉXICO S.A. DE C.V. AVENIDA SANTA FE NO. 6 UBICADO EN PARQUE OPCIÓN. CARRETERA ST, KM 57.8 QRO - SLP, SAN JOSÉ ITURBIDE, GUANAJUATO; MÉXICO.

AR ... 601211, ... ‹Ферреро Руссия› ... 8 800 7007 600. ... 03.2020

AZ «Xəbərdarlıq, oxuyun və əməl edin: kiçik hissələri nəfəs vəqida orqanlara düşəbilər »

BG ВНИМАНИЕ, ПРОЧЕТИ И ЗАПАЗИ: Съдържа малки части, които могат да бъдат погълнати или вдишани.

CS UPOZORNĚNÍ, čtěte a uschovejte: Malé části by mohly být spolknuty nebo vdechnuty.

DA Advarsel, læs og opbevar: Smådele kan sætte sig fast i hals eller næse.

DE Lesen und aufbewahren: WARNHINWEIS! Nicht für Kinder unter 3 Jahren geeignet, da Spielzeug oder Kleinteile verschluckt oder eingeatmet werden können.

EL ΠΡΟΣΟΧΗ: να διαβάσετε και να φυλάξετε. Περιέχει μικρά κομμάτια που μπορεί να καταπιούν ή να αισπνεύσουν.

EN WARNING, read and keep: Toy not suitable for children under 3 years. Small parts might be swallowed or inhaled.

ES ATENCIÓN, lea y guarde: Juguete no apto para menores de 3 años. Las partes pequeñas podrían ser ingeridas o inhaladas.

ET TÄHELEPANU! LOE LÄBI JA HOIA ALLES: need veivad sattuda lastele suhu või hingamisteedesse ja põhjustada õnnetuse.

FI HUOMIO, lue ja säilytä: Pienet osat voivat juuttua kurkkuun tai nenään.

FR ATTENTION, à lire et à conserver: Les petites pièces pourraient être avalées ou inhalées.

HR UPOZORENJE, PROČITATI I SAČUVATI: Sitne dijelove moguće je slučajno progutati ili udahnuti.

HU FIGYELEM, olvassa el és őrizze meg! Az apró alkotórészek könnyen beszippanthatók vagy lenyelhetők.

KA გაფრთხილება, წაიკითხეთ და შეინახეთ: პატარა ნაწილები შესაძლებელია გადაყლაპოთ ან ჩაისუნთქოთ.

KK Дəрдооч: Импортчу, импортчу жəна дəрдооч тарабынан ыйгарым укукту адак «Ферреро Руссия» ЖАК, жайғашкан жери: Россия, 601211, Владимирск ин, Собинск р-ну, Ворша к., «Ферреро» кондитердик фабрикасы, тел. 8 800 7007 600. Итаямда жасалған. Жасалған куну: 03.2020.

LT DĖMESIO! PERSKAITYK IR SAUGOK: mažas detales gali praryti arba įkvėpti.

LV UZMANĪBU, IZLASI ETUN SAGLABAJIET: jo pastāv iespēja, ka rotaļlietas sīkās detaļas var iekļūt elpošanas ceļos.

MK ВНИМАНИЕ, ЧИТАЈ И ЗАЧУВАЈ: Ситните делови можат да бидат проголтани или вдишани.

NL OPGELET, lezen en bewaren: De kleine stukjes kunnen ingeslikt of opgesnoven worden.

NO Advarsel, les og behold: Små deler kan sette seg fast i halsen eller nesen.

PL UWAGA, przeczytaj i zachowaj: Małe części mogą zostać połknięte lub dostać się do dróg oddechowych.

PT ATENÇÃO, leia e guarde: As peças pequenas poderiam ser ingeridas ou inaladas.

RO-MD ATENȚIE, DE CITIT ȘI REȚINUT: Părțile mici pot fi înghițite sau inhalate.

RU-KZ-BY Игрушка "Kinder". Уполномоченное изготовителем лицо, импортер: ЗАО «Ферреро Руссия», Россия, 601211, Владимирская обл., Собинский р-н, с. Ворша, Кондитерская фабрика «Ферреро», тел. 8 800 7007 600. Дата изготовления: 03.2020. "Kinder" ойнчылары. Өндірушінің уәлетті тұлғасы, импортшысы: «Ферреро Руссия» ЖАК, Ресей, 601211, Владимирск облысы, Собин ауданы, Ворша ауылы, «Ферреро» Кондитердік фабрикасы, тел. 8 800 7007 600. Қытайда өндірілген. Өндіру датасы: 03.2020.

SK UPOZORNENIE, prečítať a uchovať: Maléčasti by mohli byť prehltnuté alebo vdýchnuté.

SL OPOZORILO, PREBERITE IN SHRANITE: Majhne delce bi lahko pogoltnili ali vdihnili.

SQ KUJDES, LEXO DHE KUJTO: Pjesët e vogla mund të gëlltiten ose futen në rrugët e frymëmarrjes.

SR UPOZORENJE, PROČITAJ I SAČUVAJ: Sitni delovi se mogu progutati ili udahnuti.

SV VARNING, läs och behåll: Leksak ej lämplig för barn under 3 år. Små delar kan fastna i halsen eller näsan.

TR DİKKAT, okuyun ve saklayın: Küçük parçalar yutulabilir veya nefes borusuna kaçabilir.

UA Колекційна іграшка «Kinder». Номер партії співпадає з датою виробництва. Дата виробництва: 03.2020. Імпортер, адреса: див. інформацію на упаковці. Строк придатності необмежений.

هشدار، بخوانید و نگهدارید: اجسام کوچک ممکن است بلعیده یا استنشاق شوند.

العربية - اقرأ واحفظ: لعبة غير مناسبة للأطفال الذين يقل سنهم عن ٣ سنوات لانه يمكن إبتلاع أو إستنشاق الأجزاء الصغيرة.

注意：請閱讀及保存 此玩具不適合三歲以下小孩，其中細小部件小孩可能吞下或吸入。

注意：请阅读及保存 此玩具不适合三岁以下小孩，其中细小部件小孩可能吞下或吸入。

本玩具符合 GB6675-2003 及 GB6296.5-2005.

LEC 008
79013029

Confused yet? You should be. Crammed into 120cm² is a riot of blood red and jet black scripts, gnomic texts, strange diacritics and mysterious symbols. Scan your eye over the text more closely and you are likely to find a few words that look familiar. For me, and for most readers of this book, the most familiar is marked with an 'EN' for English and announces, with a Lilliputian gravity:

> WARNING, read and keep: Toy not suitable for children under 3 years. Small parts might be swallowed or inhaled.

It's a reasonable thing to warn of. The toys are indeed minuscule. I'm not sure how many other readers actually keep the sheet, but I haven't just kept it, I have collected multiple versions of this text that has become for me a source of beguiling, and sometimes baffling, mysteries.

On loving the languages I do not understand

As an eight-year-old waiting my turn in my trampoline class, I used to read the translated warning messages printed on the crash pads. I don't even remember what the message warned of. I do remember though that one of the languages was German and contained the word *Rahmenpolster*. I'd mouth the word again and again: *Rahmenpolster*, *Rahmenpolster*, *Rahmenpolster*. It barely mattered what the word actually meant (I only recently discovered that it refers to a soft protective coating over a metal frame).

A few years later, on a family holiday in Greece, I taught myself to read the language, revelling in spelling out street signs while never learning a single useful spoken phrase. As I grew, it became a matter of fierce pride to me that I could tell the difference between written Japanese and Chinese, that I could spot Turkish at twenty paces, that I knew 'æ' and 'ø' can never be found in Swedish.

The sounds of foreign tongues also called to me. Perhaps I was rebelling against my parents' post-war suspicion of Germany, when I came to find the precise, compounded diction of that language attractive. I learned to distinguish the rising tones of Cantonese, heard in my local Chinese restaurant, from the less tonally varied cadences of Mandarin. The pronounced gutturals of Arabic offered me a full-blooded distinction to the more familiar, and less throaty, Hebrew sounds I heard in synagogue. One of my proudest moments was when, on a trip to Australia a few years ago, I managed to work out that a broadcast on public radio was in Estonian, rather than the similar-sounding Finnish (the key was that it mentioned the Estonian newspaper *Postimees*).

Of course, I have also learned to read, speak and write languages other than English. I loved reading the work of Gabriel García Márquez in my A-Level Spanish class and took a perverse pleasure in the ludicrously formal signoffs I was taught in my French for Business AS-Level. I learned enough spoken Mandarin to have a basic conversation on my travels in China when I was nineteen. At the age of 30 I built on my basic modern Hebrew to get to a level where I could follow and contribute to academic seminars. I'm currently working through lessons in Finnish – a fiendishly complex tongue whose sounds I adore – on the Duolingo app.

Yet I have never achieved fluency in anything other than English. I don't need to – and that's the curse of the native English-speaker. While my life has been enriched by the learning of foreign languages, if I hadn't, my everyday life would not have been negatively impacted. I have the luxury of being able to decide that, since I can't keep up all my languages, I keep up none of them, allowing my knowledge to slowly erode. I don't face the lingering fear of being cut off from the world that a monoglot speaker of, say, Lithuanian might face. Nor do I live somewhere where casual bi- or trilingualism is the norm, as in parts of Africa, India and Asia.

However much I might love the English language – its bizarre Germanic-Romance hybridity, its ridiculous spelling, its innumerable syntactical oddities – there is a shaming blandness to being a native English-speaker. The easy facility with which a group of Danes or Dutch effortlessly switch to English if even one speaker joins them, always causes me embarrassment. I envy those speakers of minority British languages such as Welsh or Gaelic who form the last redoubt against the linguistic levelling of these islands. The bog-standard English that I speak with a faint London accent may strike locals as enchanting when I travel in the American Midwest, but it lacks the dialectal distinctiveness of Geordie or the luxuriant burr of West Country English.

Kinder Egg linguistics

For me, the languages I find in translated messages on everyday products offer a tantalising glimpse of the linguistic pleasures available outside the English-speaking world. Before I encountered the Kinder Egg message, the most diversity I ever found was on the list of local distributors found on boxes of Kleenex tissues. But they had nothing on Kinder Eggs – indeed, Kleenex conflate Danish, Norwegian and Swedish into one language, using a '/' to offer individual alternatives to particular words. I had never seen Georgian, Azerbaijani or Latvian on product packaging until I discovered Kinder Eggs.

Packed into one tiny slip of paper are 37 different languages, in eight different scripts. These are, in order of appearance:

[Side one]

Armenian (1)

Azerbaijani

Bulgarian

Czech

Danish

German

Greek

English

Spanish

Estonian

Finnish

French

Croatian

Hungarian

Armenian (2)

Italian

Georgian

Kyrgyz

[Side two]

Lithuanian

Latvian

Macedonian

Dutch

Norwegian

Polish

Portuguese

Romanian

Russian

Kazakh

Slovak

Slovene

Albanian

Serbian

Swedish

Turkish

Ukrainian

Persian

Arabic

Chinese (Traditional characters)

Chinese (Simplified characters)

Take a closer look at it and you will find inconsistencies and mysteries aplenty:

- Which is the original version of the message? Given that Ferrero, the company that produces the Eggs, is based in Italy, is Italian the mother of all the translations?
- What do the two-letter codes before each message refer to?

- Why do some messages mention under-3s (including the English one) whereas others appear not to?
- There seem to be two Armenian texts, one including the message and the other including some kind of address. The warning message is written all in capital letters in Armenian script and marked with the code 'HY'. The address text is written in lower case and marked with the code 'AR'. Why? Why? Why?
- Some languages print the word 'WARNING' in capitals and others do not. In Danish and Norwegian it is *Adversel* and in Swedish *VARNING*. Do some languages prohibit the use of all-caps words?

Stare hard enough at the warning message sheet, and it dissolves into anarchy, chaos and brain-melting puzzles. And there's more: some toys come with extra messages specific to them. The mini slingshot I found in one Egg, for example, includes a multilingual warning not to aim at the eyes or face.

Something odd also happens the more you delve into the world of Kinder Egg linguistics: you start to realise what *isn't* there. How many other versions exist? Where are they used? Who decides on their content? Why is it that the sheet of paper used in Europe includes all EU official languages except for two (Irish and Maltese)? Who decided not to include them? And given that millions speak 'minority' European languages like Catalan, there is a strong case for including them too. In fact, there are 5,000–6,000 languages spoken in the world today, together with innumerable dialects. The Kinder Egg message can only be translated into a fraction of them. When looked at in this way, the message sheet starts to look oddly impoverished. Why should a multilingual Dane need a specific message in Danish while a monolingual speaker of one of the indigenous languages of Greenland (an autonomous Danish territory) not be provided with a translation into his or her own language?

This message, so brutally short, legalistic and commanding, also contains hidden ambiguities:

- 'WARNING, read and keep': Who is being warned? Why do we need to keep the message? Where should we keep it?
- 'Toy not suitable for children under 3 years': How is suitability to be understood here?
- 'Small parts might be swallowed or inhaled': By whom and under what conditions?

The 'obviousness' of the message depends on all kinds of cultural and linguistic assumptions. Look closer and these assumptions evaporate into nothingness, leaving only a disembodied voice, addressing someone somewhere about something for some reason.

I don't blame the manufacturers for this confusion and I don't see it as a bad thing. In fact, I revel in this glorious muddle. For it is nothing but a manifestation of the ways in which language seduces and bamboozles. The creators of the Kinder Egg warning message were trying to communicate something simple to us, but they ended up creating a sheet of paper of byzantine complexity.

Language is never simple and so communication is never simple. Despite that, using language to try to communicate is also just what humans do. We are driven to connect with each other. And it was the need to connect that drove me to write this book ...

Reaching out

Kinder Eggs and I have a history. I first came out to the public as a warning message-lover at a talk I gave at the 2017 Boring Conference in London. In preparation for the talk, I commissioned translations of the warning message into more languages. I started with Irish and Maltese, in order to complete the set of EU languages. After that I found it hard to stop: I collected Luxembourgish, Cornish, Welsh and then Biblical Hebrew. At the end of the talk I led the audience in a joke pledge to never buy another Kinder Egg until they included a translation of the warning message into Cornish.

In 2018 I recorded a podcast for the BBC Boring Talks series and added yet more languages to the collection. I also included an appeal for listeners to send me warning message sheets from around the world, and listeners in South Africa, Brunei and Nepal duly obliged.

Every so often, following the release of the podcast, I'd receive an email offering me a translation into a new language. I received one such email in late March 2020, in the first phase of the Covid-19 pandemic. The sender inquired whether I would be interested in a recording of the warning message into Shanghainese (it could only be a recording as the language is rarely written down). In the end, the offer didn't pan out, but it still flicked some kind of switch in my brain. In a time of disconnection, commissioning translations would bring me connection, yet the translations themselves would be unreadable to me. Could there be a better metaphor for the human yearning to reach out to others and the limits of doing so?

Another thought seized me: for some years I had been writing and researching about the worst aspects of humanity. I had published two books that went to very dark places, exploring racism, antisemitism, Holocaust denial and other forms of denialism. I had argued that we needed to come to terms with the fact that human diversity isn't always something to celebrate, since human beings hold to a wide range of incompatible moralities and desires. I still believe this, but in 2020 I had a strong yearning to demonstrate the other side of the coin, that human diversity can be a wonderful thing. To write about linguistic diversity during challenging times reminded me that language is the most amazing thing that human beings have created.

So spring and summer 2020 saw me firing off email after email: to language promotion officers in the Channel Islands, to professors of Sumerian, to Romani rights activists, to creators of invented languages, and to almost everyone I could think of in my address book who spoke a language that wasn't to be found on the original warning message slip. Some never replied, a few frostily refused, but the majority agreed and many more went further: sending me the translations by return, recommending experts in other languages, offering me reams of explanations as to word choice. I posted the results of my searches on my blog and on social media. As my collection grew, so people would write to me explaining how much they enjoyed the project and encouraging me to keep going.

However much translating the Kinder Egg warning message into multiple tongues might seem a pointless project to some, other people just get it. Reading languages you do not understand is an underrated pleasure. I'm not the only person to find the experience of seeing a familiar message rendered unfamiliar an enchanting one. And my joy in incomprehension is all the greater when the translation appears in a script I've never previously encountered, features unusual diacritics, or just looks plain weird.

Becoming a language fan

I'm a language fan. To be one you don't need to be trained in linguistics, nor do you have to be multilingual (after all, you can be a tone-deaf fan of Mozart). All language fandom requires is that you find it thrilling that there are more tongues in the world than one person could ever speak. You have to enjoy the experience of not being able to understand speech and writing. And above all, you have to view language as humanity's most magnificent creation.

This book will try to convince you to become a language fan too (if you aren't one already). I also have a serious agenda: my experience of reaching out to linguists and speakers of a vast array of languages across the world has taught me that the myth of Babel needs to be turned on its head: the splintering of human language into multiple tongues is not a metaphor for the fall of man into conflict and division. Rather, it is a metaphor for a different kind of unity. A world that speaks in one language could only be united in oppressive ways, forcing us to speak so plainly that all creativity and nuance is lost. In contrast, a world that speaks in many languages is one in which human individuality and invention can flourish. There is unity here too; unity in incomprehension. When I encounter a language I don't understand I am reminded of the amazing tendency of human beings to forge new paths, to do things in different ways.

In the modern world this unifying Babel is under threat. Around half the world's languages are classified as seriously endangered and some estimates suggest that by the end of the century, 90% of our languages will have lost their last living native speaker. Globalisation, the mass media, migration to big cities and the centralised modern nation state have all contributed to this erosion. Linguistic diversity is linked to biodiversity, as the same forces threaten both. Just as we need to treasure and protect the ecological diversity of the natural world, so should we guard the diversity of the human world. Translations of the warning message into endangered or lesser-known languages remind us that these languages live, they exist and should not be erased.

One of the ways we can learn to appreciate linguistic diversity is by challenging some of the myths we hold about language. Language is never an exact expression of our thoughts and intentions, languages are never entirely coherent things, translation is never an exact science. Rather, to speak is to engage in a creative act, drawing on systems of signs that can never be fixed. We are always improvising, contributing to the never-ending process of linguistic evolution. Part of the beauty of language is that it can never simply be a 'tool' of communication; it is always just out of reach. Any attempt to raise one language up over another, to see a language as a fixed, defined thing, will always end up in someone, somewhere getting silenced.

The same is true for the categories we create using language. If we delude ourselves that categories like 'nations' are natural phenomena to which we simply apply names, then we pave the way for attempts to use them to exclude people, to treat some people as 'naturally' belonging to them and to treat others as unnatural outsiders. Fortunately, language has an impish habit of subverting our attempts to do so. However much we try to pin the butterfly, to hammer down the world into neat divisions, something always resists our control: the unruly ability of language to burst human boundaries.

Revealing the ambiguities in the warning message, the messy process through which it has been translated and the challenges in communicating it, also makes a powerful statement: we refuse to silence the glorious babble of humanity, we refuse to treat any language, any nation, any state, as deserving of a louder voice, a bigger platform.

This, then, is a book about Kinder Surprise Eggs and it is not about Kinder Surprise Eggs at all. It is an investigation into the apparently trivial mysteries contained in a mundane slip of paper hidden inside a chocolate egg. When read correctly, the message sheet communicates another message beyond ensuring you don't inadvertently harm small children.

It is not just a message, it is the <u>M</u>essage, and that is how I will refer to it from now on.

Just as we break open the chocolate egg to reveal the treat inside, so I will break apart the apparent mundanity of the Message to reveal the wonderful, messy and bewildering reality of what language is. This is the kind of treat that can be enjoyed by human beings of any age.

Part

Set the controls for the heart of the Message

Chapter 1

The Message

On the liminality of Kinder Surprise Eggs

How human it is to create something so complex!

Kinder Surprise Eggs are certainly complex things. Regular eggs have an inedible shell within which edible life gestates. The Kinder Surprise Egg has an inedible outer foil wrapped around an edible chocolate shell, containing a yolk-coloured but inedible capsule, that itself encloses further inedible objects. The Egg is what anthropologists would call a *liminal* object; one that straddles the boundary between edible and inedible.

Research suggests that children do have the ability to understand the 'double nature' of the Eggs.[1] However, in some countries, most notably the United States, the liminal nature of an object like this is intolerable. In the US, after long legal battles, the Food and Drug Administration decreed in the 1990s that confectionery cannot contain inedible objects.[2]

The approach taken in other parts of the world, including within Europe, is to alert responsible adults to liminality. By legally mandating that warnings be included on and within the Egg, the adult purchaser will understand that special care should be taken to manage the dangers of an object that is both one thing and another thing.

Language – specifically written language – must bear a massive weight of responsibility here. Product warnings are strange things. Warnings contradict the temptations of products designed to be irresistibly tempting. They may tell the consumer not to use something they have actually bought (like cigarettes). Warnings can also be expressions of a kind of fear from the manufacturer. In the US, the annual 'Wacky Warning Label Contest' is both funny – one example is a fishing lure marked 'Warning, harmful if swallowed' – and draws attention to the over-litigious nature of American society that leads manufacturers to try to anticipate any conceivable misuse of their product.[3]

Warnings are expressions of an impersonal form of care. The anthropologist Margaret Mead is supposed to have said that the first sign of civilization in ancient culture was a broken femur that had healed, because this shows that someone stayed to help the victim recover. Whether or not she actually said this or it is historically accurate – and there is some doubt about both[4] – is a moot point; what's important here is that the capacity to care goes way back and way deep. To help someone recover from a broken femur, in ancient times or today, requires a degree of intimacy, even if it is just a doctor or nurse putting the leg into a splint. In contrast, written warning messages are distanced from the body. We don't know the people who wrote them, and they do not know who will read them. If we fail to heed warning messages, their authors will not have the ability to care for us.

There is a whole body of academic literature on the construction of warning messages, that draws on psychology, law and graphic design.[5] Ferrero appear to have adhered to best practice in constructing the Message: it conforms to various international and national legal regulations (some of which will be discussed later in the book). It includes both visual and written elements in the warning. It clearly identifies the nature of the hazard and the consequences for not avoiding it. The font is similar or identical to Helvetica; one that is frequently used on official signs and messages and is noted for its clarity and simplicity.

The biggest challenge to the Message's efficacy is something that the manufacturers can do very little about: will the Message be read? After all, it is a competitor in a crowded market for *attention*.

Paying attention

When you first heard about this book, you might have found its premise amusing. A whole book on the warning messages in Kinder Surprise Eggs! The reason this seems funny is that the Message is usually among the many things in our lives that we relegate to the background. Other warnings might intrude into our life in ways that grab our attention, such as error messages – both visual and aural – on our computers or flashing accident lights on the motorway. The Kinder Surprise Egg cannot intervene in our lives in such a visceral fashion. It is one of the many objects in our lives that are festooned with text and that we do not pay too much attention to.[6] Indeed, we *cannot* pay attention to them, since to do so would consume most of our lives. How would we ever cook dinner if we assiduously read the information on every component of the ingredients? One of the reasons why Obsessive-Compulsive Disorder is such a serious condition is that the sufferer is constantly paying too much close attention to the minutiae of everyday life.

The writer Georges Perec, in an essay first published in 1973, suggested that we needed to focus our attention on the ordinary, urging the reader to, among other things, 'question your teaspoons'.[7] Such attention can be a source of pleasure and a form of politics. As Perec argued:

> In our haste to measure the historic, significant and revelatory, let's not leave aside the essential, the truly intolerable, the truly inadmissible. What is scandalous isn't the pit explosion, it's working in coalmines.[8]

I am not going to claim that paying attention to the Message could change the world. However, the Message could help us reflect on the impossibility of bearing the burdens of responsibility that modern life places upon us. To buy a Kinder Surprise Egg for a small child is just one of those occasions when information is piled on us and, should we fail to read it closely or at all, it is we who will bear the consequences.

But let's, for the moment, assume that most adults who buy Kinder Surprise Eggs were assiduous readers of the Message; that they seek out the version in their language and study it carefully, even keeping the Message indefinitely as they are told to do.

There would still be a problem.

That problem's name is language. And it is beyond the ability of even the most experienced writer of warning messages to solve.

The slipperiness of language

To speak or to write is not a simple process in which a coherent message from our brain is transferred to someone else's brain. That we are all meaning-making creatures doesn't imply that we share an identical understanding of the system through which we make meaning. The capacity for language knits us humans together, but that doesn't mean anyone 'owns' a language in its entirety. Nor are our individual and collective assumptions completely known to us.

The connection of language to the world beyond us is slippery and often tenuous. It has never been particularly controversial to note that the association of words to things is arbitrary (outside of onomatopoeia); the word 'toy' is not a property of toys themselves. In the early twentieth century, the Swiss linguist Ferdinand de Saussure went further than this, arguing that words – known as 'signs' – do not refer to things themselves, they refer to the mental concept of the things themselves. The sign is a combination of the 'signifier' (a sound) and the 'signified' (a concept).

Saussure's work was a major contributor to a wider trend in twentieth-century humanities and the social sciences, known as the 'linguistic turn'. The nature of language and how it shapes our world became *the* preoccupation for a host of disciplines. One of the fundamental questions is whether we can exist outside language in the first place: is there a world outside the sign? The intellectual currents known as postmodernism and post-structuralism, and their advocates such as Jacques Derrida and Jean Baudrillard, are often accused of treating the world as a purely linguistic construct with no intrinsic meaning. Certainly, their determination to reveal the arbitrariness of the connection between signifier and signified seems to treat meaning itself as equally arbitrary.

But you don't have to be a dyed-in-the-wool postmodernist to recognise that meaning is an exceptionally slippery thing. We cannot get inside one another's heads and know for sure that our own signifieds are the same as other people's signifieds. All of us have known the anxiety of not being sure that the other understands what we are trying to say in the way we want to be understood. The fact that, through language, human beings can cooperate and get things done in the world is a kind of miracle.

The social sciences have revealed the messy process through which language works on an everyday basis. Detailed analysis of mundane language use shows, for example, how political talk involves a constant process of knitting together contradictory 'interpretive repertoires'.[9] Look in detail at conversation and you find an astonishing ability to turn fragments of talk into a meaningful dialogue. When I was doing postgraduate work, a fellow student analysed a conversation between a 'psychic' and her client. Pretty much everything the psychic said turned out to be incorrect, but she and her client 'worked' to turn the encounter into something that was revelatory. Conversation analysts have shown how our talk involves all kinds of implicit assumptions that we share without realising it. Harvey Sacks, a pioneer of this methodology, focused on the beginning of a story by a young girl – 'The baby cried. The mommy picked it up' – in order to reveal the implicit 'rules' through which we find it 'obvious' that the baby is the mother's baby.[10]

The Message is suffused with assumptions: that the warning is addressed to the reader; that 'read and keep' refers to the Message itself; that 'toy not suitable' refers to the toy inside the egg; that 'small parts' refers to the small parts of the toy. The confidence of Ferrero that the Message is intelligible shows how far we rely on rules that were never explained to any of us. While we might be able to assume that the reader understands some aspects of the Message, there is much else that seems to rest on less solid ground. For example, there is the presumption of the unknown writers of the Message that they can and should be obeyed. Then there is the assumption that pointing out the danger of the toy to under-3-year-olds necessarily implies that the adult reader will not accept this risk. Indeed, the explicit mention of 3 years as the cut-off point for suitability implies a process of child development where all children progress at the same rate.

Reading and writing the Message

Since we are constantly misunderstanding each other in talk, we rely on processes of 'repair' that put conversation back on track when mutual understanding breaks down. The Message is not a contribution to a conversation. It cannot be clarified. The differences between the assumptions of the writer and reader cannot be made explicit.

The literary theorist Roland Barthes distinguished between 'readerly' and 'writerly' texts.[11] In the former, readers passively consume texts suffused with common-sense meanings. In the latter, the text is open for the reader to 'write' the text, to produce new meanings. No doubt Barthes would have seen the Message as eminently readerly. We cannot be so sure. The Message may be being rewritten all the time.

On top of this unstable meaning-making, Ferrero also have multiple languages to contend with. At one level, the challenge is the same with the Message in every language. No natural language can 'solve' the problem of language's fundamental instability (although some 'constructed' languages have tried, as we shall see later in this book). But the nature of the challenge can be different in different languages. And the challenge is compounded by the challenge of translation itself.

Translation is a work of *re*creation, an act of writing, a strange alchemical process whose task, according to Walter Benjamin, is 'to release in [the translator's] own language that pure language which is under the spell of another, to liberate the language imprisoned in a work in his re-creation of that work'.[12] That may sound a little overblown when it comes to a technical translation of a short message, but the fundamental task of translation is daunting whatever you are translating. As the translator David Bellos has written:

> [T]he practice of translation rests on two presuppositions. The first is that we are all different – we speak different tongues and see the world in ways that are deeply influenced by the particular features of the tongue that we speak. The second is that we are all the same – that we can share the same broad and narrow kinds of feelings, information, understandings, and so forth. Without both of these suppositions, translation could not exist. Nor could anything we would like to call social life. Translation is another name for the human condition.[13]

Even if we speak the same language we all have to face the dual nature of the human condition. Indeed, George Steiner argued that translation is something that we do *within* languages as well; speakers of the same language cannot assume perfect understanding of each other, they have to work at understanding the other.[14] Ferrero's challenge is all the greater for having to confront the human condition on a tiny piece of paper, in multiple languages – and with human lives at stake.

The scale of the challenge makes me even more obsessed with the Message. It also helps me view Ferrero, a multinational corporation, with indulgence; to see it as irreducibly human. They are trying, against almost impossible odds, to tell purchasers of products they themselves made, who are scattered across the world, to take care and avoid harming their children. The only tool they have available is a monologue forged out of multiple written languages. That tool is imperfect and out of their control. And they are simultaneously trying to communicate in the same packaging a radically different message: that this product will entice and delight small children.

This book revels in the resulting contradictory, confusing, slippery result. The warning Message sheet is a tiny monument to the heroic attempts and desperate failures inherent in humanity's reliance on language. It is an attempt to control that which cannot be controlled. Its limitations are all our limitations.

So I hereby name the piece of paper on which the Message is inscribed the *Manuscript*. It is an ancient tome, on which the story of language itself can be read.

Chapter 2

The Manuscript

Transcribing the Manuscript

I paid the Manuscript the highest honour I could – I wrote it.

Or rather I transcribed the Manuscript on my laptop, paying close attention to it in a manner it has likely never received before at the hands of anyone outside Ferrero. While I might have strayed into auto-pilot when transcribing English, I could not do so with the other languages. My English keyboard lacks the letters from other scripts and the diacritics and additional letters in some Latin-based scripts. I had to find keyboard shortcuts and use online keyboards to write them, which was an arduous yet enthralling process. My attention never wandered.

Transcription forced me to be humble in the faces of languages I could not understand. I was obliged to pay attention to minuscule differences between letters as I never knew if an apparently tiny error could render an entire Message nonsensical. The font size is so small that some differences became almost microscopic. Georgian was a particular challenge. Working out whether a word contained a 'ბ' ('b') or a 'გ' ('g') required distinguishing between a hook or a diagonal line, a difference of a fraction of a millimetre. The stakes were high. In one of the two Armenian Messages you find the word *Հրուշակեղենիգործարամ* which transliterates as *hrushakeghenigordzaram* or 'confectionery'. Mistake the third letter 'ռ' for a 'ń' and you have *Հրուշակեղենիգործառամ, hrrrwshakeghenigordzaram* or 'fireworks'. The boundary between sense and nonsense comes down to the presence of a tiny hook at the bottom of a line.

It took me several attempts – pasting and re-pasting them into Google Translate as I went, to check that what I had transcribed made sense – to get the transcription right. I was left in awe at human visual acuity, at those who could read Georgian and Armenian fluently, and at myself for being able to pull off a similar trick in English.

In the end, I didn't manage to transcribe everything. I failed with Arabic and Persian; not because their alphabets are particularly complicated, but because letters are joined together and I found it impossible to separate them. Chinese was also a step too far. To use a Chinese dictionary to identify a particular character, you need to know a certain number of characters already, since they are sorted by 'radicals', segments that are common to sets of them. So I resorted to paying native speakers who transcribed them for me.

Writing the Manuscript ensured that I came to know it, to understand and appreciate its intricate details. Today the Manuscript is no longer a foreign land, though its expanses still contain mysterious territories. For truly committed Manuscript fans (and those who aspire to be) I have included a detailed journey round its two sides in the Appendix. For the rest, the most important thing to appreciate is that this tiny sheet of paper does not contain a simple recitation of the same Message into multiple languages. Rather, it is a much more nuanced, complicated and sometimes bewildering document.

The Manuscript contains languages from six language families (by far the most common being Indo-European, with

27 languages), written in seven different scripts. Across the world, at least three and a half billion people are native speakers of at least one language found on the Manuscript.[1] The least spoken is Estonian, with just over 1 million native speakers, and the most is Mandarin Chinese, where nearly 1 billion have command of the language. Over 160 countries use at least one Message language as an official or *de facto* national language.

While the Manuscript is undoubtedly a linguistically diverse document, it is also stylistically diverse. The 34 Messages come in twelve different varieties. Some of them are unique, such as Hungarian, where 'warning' is capitalised and 'read and keep' is lower case followed by an exclamation mark. Others are more common, such as the nine instances in which the entire Message is capitalised (Bulgarian, Croatian, Armenian, Latvian, Macedonian, Romanian, Slovene, Albanian, Serbian). There are two Chinese Messages, one in simplified characters and one in traditional characters. Only seven Messages mention the age of 3: German, English, Spanish, Swedish, Arabic and the two Chinese. The English Message is in a group of three, alongside Spanish and Swedish, where the age of 3 is mentioned, 'warning' is capitalised and 'read and keep' is in lower case.

The Manuscript also contains sections that are not actually Messages at all. There are importer and manufacturer details in Kyrgyz, Russian, Kazakh and Ukrainian – but no actual Message in these languages. There are two Armenian sections, one of which is a Message and one of which gives importer information.

The complexity of the Manuscript is such that at least one error has crept in. The eighth word in the Estonian Message should read *võivad*. Instead, the left of the 'o' is bisected by a tiny line, forming a new letter that appears neither in Estonian nor in any other alphabet. This error has appeared in multiple versions of the Manuscript. Another oddity – that I cannot definitely state is an error – is that recent versions of the Azerbaijani Message treat certain combinations of letters as 'ligatures', pushing them together in the same way that the Danish 'æ' does 'a' and 'e'. So 'ə' and 'l' are treated as ligatures in the Azerbaijani Message. These ligatures are not part of standard Azerbaijani script and I cannot reproduce them typographically here. Why they appear that way on the Manuscript is a mystery I cannot solve.

No doubt you are now thinking what I am thinking: why did Ferrero not use the same Message content, reproducing it identically across all the languages? Why is the 3-year minimum age only mentioned in seven Messages? What is the reason for the multiple tiny typographical differences?

But, as I discovered, the more appropriate question was: why do I feel that I need to know?

In search of the Codex

On my journey around the Manuscript, I started to fantasise about a great tome, a 'Codex', in which all Messages past and present were recorded. In its margins were glosses explaining the choices that were made to include or exclude a particular word or detail. On the Codex's illustrious pages, the names of those who write the Messages would be inscribed for all eternity.

If the Codex did exist, it would likely be maintained by Ferrero, the author of all the Messages.

Ferrero are a large multinational who, in addition to Kinder products, own brands such as Nutella, Ferrero Rocher and Tic-Tac, as well as all or part of many more brands and companies worldwide. As a corporation, they seem to have a genius in creating and marketing instantly identifiable products. Even when they get it 'wrong' and their global vastness means they don't tailor their branding to local markets correctly, they seem to get it right. In the UK, if you mention Ferrero Rocher (or even just the name Ferrero) in conversation you will likely get the response: 'With these Rocher you are really spoiling us!' This is a reference to an advert for the chocolates that aired in the 1990s featuring a suave ambassador whose good taste 'captivates' his guests and who orders his butler to bring a massive pyramid of Rochers into one of his cocktail parties. Ferrero didn't intend for the advert to be seen as kitsch and unintentionally funny, but they benefited from it all the same: everyone in the UK knows about Ferrero Rocher and many view the product affectionately.

Ferrero was born in 1946, when a Piedmontese confectioner in the town of Alba named Pietro Ferrero was struggling to respond to post-war shortages. He concocted a creamy paste from hazelnuts (a common local crop) and cocoa, based on a local confectionery called *gianduja*. His brother Giovanni assisted with the distributing and marketing of what was originally called *Pasta Gianduja*. It rapidly 'spread' across Italy and, in the 1950s, to other European countries. The spread was renamed Nutella in 1964.

The company now has factories in twenty countries and offices in many more. In 2014, the Italian food writer Gigi Padovani noted that Ferrero uses 120,000 metric tons of cocoa per year and sells 1.1 million metric tons of products per year.[2]

Kinder Surprise Eggs were co-created by Michele Ferrero (Pietro's son) and William Salice in the late 1960s and were launched in 1974. They were based on an Italian tradition of Easter eggs containing toys. Today they are only one product in the Kinder line, which also includes standalone chocolate bars. In 2001 Kinder Surprise Eggs were joined by the Kinder Joy, which are similar in size to the Surprise Eggs, but are enclosed in a hard plastic shell and divided into two sections, one containing a chocolate paste and the other a toy. It was launched in the US in 2018, where Kinder Surprise Eggs still cannot be sold.

Ferrero remains a family business. Pietro Ferrero died in 1949, after which his son Michele took over as the company expanded out from Italy. In 1997 Giovanni Ferrero, Pietro's grandson, became joint CEO alongside his brother, also called Pietro. After Pietro's death in a cycling accident in South Africa in 2011 and Michele Ferrero's death in 2015, Giovanni, Italy's richest man, has been in sole charge.

The company is now headquartered in Luxembourg and Italians are only a minority of its global workforce. But while Ferrero resembles other global multinationals in many respects, its heart remains in Alba, which is something of a company town. Its factory in the city stretches over 400,000 square metres and it is responsible for building leisure facilities and public amenities in the region, as well as supporting local and international causes via its Foundation.[3]

If there is a Codex, it might well be found in Alba. Ferrero politely declined my request to open up their secrets to me. This was understandable. The company are not in the Message business, they are in the confectionery business. To draw attention to the Message is to draw attention away from their actual products.

That doesn't mean that Ferrero disapprove of those of us

who love the Message. In fact, they are a company that displays considerable indulgence towards those who love its products.

Kinder Surprise Eggs attract a thriving collectors' subculture. Look on eBay and you will find toys and other paraphernalia for sale. In Germany and some other countries (less so the UK) there are conventions, books and catalogues produced by collectors. So varied is the range of Eggs and contents, that collectors specialise in different things. One German website identified at least eleven separate items collected by Kinder Surprise fans.[4] Some of them, such as the toys themselves, have been collected since the Eggs were first produced in the 1970s, and the warning messages have existed and been collected since 1989. They are not the only slips of paper that Kinder fans collect. The package insert or *Beipackzettel* – known universally among Kinder fans as the 'BPZ' – have been collected since the mid-1980s. The outer foils are also collected, although it is challenging to peel them off the Eggs without damage.

I was tantalised by the possibility that there were fellow Manuscript fans in the world. I began to reach out to prominent figures within the Kinder collecting subculture. I swiftly found out two important things:

First, Ferrero's attitude to Kinder collectors is benign. While they don't seek to feed the subculture, nor do they do anything to prevent it from flourishing. Images of their products are published in a profusion of collectors' guides, books and websites.

The second thing I found out is that if I was interested in the warning messages, there was one particular website to visit.

And that's how I discovered that a Codex did indeed exist.

The real Codex

The Codex is part of a sprawling website called 'Helmut's Sammlerseiten' (Helmut's collector-site).[5] It's run by a team led by Helmut Henze, a German Kinder Surprise collector. The site attempts to catalogue every Kinder toy, sticker, BPZ – and every Manuscript too. The Manuscripts are catalogued in the section *Warnhinweiszettel (WHZ)* ('warning notice slip'). There are hundreds of variants listed on the Codex, including scans of each one, and they date all the way back to 1989. New ones are added soon after publication.

Finally I could trace the history of the Manuscript back to the original! It soon became clear, though, that the Codex isn't completely comprehensive – its coverage is restricted mainly to Manuscripts found in Europe. Moreover, while the Codex has been compiled by seasoned Kinder collectors, they don't appear to have any more information than I do about the 'why' of the decisions made by Ferrero.

Still, the Codex confirmed that 1989 appears to be the first year in which a separate Manuscript was included in the Eggs. While there might have been Italian Manuscripts around at the time, their first recorded Message is in German and looked like this:

Lesen und aufbewahren:
Spielzeug nicht für Kinder unter 3 Jahren geeignet, da Kleinteile verschluckbar.

The first multilingual Manuscripts, published in 1989 or 1990, featured ten languages,[6] including the first recorded English Message:

Please read and keep: the surprise is not suitable for children under 36 months. Could be swallowed.

I managed to buy an early Manuscript on eBay from a Czech dealer. The thrill of holding in my hand this delicate flower was intoxicating. At 6.5 by 3.3cm it is smaller than the Manuscript I know and love today and is printed on rough blue paper. That such a thing could have survived to our days seems a miracle.

Time marches on. Over the last 30 years the Manuscripts progressively added languages and other details. There have been times when languages no longer found on the Manuscript were included, such as Japanese. As recently as 2012, Ukrainian, Russian and Kazakh Messages (not just product information) could be found.

The wording of the Messages has also been tweaked and adjusted. There was a brief period in the early 1990s when the minimum age was set at 5 rather than 3 years. But the Manuscript as we know it today seems to have stabilised in about 2014. Subsequent changes have been restricted to tweaks in formatting and things such as addresses, rather than the Messages themselves. I have to confess that, one night during the writing of this book, I had an anxiety dream that the Manuscript had completely changed – and my own manuscript had already gone to press. If this were to happen, it would be as if the face of an old friend had been replaced with that of another. I would adjust but it would be hard.

There are, though, separate versions of the Manuscript in Asia that include languages such as Vietnamese, Korean and Thai. Some Eggs also include additional Manuscripts giving additional warnings for some toys. The outer wrappers of the

Eggs contain Messages too, which are slightly different to the ones on the Manuscript, such as:

WARNING: TOY INSIDE. SMALL PARTS. ADULT SUPERVISION RECOMMENDED.

The Manuscript is always under construction. It makes little sense to talk about an 'original'. One thing I found by using the Codex to compare the minute changes in the various Messages over time, is that particular versions can change while others stay the same. If there was an original template, it has now been lost as the Messages follow their own paths through time and space.

The boundaries of knowledge

The Codex and my own research helped me understand the diversity of Messages across time and space. Much is still mysterious though. We appear to be approaching the boundaries of what is knowable.

There are precedents for attempting to understand a document without fully understanding who the author was or what their motivations were. Scholars of ancient literature have demonstrated that, through minute attention to detail, it is possible to infer a surprising amount about works whose authorship is mysterious. Since the nineteenth century, biblical scholarship has shown that the Bible is the work of several authors. The 'documentary hypothesis' suggests that the Pentateuch (the first five books of the Bible) was compiled from four separate sources, known as the Jahwist, Elohist, Deuteronomist and Priestly sources. While this hypothesis is still vigorously debated, the principle that the traces of separate authorship can be found through detailed textual analysis remains the scholarly consensus.

Can we perform a similar analysis on the Manuscript? Certainly, there is much that we can infer if we look closely at the document. We can, for example, speculate that the Messages in Norwegian and Danish – which are closely related languages – may well have been written by the same person or translation agency, since they both print 'warning, read and keep' in sentence case. In the following chapters I will also explain how some of the choices made by the writers of the Manuscript can be explained by wider geopolitical developments and that we can find traces of the Message in manuscripts and documents created by organisations other than Ferrero.

As with the Bible or the works of Homer, we will never achieve full knowledge. Does this matter, though? Does being obsessed with the Message necessarily mean that I must possess it and uncover all its secrets?

The subversiveness of fandom

What does it mean to love a text? How, indeed, can we develop a relationship with something that resists any kind of relationship with us? These are the questions that the fan has to confront.

The word 'fan' often has negative connotations; the etymology of the word, which stems from 'fanatic', associates the fan with excessive enthusiasm. The fan can be a dangerous individual, motivated by blind love to destroy any rivals to the object of that love. The distance between the fan and the love object can be maddening to the point that it is reduced to fantasy. There is a certain sort of fan for whom only complete possession will do; the kind of fan that stalks the love object and empties their bins at the dead of night in order to learn their most intimate details. Or, at least, that is the stereotype of the rabid fan – and, in fairness, they are not unknown.

Fandom is often a gendered category. Female fans – from Frank Sinatra's Bobby-soxers to K-Pop fans today – are often dismissed as over-emotional, sexually frustrated, uncritical slaves to idols who are little more than products of the entertainment industry. That's one of the reasons why members of some music scenes – particularly male ones – are often keen to emphasise their knowledge, connoisseurship and distance from the commercial 'mainstream'. It's also why, as far as I can see, Kinder connoisseurs tend to see themselves as 'collectors' rather than as fans.

Yet the fan can be a subversive figure. Fans *create* things. For decades, TV and film sci-fi fans have been writing stories, making music and even their own films that take commercial shows as the starting point for creative adventures. The most astonishing example of this is 'slash' fiction, which depicts male stars of TV shows in gay romantic relationships. To be a fan is not to passively consume, it is to use media for one's own purposes. The fact that the fan can only know the object of their love to a limited degree acts as a springboard to a different kind of relationship.

One of the most dramatic examples of the power of the fan is the Jewish tradition known as *Midrash*.[7] Midrash is a form of textual interpretation that, when applied to biblical texts, both clarifies meaning and expands it in new directions. The Bible is full of inconsistencies, contradictions and ambiguities. Modern textual criticism has identified places where scribal errors have led to 'mistakes' in the text. In Midrash, the text of the Bible contains no errors; all is for a purpose. By engaging in the Midrashic process we build on and enrich the text in all its holiness. For example, in Genesis chapter 37, which recounts Joseph's brothers selling him into slavery, the text implies that they sold him to passing Ishmaelites and then it describes them as selling Joseph to Midianites. Rather than putting this down to bad editing, the Midrash offers various sophisticated ways of reconciling this contradiction, expanding the story to a complex plot featuring two different sets of traders passing by.

What Midrash shows is that it is possible to love a text without being a slave to it. By playing with the text and delving into it we do it honour. Similarly, postmodern philosophers have talked about 'the death of the author', the abandonment of the quest to find the one originator who produces meaning. Instead, they see texts as always open to new meanings, as artefacts whose interpretation is always open. Such philosophising is often couched in obscure, infuriating language and is sometimes seen as an abdication of responsibility to actually understand the text. It is better viewed as an invitation to release oneself from participating in endless shaggy dog stories about who wrote what and why.

The Message and the Manuscript are ours, not Ferrero's, and we are free to do with them what we will. Once a message is out in the world, it is no longer the creator's property, whatever copyright law might say. However much I want to understand the Message's nuances and its history, the limits of my knowledge are actually my starting point.

In 2017, the comic artist R. Sikoryak turned the voluminously legalistic iTunes terms and conditions into a surreal graphic novel.[8] The project both satirised the ludicrously lengthy document and used it to create a thing of beauty. In the same way, to insist on the Message's aesthetic qualities helps us to tell a different story about modern industrialised society. There is a long intellectual tradition that highlights the manifold ways in which bureaucracies can cause tremendous harm, while the individual perpetrators become just cogs in a machine. Hannah Arendt famously called this the 'banality of evil'. Choosing to see the Message as an aesthetic object demonstrates that there can be a 'banality of beauty' too.

From Message fan to language fan

While I admire Kinder collectors, I couldn't become part of their culture. Collecting simply isn't *enough* for me. The work of cataloguing that the writers of the Codex have undertaken is extraordinary. But it doesn't draw on the most creative aspects of fan culture.

The collectors I contacted also seemed to pick up on a sense that I wasn't quite one of them. Again and again, an enthusiastic first email response would be followed by an embarrassed silence when I wrote again to clarify what my interests were. For example, I tried very hard to contact one of the greatest collectors of Manuscripts, a German gentleman whose finds make up much of the Codex's archive. The Codex personnel never responded to requests for assistance (on this matter or on anything else). One collector I was in touch with did in fact know the Manuscript collector and contacted him on my behalf, but he had no interest in speaking to me and he has recently sold his collection.

This made me realise that, not only was I more of a fan than a collector, my interest exceeded the object itself. I am interested in the Message and the Manuscript as a fascinating example of language in action; and the diversity of languages in action in particular. More than anything, I am a language fan, and it is as a language fan that I will proceed first to explore the delights of the Message even further, and then to go beyond it, to a land where even greater pleasures await ...

So while I never found *the* original Message, I have found *my* original Message. The English Message that I quoted in the first chapter was the starting point on my journey; the Message that led me to discover all the other Messages. With a few exceptions, it is also the Message from which the translations presented in the rest of this book were produced. Even if, in reality, this particular version of the English Message is one of many different Messages produced by Ferrero, it has become the progenitor of a whole host of new Messages. In this way, my original, while it is not the only original, may usher in a whole new epoch nonetheless.

Part

The multilingual Message

Chapter 3

Learning to be superficial

Unlearning profundity

What does it mean to be a language fan?

In my case, becoming a language fan required me to do a fair amount of unlearning, to adopt an attitude to language that was different to the attitude I was taught to take.

As an undergraduate and then a postgraduate, the education I received as a social scientist was imbued with the spirit of the 'linguistic turn' discussed in Chapter 1. I was, above all, taught that language was *important*; understanding it was the key to understanding the world humans have built.

Language has always been one of the main focuses of speculation and scholarship across a wide range of disciplines – linguistics, philosophy, neuroscience, sociology, psychology and more. What binds this sprawling realm of research and speculation together is an assumption that language is not just important, it is complex and multi-layered. Whether a scholar is engaged in research on verb forms in Armenian or in profound speculations about what language is in the first place, the guiding assumption will be the same: to understand the secrets that language holds, we must mine it; we must delve deeply into its mysteries.

The debates on the nature of language that have spread across the humanities and the natural and social sciences in recent decades and centuries are debates about core issues: Is language an 'instinct' as Steven Pinker has famously put it? Are we born with an inbuilt 'universal grammar' that predisposes us to pick up languages as children, as Noam Chomsky has argued? When did humans first develop languages, what did they sound like and what was their evolutionary advantage? Do different languages determine how we see the world, as the 'Sapir-Whorf hypothesis' insists? How far can language express the 'inner states' within the speaker's self? What is 'meaning' and how far can language carry it?

There is a profound split between the instinctive ease with which we use language on a daily basis and the difficulty of studying it. For me, this has made me shy away from directly addressing language as an issue in my own writing. I have tried to keep my love of words, grammar and the diversity of language away from the work I was trained to do.

But what if we could find a way to merge the two? What if it were possible to immerse oneself in the sea of language without being dragged down by questions of great profundity? What if it were possible to 'bracket out' the deep questions, by acknowledging that they exist, but proceeding as if they didn't?

What I am talking about here is a 'superficial' approach to language.

Loving language for its own sake

Superficiality gets a bad press generally and within academia it is one of the worst things to be accused of. By making the case for a proudly superficial perspective, that doesn't mean that I think research on language is unimportant. Rather, I am suggesting a complementary perspective that revels in languages' 'surface' features. This is an *aesthetic* approach that draws attention to how we might enjoy the experience of engaging with the sounds and written forms of languages. In particular, I am interested in the aesthetics of *the languages we do not understand.*

Too often, the languages we do not understand are treated as a kind of dead space, perhaps a source of frustration when trying to communicate in a foreign country. They can be a kind of reproach, a reminder of ignorance. We must either learn the languages we do not understand or find ways to work around them. But what if we tried to take pleasure in them instead, without feeling any pressure to 'solve' the languages we do not understand by learning to speak them?

Perhaps we could learn to relate to the languages we do not speak with the same easy familiarity with which we relate to the languages that we do speak. With our native languages we are constantly creating without even noticing. Each of us has our own distinctive 'idiolect', a way of speaking distinctive to us and that we often haven't developed consciously. We form sentences on the fly, we mangle words and produce neologisms, we play, we shout and we cry. Why shouldn't the languages we do not speak be subject to the same effortless entitlement?

The language fan is therefore someone who embraces this superficial approach to language. The language fan feels awe at the ability of others to speak languages s/he will never understand. The language fan doesn't necessarily like all languages equally but combines a respect for the 'genre' with a taste for particular kinds or aspects of language. The language fan can and should be someone who intervenes in the object of their love: collecting details, learning words and phrases and seeking out translations.

Above all, the language fan shouldn't feel the need to justify the existence of the object of their love. For a language fan, serious arguments about the 'value' of this or that language should be beside the point.

There is an *excess* to language in that we have many more ways of saying something than we actually need. And even though we can choose from a bounteous linguistic buffet, we still create language anew all the time.

The beauty of compocorance

Sometime in the Second World War, my maternal grandfather was bickering with an army comrade, who eventually threw his hands up in frustration and uttered the immortal words:

'Oh you're so ... compocorant!'

I grew up with the word compocorant. My mother was and is particularly fond of it and uses it to describe the adorable ways in which small children can be bossy and pernickety. My daughter was particularly compocorant as a toddler. Even though I have a penchant for etymology, I had never investigated the root of the word until my late 30s. To my surprise, I couldn't find any trace of it online. Somehow, as the family story had been passed down to me, I never twigged that the whole point of the tale was that the word didn't actually exist. It was an unintentional malapropism; a failed attempt to accuse my grandfather of pedantry and stubbornness. Yet how could I have known? I had heard the term compocorant all the time, particularly after I became a father. It had become a 'real' word, regardless of its origins. And it continues to be a word to me today. Perhaps after this book has been published, and I release compocorant to the world, it will become part of the English language beyond the bounds of my family (it will certainly turn up online eventually, via Google Books).

Compocorant works because it sounds just right. It seems to signal a cluster of related terms, taking on their meaning without actually becoming them: contrary, confrontational, comportment, truculent, punctilious, intractable ... I hear echoes of compocorance in all of these. My grandfather's comrade was seduced by language's surface sheen to push his linguistic abilities beyond their limits. In doing so, he planted the seed of a new word, a new meaning, a new way of describing a particular kind of childish behaviour.

As a language fan, I am drawn to language's surfaces, its trace associations, its glint and shine, rather than its weighty depths. Scholarly deliberations about the nature of language seem to me to be an irrelevance as a language fan. I can't judge whether Noam Chomsky's arguments regarding humanity's innate capacity for grammar are correct or not, but I can say that the search for the fundamental deep structures of human language doesn't help us appreciate their gorgeous surface features. Similarly, the hotly contested issue of 'linguistic relativity' – how far each language encodes a separate way of viewing and relating to the world – doesn't help us appreciate how the amazing variety of languages might be an intrinsically wonderful thing, even if they might be 'all the same' at some level.

By getting comfortable with enjoying languages without actually learning them, the language fan is also released from toil and anxiety. I enjoy reading about and hearing examples of the many languages of the Caucasus, but learning them would be a passport to misery. The languages of the Circassian people, such as Adyghe, have a legendarily huge range of consonants (50 or 60), including some unique to those languages. This makes it wonderful to listen to but intimidating for an English-speaker to learn. It would be great to speak Georgian, which delights in consonant clusters, an intricate grammar and a unique writing system, but I never will. And while I have learned enough Mandarin Chinese to be able to pronounce its four tones, I am happy to revel in, rather than attempting to reproduce, the music of the six Vietnamese tones.

One of my favourite online language resources, Wikitongues, records videos of speakers talking in a huge range of languages.[1] They are rarely translated and perhaps that's the point – we should enjoy their sounds regardless of what they mean. I have taken a similar approach in this book: when I present a Message in a non-Latin alphabet I usually leave it untransliterated; I rarely delve into the specific meanings of particular versions of the Message.

Yet not understanding a language is more complicated than one might think. We are meaning-inferring creatures as much as we are meaning-making ones. We can't help ourselves. The sounds made by humans when they talk produce meaning in the receiver, even when they don't understand what the words mean.

We hear the languages we do not speak through the aural lens of those we do speak. The constructed language Klingon (first developed for *Star Trek* but subsequently developed as a language in its own right) was designed to be full of guttural and 'ejective' sounds because for speakers of English, these sounds can signify as warlike and confrontational – and the Klingons are just that. But a speaker of Arabic or a Caucasian language would be entirely justified in hearing Klingon differently and might even be insulted by the idea that such sounds are violent ones.

While we have to acknowledge our own prejudices, we can also choose to enjoy our partial hearings. By becoming comfortable with our ignorance, unfamiliar sounds can become familiar sounds, even when the words mean nothing to you. After all, we can distinguish the sounds of particular birds even though no human truly understands their meaning.

As the writer R. Murray Schafer argued, humans inhabit a 'soundscape' that moulds us in often imperceptible ways.[2] Speech occupies part of that soundscape, even when it is speech that is incomprehensible to us. On my travels I have bathed in the call to prayer in Egypt, the precise politeness of Japanese train station announcements, the beery chanting of German football fans; all of them told me that I was *here*, outside my familiar English-speaking environment.

The linguistic landscape

That ability to connote 'hereness' is even more pronounced with written scripts. The visual landscape of cities and countries is indelibly marked by written language. And we can delight in the sight of writing we cannot read just as we can find pleasure in the sounds we cannot decode. Written language helps to shape what has been called the 'linguistic landscape', the sign-rich environment that city-dwellers inhabit.[3] On visits to Hong Kong, China and Japan I have found myself in awe of the people all around me who are somehow able to find instant meaning in what to me looks like a chaos of characters. I am endlessly drawn to the most complex characters, marvelling at how anyone could ever learn them. That I find the Chinese Message a little intimidating is high praise indeed:

注意：請閱讀及保存 此玩具不適合三歲以下小孩，其中含細
小配件，小心勿讓小孩吞食或吸入。

Japanese adds a dose of anarchy to the intimidation. The language uses characters, adopted originally from Chinese, and adds to them two further scripts that denote particular syllables, *hiragana* and *katakana*. While this combination of writing systems makes Japanese instantly recognisable, when you can't read it, the writing system seems to be constantly on the verge of breaking down, alternately freeing itself from and chaining itself to the characters:

必ず読んで保管してください: 部品類をあやまって口に入れ
たり飲み込んだりする危険があるので、オモチャを3才以下の
お子様には与えないでください。[4]

You don't have to visit the countries themselves to be drawn to foreign scripts. In and of themselves, scripts can be beautiful in ways that need little further justification. Take, for example, the Georgian Message:

გაფრთხილება, წაითხეთ და შეინახეთ: პატარა
ნაწილები შეიძლება ბავშვს გადააყლაპოს ან
გადააცდეს.

Those loops and curves! Those jaunty hooks, jagged lines and pointy bits! Georgian's elegance is combined with a complete lack of clues as to how it is to be pronounced. Although examples have been found dating back to the fifth century, its origin is unclear and while it might have been inspired by

Greek or Semitic alphabets, those who read such scripts will find nothing familiar to grasp.

Georgian has a silky flow to it, a succession of rolling waves. But that's nothing compared to the Arabic version of the Message:

العربية – إقرأ وإحفظ: لعبة غير مناسبة للأطفال الذين يقل سنهم عن 3
سنوات لانه يمكن إبتلاع أو إستنشاق الاجزاء الصغيرة.

Few written scripts capture the pleasure of writing better than Arabic. The fluency with which letters are cursively joined together, the elegant flourishes, the abruptness with which curves are halted and freestanding lines and dots added – you can almost feel what it would be like to write Arabic with quill and parchment, or at least a snow-white notepad and fountain pen.

In contrast, what Thai lacks in flow, it gains in elegance, festooned as it is with dainty filigrees and poised, rounded-off curves:

คำเตือน, โปรดอ่านและระวัง : ของเล่นไม่เหมาะสำหรับเด็ก
ที่ อายุต่ำกว่า 3 ปี เนื่องจากชิ้น ส่วนเล็กๆ อาจถูกกลืนหรือสูด
เข้าไป[5]

In praise of diacritics

My avid reading of the Manuscript has made me realise how dull English writing is. It's not that I don't adore the language itself, it's just that it lacks something that many other languages that use the Latin alphabet have – diacritics, the tiny marks that modify letters in many alphabets.

Ťhíṣ šöřť óf ţhĩňǧ.

Diacritics are counted as separate letters in some alphabets – 'ñ' appears after 'n' in a Spanish dictionary, for example – or they may indicate the modification of the sound of a particular letter. Diacritics complicate computer keyboards and cause frustration to those who need to type a foreign word into a text message on their phone or computer.[6]

Diacritics can also be used as a source of play and allusion. One example is the 'heavy metal umlaut', where the diacritic is used to import a patina of Teutonic hardness to metal band names. It's hard to think of Motörhead without the dotted 'o' and the Gothic typeface, and other bands such as Queensrÿche and Mötley Crüe have also turned to the umlaut for their logos. Spın̈al Tap satirised the metal umlaut by placing it over the 'n', which no existing language ever does, also including a dotless 'ı', which is at least found in Turkish.

My favourite diacritic cannot be found in any online typeface. In Hergé's *The Calculus Affair*, Tintin and Captain Haddock travel to the capital of Borduria, Szohôd, to rescue Professor Calculus from the clutches of the chief of police, Colonel Sponsz. Borduria is run by a Stalinesque dictator called Marshal Kûrvi-Tasch. The dictator's curvy 'tache is a symbol of the nation, appearing not just on the nation's flag, but as a modified circumflex in the Bordurian language (which is ubiquitous on street signs). It's a brilliant satire of how scripts can bear the imprint of the countries that write in them, and on how that script marks the physical space of the city. Interestingly, in the French original, Marshal Kûrvi-Tasch is Marshal Plekszy-Gladz (i.e. 'Plexiglas'). While the curvy 'tache is similarly omnipresent in the original French version of the book, Hergé clearly saw no need to belabour the point in the dictator's name or include a circumflex in it. But then,

French is a language that uses the circumflex, so a French speaker will likely find them less visually arresting.

English is plain vanilla diacritic-wise. Our letters are unadorned and cause no problems to users of other Latin keyboards. While Italian and Dutch are also diacritic-less on the Manuscript, at least they do use them in other texts. English also lacks 'ligatures', the collided letters found in some alphabets, such as the Danish 'æ'. We long ago dropped the distinctive 'ð' and 'þ', denoting the two ways of pronouncing 'th', which are only found today in Faroese ('ð' only) and Icelandic (both 'ð' and 'þ'). We lack the quirky splendour of unique letters like the Maltese 'Ħ' or the Azerbaijani 'ə'. We are dull.

Just as we hear other languages through ears shaped by our own language, so we see other languages through what our eyes are accustomed to read. Perhaps the only advantage of English's plainness is that the many Latin scripts that use diacritics always read as thrillingly 'other'. To me, for example, Hungarian always looks belligerent and proud (it helps that, as a non-Indo-European language, its words are mostly unrecognisable to an English-speaker). I once had an article I wrote on heavy metal published in a Hungarian-language journal and I was delighted by how the script seemed to match the subject matter. The Hungarian Message seems to me to be taking no prisoners in the emphatic nature of its warning:

FIGYELEM, olvassa el és őrizze meg! Az apró alkotórészek könnyen beszippanthatók vagy lenyelhetők.

Of course, I do try to ensure that the connotations that written Hungarian hold for me do not 'bleed' into my view of

Hungary and Hungarians themselves. I do not, rest assured, see Hungarians as intrinsically belligerent (the Hungarian I know best is a complete pussycat). While I might see Hungarian script as badass, a Hungarian will most likely see it as just writing.

I am also drawn to Czech, which glories in reversed circumflexes such as 'ř'. This denotes Czech's semi-legendary 'raised alveolar non-sonorant trill'; a sound found in very few other languages. It is actually one of the few Czech letters that foreigners are obliged to tackle due to its appearance in the name of the composer Dvořák. Neither I nor most English speakers can easily pronounce its bewildering sound combination of a trilled 'r' and a 'j'. Yet I love watching videos of Czechs doing so, and I am thankful to live in a world where such a confounding sound can occur.[7] The reversed circumflex is, for me at least, a slice of sonic strangeness and, while there is unfortunately no 'ř' in the Czech Message, its other diacritics still tantalise:

> UPOZORNĚNI, čtěte a uschovejte: Malé části by mohly
> být spolknuty nebo vdechnuty.

Whether they use diacritics or not, there is a certain tentativeness in Latin alphabets. The versions of the Latin alphabet that emerged over the last few centuries tended to add diacritics rather than going the whole hog and creating a new letter. We Latin script users can be obstinate in our refusal to adapt our alphabets to sound changes and developments in the language. English is an extreme example here – every word in this sentence so far could be pronounced in more than one way. But even in those languages that do use diacritics, spelling and pronunciation can be miles apart. Danish may have an 'å', 'æ' and 'ø' but it doesn't stop Danes swallowing consonants to such a degree that words can be a confusion of vowels. I once stayed in the suburb of Hvidøre in Copenhagen and never mastered the name of the place, other than it approximated to 'ee-orgh-er'.

A set of writing conventions that is regular and accurate enough to capture the way a language actually sounds is known as 'phonemic orthography'. There are some Latin scripts that achieve something close to this, such as Albanian and Finnish. These were developed relatively recently, as the languages have only been written for a few centuries. Albanian began to be written from the sixteenth century and spelling was codified in the nineteenth and twentieth centuries. That means that the language hasn't had much of a chance to depart from written conventions. English and French, in contrast, have been written for over one thousand years, undergoing multiple changes in sound and vocabulary, with the written language barely keeping up.

As a general rule, I am pessimistic about the chances of speaking the Latin-script Messages without knowledge of the language. After all, I still need to know what the spelling conventions actually refer to. *Vogla*, the Albanian Message word for 'small', looks pretty easy, but when I looked up the spelling rules, it is actually pronounced something like 'vorglow'. *Osat*, the Finnish for 'parts', is pronounced closer to 'osut'.

I don't mind the confusion. In fact, my lack of knowledge of many languages written in Latin scripts, and my caution in trying to pronounce them, helps me to focus better on the aesthetics of how they look on the page. Unlike non-Latin scripts, my familiarity with the core of the alphabet forces me to pay closer attention to the quirks of the diacritics and spelling. For example, Latvian, to me, is indelibly marked by an upper horizontal line known as a 'macron':

UZMANIBU, IZLASIET UN SAGLABAJIET: jo pastāv iespēja, ka rotaļlietas sīkās detaļas var iekļūt elpošanas ceļos.

I don't know how to pronounce words like *pastāv* correctly, but I appreciate the way they help me 'see' Latvian. They create the impression of a language that is trying to flatten itself, to make itself measured and restrained. At first glance, Latvian's Baltic neighbour Estonian also appears to indulge in these flattening diacritics. A closer look, though, reveals a quirky difference:

TÄHELEPANU! LOE LÄBI JA HOIA ALLES: need võivad sattuda lastele suhu või hingamisteedesse ja põhjustada õnnetuse.

The Estonian 'õ' is a Latvian macron gone a bit mischievous, a jaunty furrowed brow. Contrast this with the Hungarian 'ő', which is an umlaut gone a bit bolshy.

Of course, these letters do have sounds. The Latvian macron denotes a 'long' vowel length. The wonky Estonian furrowed brow is a 'tilde' and when added to an Estonian 'o' it makes the vowel sound as though it were being pronounced through the nose. The Hungarian aggressive umlaut is a doubled acute accent and denotes a long vowel. Such prosaic explanations do not negate the instinctive reactions a non-speaker of Hungarian, Estonian or Latvian might have towards those scripts.

The tendency of Latin scripts to adapt themselves to new languages via the use of diacritics has its limits. In adapting Latin script to Vietnamese at the urging of colonial powers, this tonal language with a phonemic inventory very different to any European language required a bewildering array of accents and diacritics:

> Cảnh báo (yêu cầu đọc và lưu giữ): Đồ chơi trong sản phẩm này không phù hợp cho trẻ em dưới 3 tuổi. Trẻ có thể nuốt hoặc hít phải các mảnh nhỏ.

One cannot help thinking that Vietnamese might have benefited from an entirely new script, or at least some new letters. The Korean *Hangul* alphabet, created by King Sejong in the fifteenth century, is unique to the language. It forms letters into blocks, denoting separate syllables, and seems to reinforce the separateness of the language and its people:

> 경고, 잘 읽고 보관하시요. 3세 미만의 어린이는 사용할 수 없음. 작은 부품이 포함되어 있어 삼키거나 입 안에 넣지 않도록 주의.[8]

The agility of Cyrillic

When Cyrillic alphabets (first used in Slavic languages such as Russian and Bulgarian) are applied to new languages, there is usually a much less reticent attitude to creative additions than with Latin scripts. While diacritics are used to specify sound changes, it is common to create whole new letters or to radically modify existing ones.

Perhaps this propensity to add to the alphabet stems from the hybrid character of Cyrillic itself. A reader of a Latin script will immediately notice familiar letters. That's because Cyrillic (which was developed in what is now Bulgaria, then part of the Byzantine Empire, in the ninth century) owes much to the Greek alphabet, to which Latin script also owes a debt. Take the Bulgarian Message:

ВНИМАНИЕ, ПРОЧЕТИ И ЗАПАЗИ: Съдържа малки части, които могат да бъдат погълнати или вдишани.

Compare this to the Greek:

ΠΡΟΣΟΧΗ: υα διαβάσετε και υα φυλάξετε. Περιέχει μικρά κομματια που μπορεί υα καταπιούν η υα ειοπνεύσουν.

I find the simultaneous familiar and alien features of Cyrillic and Greek disconcerting. I cannot separate my reactions to Greek from its antiquity, its civilizational importance and my shame at my own lack of a classical education. The associations that Cyrillic has for me changed over the course of the research I did for this book. My previous encounters with Russian left me with frustration because I could read some letters but not all. These days, while my ignorance is undimmed, I am more likely to see Cyrillic as a typographical treasure trove.

While the various Slavic languages that use Cyrillic alphabets are broadly similar, there are plenty of idiosyncratic letters. Take the final, 2013 versions of the now sadly-defunct Russian and Ukrainian Messages:

ВНИМАНИЕ! Прочитайте и сохраните: игрушку не предназначена для детей младше 3-х лет, мелкие детали могут быть проглочены или попасть в дыхательные пути. Рекомендуется наблюдение взрослых.

Обережно, прочитайте та збережіть: Діти можуть проковтнути чи вдихнути дрібні деталі.

These look like different languages written in the same script. Yet Ukrainian – the second Message – includes an 'I' in the word for 'keep', *ЗБЕРЕЖІТЬ*. That letter is not used in Russian, although it is used in Belarusian and Rusyn. The 'J' in the Macedonian 'read and keep', *ЧИТАЈ И ЗАЧУВАЈ*, is found elsewhere only in Serbian Cyrillic and denotes a 'y' sound. The Serbian Cyrillic Message (found in earlier versions of the Manuscript) includes the word *млађој* ('younger) and contains not just a 'j' but the unique 'ђ', denoting 'dje'.

Things get even more fun when you consider the multiple non-Slavic languages that use Cyrillic scripts. The Russian and Soviet empires attempted to integrate non-Slavic peoples into the expanding state through adapting Cyrillic for languages in the Iranian, Turkic, Caucasian, Uralic, Mongolian and other language families. That meant finding ways to represent new inventories of phonemes utterly distinct from Slavic ones. A Message in Kazakh, a Turkic language, has not been included in the Manuscript since 2013. When it first appeared, in 1998, it looked like this:

НАЗАР! ОЙЫНШЫҚТЫ ҮШ ЖАСТАН КІШІ БАЛАЛАРҒА БЕУГЕ БОЛМАЙДЫ ҰСАҚ БӨЛШЕКТЕРІ ЖҰТЫЛЫП НЕМЕСЕ ТЫНЫП ҚАЛУЫ МҮМКІН.

The Kazakh Message word for 'swallowed', *ЖҰТЫЛЫП*, contains the unique character 'Ұ', denoting something like an 'oo'.

Warning! Superficiality failure imminent!

In the end though, I didn't manage to achieve true superficiality.

However much it might be possible to appreciate written languages in their own terms – enjoying the aesthetics of scripts, appreciating the associations they trigger while recognising that these are yours alone – it is hard not to fall prey to the urge to decode. Perhaps the easy familiarity I developed with the various Message languages was a consequence of knowing that they all, ultimately, meant something broadly similar. Yet somewhere in my subconscious lurked the anxiety that the Messages might be profoundly different from each other. Maybe my closeness to the Messages was built on a lie.

What finally led me to confront this unnerving feeling was, ironically, a growing discomfort with the *English* Message. My son was telling me about Latin grammar one day when the question that had been brewing for some time hit me:

What sort of word is 'warning'?

The word is a present participle. In the English Message it also seems to act like a verb, carrying some of the sense of an imperative. It is followed by two imperative verbs: 'read and keep'. Should we parse 'warning' as 'be warned'?

'Warning' is an example of what linguists call 'nominalisation' – the process through which a noun is created from an adjective or verb. Words like 'decision', 'difficulty', 'reaction' and 'swimming' are all nominalisations. They are particularly important in highly formalised uses of language, such as within academia or bureaucracies. Nominalisation creates distance from the active forms of verbs, producing a 'cooler' style. For example, 'A decision was made by Ferrero to ...' rather than 'Ferrero decided to ...'; or 'The public reaction to the new Kinder toy designs has been positive' rather than 'The public reacted positively to the new Kinder toy designs'. Stylistically, nominalisation can have the effect of asserting impersonal authority.

It was only in conversation with Yaron Matras, Emeritus Professor of Linguistics at the University of Manchester, that I managed to pin down why this particular nominalisation has such a strange effect. Yaron pointed out an obvious fact: the term 'warning' draws attention to itself; it is 'self-reflexive', even solipsistic. 'Warning' is a speech act that goes beyond simply conveying information to 'performing' it. The best way to parse it is '[this is a] Warning'. It doesn't draw attention to anything but itself. Indeed, the German Message goes even further by using the term *Warnhinweis*, meaning 'warning message'.

Why does a warning message need to tell the reader it is a warning message? After all, it is clear after the first few words what the message is about. Perhaps the purpose is to draw attention to the author of the message. 'Warning' claims the status of being 'the one who can warn'. Against this linguistic authority, what can the reader do but obey?

However, as Yaron also pointed out to me, there is an alternative that reaches out to the reader, rather than emphasising the authority of the author. And that word can be found on the very same page as 'Warning': the Spanish, French and Italian Messages start with *Atención, Attention* and *Attenzione* respectively. Turn over the page and the other two Romance languages in the Manuscript, Portuguese and Romanian, begin with *Atenção* and *Atenție*. All these are nominalisations too but they are subtly different to 'Warning' in that they signal something that the reader must do – pay attention – rather than something that the author has done.

Etymologically, the word 'warning' comes from the Germanic branch of Indo-European – its Old English ancestor was *warenung*. Romance languages are less likely to include words from the Germanic branch, at least in this case. Words signalling attention in Romance languages derive from the Latin noun *attentio*. English, being a hybrid of Germanic and Romance, has both options. However, Romance languages do include words that translate more closely to 'warning' in the sense of a warning notice, such as the French *avertissement* and the Romanian *avertizare*. That they are not used on the Manuscript suggests that the choice of attention-based warning words is the result of a subtly fundamental distinction between how these languages 'do' warnings.

How do we account for this distinction? Yaron suggested that I test the hypothesis that southern and northern European languages might each form a *sprachbund*, the linguistic term for a zone within which various languages – including unrelated ones – come to share common features. Perhaps the northern sprachbund might have a more developed bureaucratic language than the southern one.

Aside from English and German, three other northern European languages use 'warning'. The Swedish Message begins *Varning*. At first sight, the Norwegian and Danish *Advarsel* seems to have a strangely Romance tinge to it. This is a coincidence, though, as the root of the word is *var*.

Yet some other northern languages do not follow this pattern. The Dutch *Opgelet* translates closer to 'attention', even though the language contains the word *waarschuwing*. Dutch is the only Germanic language on the Manuscript to depart from this pattern. Elsewhere in northern Europe, Finnish, Estonian, Latvian and Lithuanian lean closer in translation to 'attention' rather than 'warning'. On the other hand, in Central Europe and the Balkans, Hungarian, Czech, Slovak, Bulgarian, Serbian, Slovene and Croatian offer 'warning'. In southern Europe, the Albanian *Kujdes*, the Turkish *Dikkat* and the Greek *Προσοχη* do indeed translate closer to 'attention/caution' than 'warning', even though all these languages do contain words that are similar to the latter.

So are there separate northern and southern warning message sprachbunds? The answer seems to be ... sort of. What is certainly true is that the further north you go in Europe – although not the further north-east you go – the sterner the Message becomes.

Another striking thing about the English Message is its condensed language. It says 'Small parts might be swallowed ...' rather than 'The small parts might be swallowed ...'. This is a language shorn of articles like 'the'; it is stripped down to its bare bones. But Romance languages appear to be different. French speaks of *Les petites pièces* and Spanish, Portuguese and Italian also use 'the'. In these languages, the definite article is grammatically necessary to indicate the whole of something. Romanian, for some reason, does not include the definite article in its message.

In total, I identified nineteen Message languages that have articles of some kind.[9] I then looked to see which of these languages used them in their Messages. Other than the four out of five Romance languages, the only other two were Arabic and Dutch. That makes Dutch an outlier among the Germanic languages in using 'the' (just as it is an outlier in not using 'warning').

In total then, thirteen Messages that could use articles, do not do so here. Yet what had I actually discovered? I knew that an article-less English is a feature of instructions, warning messages and the like. Does that style exist in the other twelve article-less Messages? And does it exist for Dutch and Arabic and the Romance languages?

I eventually realised that these questions are part of one bigger question: how far were the translations of the Message guided by linguistic necessity or by stylistic choice?

And just like that, I found myself going deep. Deep into fundamental questions about what translation is and how far words in one language can be mapped onto words in another. Deep into the uncertainties that arise when a non-speaker of a language tries to understand something of its nuances.

The secrets of style

The more familiar I became with the Manuscript, the more I speculated about its non-superficial qualities and its secrets. This is the danger of being drawn into the search for meaning: I can feel entirely at home with the delightful sight of a word like Czech's warning equivalent *Upozornění*, provided I don't start wondering about what it actually means. And when I do wonder, the pleasures give way to anxiety.

Can shapes on a page ever just be shapes on a page? Can style ever just be style? Such questions led me to look again at the multiple stylistic variations that I had identified. Take the difference between Slovene:

OPOZORILO, PREBERITE IN SHRANITE: Majhne delce bi lahko pogoltnili ali vdihnili.

... and Slovak:

> UPOZORNENIE, prečítať a uchovať: Malé časti by mohli
> byť prehltnuté alebo vdýchnuté.

It isn't too difficult to see that the two messages are in related
Slavic languages, although they are not easily mutually intelligible. But is the difference between the capitalisation of the
first four words in the Slovene version and the capitalisation
of the first word only in Slovak a meaning-making distinction?
Is it a manifestation of difference in how these two languages
write formal instructions and messages? And even if there
are no essential differences and it is simply a stylistic choice,
does this imply that Slovenes and Slovaks will respond to the
Message in subtly different ways?

In contrast I found an intriguing similarity between the
Azerbaijani and Armenian Messages:

> «Xəbərdarlıq, oxuyun və əməl edin: kiçik hissələri
> nəfəs vəqida orqanlara düşəbilər»

> "ՈՒՇԱԴՐՈՒԹՅՈՒՆ, ԿԱՐԴԱԼ ԵՎ ՊԱՀԵԼ' ՓՈՔՐ
> ՄԱՍՆԻԿՆԵՐԸ ԿԱՐՈՂԵՆ ԿՈՒԼ ԳՆԱԼ ԿԱՄ
> ՆԵՐԱՇՆՉՎԵԼ":[10]

Both Messages are enclosed within quotation marks ('«' is
known as a 'guillemet' and is also found in several other
languages, including French). I wondered whether the use
of quotation marks is mandatory for this kind of message
in Azerbaijani and Armenian. Not so. I examined an additional Manuscript that gives a specific warning for a certain

kind of toy and here there were no quotation marks for Azerbaijani and Armenian. So why did they appear in the main Manuscript? Would Azerbaiijanis and Armenians respond to their Messages in the same way as I would were the English Message enclosed in quotation marks – as denoting irony and distance? Even more confusingly, Armenian also uses the guillemet, and double inverted commas are not a standard part of Armenian punctuation. So does the use of speech marks instead signal a further oddness to Armenian readers?

That Armenia and Azerbaijan have fought each other in war (most recently in 2020) adds another dimension to the puzzle. Do their Messages signal a subterranean sprachbund extending across these two linguistic communities, whose languages are unrelated?

Another feature of the Azerbaijani Message is that the sentence after the colon does not begin with a capital letter. That's also the case in the Estonian, Lithuanian and Latvian Messages. Is this a requirement of these languages or, once again, a stylistic choice? It's striking that all three languages of the Baltic States do this (despite Estonian being part of a different language family to Latvian and Lithuanian). Does this mean anything at all?

Little details such as punctuation and capitalisation are often the most chaotic aspects of written language. Despite the efforts of writers such as Lynne Truss, the 'rules' are often obscure, contradictory or non-existent. In her book on the semicolon, Cecelia Watson suggests that we abandon our search for rules in punctuation and direct close attention to the subtle impact that these tiny marks may have on meaning.[11]

The trouble is, in the case of the Message it's hard to tell what that impact might be.

Another possible agent of meaning is the font(s) in which the Messages are written. The Manuscript uses a font – which may or may not be Helvetica or something very similar – that maximises functional clarity.[12] What would the impact be on the meaning of the Message if it were printed in a different font? And how would its impact vary across languages?

To really get under the skin of the Manuscript, I would need to achieve a high degree of fluency in all its languages; a level of fluency that would help me understand the subtle associations that its wording, punctuation and style might convey. I would also need fluency in fonts, punctuation and perhaps other aspects of writing too.

Very few people have ever achieved fluency in more than a handful of languages. I could have approached a native speaker in every Manuscript language but then I would be facing another problem: is it even possible to translate the nuanced associations of one language into another? Who would I choose, anyway? An Armenian bureaucrat might view the Message in one way, and an Armenian farmer another.

... And we're back to deep questions about language again. We're back to the threat of paralysis that can result when you acknowledge that 'meaning' is never a stable, completely understandable thing.

In the end, it is hard to remain superficial where language is concerned. While I am a language fan, I cannot only be a language fan. Language fandom celebrates the playful possibilities of language, but humans also often try to do the reverse – to fix language into a stable, defined thing. The Manuscript is the product of many such attempts. Indeed, for all the superficial pleasures it supplies, it is the result of systematic efforts to turn back the tide of linguistic anarchy. And it is to these attempts that we now turn.

Chapter 4

The official version

The other messages

When the Scribes at Ferrero set out about the great work of composing the Manuscript, they faced a daunting task. Yet they were not alone in their endeavours. Some of the work had been done for them in obscure international committees.

In their document *EN71 – Safety of Toys*, the European Committee for Standardisation (CEN) issued instructions on the nature of the warnings to be placed on Ferrero's products.[1] CEN also sets standards for the translation of those warnings in another document, *PD CEN/TR 15071 Safety of Toys – National translations of warnings and instructions for use in the EN71 series*.[2] This is an essential read for any self-respecting Message fan. The pulse quickens on reading its deathless prose:

> This Technical Report contains a compilation of national translations of warnings and instructions for use, mentioned in the EN71 series of standards. The warnings and instructions for use need to be applied in accordance with the requirements and specifications of the EN71 series of standards for safety of toys and these standards should always be consulted before drawing up the text of a warning or instruction for use.[3]

The document does not offer a ready-to-use version of the Message in its entirety. What it does do is offer key terms and phrases that can be used in warning messages in all CEN-member languages. So many old friends from the Manuscript make an appearance. Hello *ВНИМАНИЕ* (Bulgarian for 'warning')! Nice to see you *Små delar* (Swedish for 'small parts')! Greetings to you *no apto para menores de* (Spanish for 'not suitable for those under ...')! These and many more words and phrases do appear in the document's collection of translations.

But when I started to examine the document more systematically and compared it to the Manuscript, I started to notice the differences. In the Dutch Message, 'warning' is *OPGELET* – the document suggests *Waarschuwing*. The Finnish Message warns *HUOMIO* – the document offers *Varoitus*. The German Message proclaims *WARNHINWEIS!* – the document proclaims *Achtung*. There were also differences in Greek, Hungarian, Latvian, Lithuanian, Polish, Romanian, Spanish and Turkish. Old friends seemed to be intermingling with strangers.

It seems that the document does not legally mandate particular words or phrases, even though the Message translations sometimes conform to its suggestions. In order to clarify what is and is not required, I turned to a couple of Kinder Surprise rivals and examined their own warnings. One is a 'Wow Egg' manufactured by a UK-based company called Meeran. This has no manuscript (it cannot be a Manuscript) but it does have a message (it cannot be a Message) in English that reads:

WARNING: Surprise toy inside contains small parts.
Not suitable for children under 3 years old.

One competitor that does have a manuscript is a 'Paw Patrol' Egg made by Zaini, an Italian confectioner based in Milan.

Their manuscript is impressive indeed, with messages in 40 languages, including some that do not appear on the Manuscript such as Icelandic. They are bunched so close together as to be almost unreadable and the English translation is hardly a model of stylistic excellence:

> WARNING: IT CONTAINS A TOY. ADULTS' SUPERVISION RECOMMENDED. NOT SUITABLE FOR CHILDREN UNDER 3 YEARS. SMALL PARTS CAN BE SWALLOWED OR INHALED.

Some of the other versions of the Zaini message contain words and phrases found in the Kinder one. But, here too, not all of them follow the EN71 translation guidelines. For example, the German 'warning' is *WARNUNG* rather than the 'official' *Achtung*. In addition, the Zaini Bulgarian, French, German, Spanish, Czech and Slovak words for warning are different to both the Kinder Message and to EN71.

These are just two examples. I found similar messages on other similar products too. None of them are identical to the Message, at least in English, but *parts* of them are identical or nearly identical. After all, how many ways are there to warn of the presence of small parts that can be swallowed or inhaled?

There clearly isn't an officially and legally mandated set of translations, despite many warning messages in many products 'shadowing' each other. Or at least there is enough latitude to ensure that Ferrero are able to compile the Message with some degree of creative freedom. The aesthetic dimension has not been completely suppressed by the legal dimension.

Official languages

In another, much broader respect, the Manuscript does conform to 'official' language in that it is based on the assumption that the various languages in which the Message appears are separate, distinguishable things. The Manuscript has no hierarchy, no categories other than alphabetical order. Arabic, Croatian and French are all the same things: separate languages with separate language communities into which a Message must be translated if it is to be understood.

But a language is not as innocent a category as the official version might have it. While humans have created their languages slowly (other than 'constructed' languages such as Esperanto), through an evolutionary process that no one ever had complete control over, the decision to classify something as a language is a much more deliberate and conscious process. This classification involves giving a language a name; speakers of a named language therefore come to understand themselves as speaking one language among other named languages.

Naming a language almost always involves downgrading the status of another way of speaking. Many of the earliest written languages bolstered that status through a reluctance to name other languages as equivalent in status. Famously, the root of the English word 'barbarian' lies in the Ancient Greek βάρβαρος, Barbaros. The term is supposedly onomatopoeic, mimicking the unintelligible 'bar bar bar' sound that non-Greeks made. For the Greeks, to speak another language was barely to speak at all; certainly such 'non-languages' did not deserve to be named.

In the age of writing, an unwritten language could also be a non-language. The prestige and power encoded in a written language was such that even invaders of a realm might adopt the language of the rulers they supplanted. The Vandal and Gothic peoples who invaded the collapsing Western Roman Empire did not spread their early Germanic languages to the shores of the Mediterranean; Latin languages held sway and, with the exception of North Africa, they remain Romance-speaking territories to this day. Nor do we have much idea what language the Huns, and their king Attila, would have spoken as they laid waste to much of Europe in the fifth century. Their language did not congeal into written bureaucracy and law; it remained protean, ungovernable and ultimately ephemeral.

The language of rulers has often had very little in common with the language of the ruled. Latin remained a language of church and state long after the fall of the Western Roman Empire. While Latin did evolve, it did so at a much slower rate than the vernacular Vulgar Latin tongues that eventually formed the basis of languages such as French and Italian. The writing of European vernaculars proceeded at an erratic rate, and even when literature might have been written in them, law and religion were often slow to yield. We still read Chaucer's fourteenth-century works in the Germanic-Romance hybrid language of Middle English, but government and law only completed the switch to English in the fifteenth and sixteenth centuries. The Florentine Italian in which Dante wrote in the fourteenth century took centuries to become the uncontested language of ruling throughout the Italian peninsula.

What we know today as separate languages were once just waystations along a 'dialect continuum', in which the spoken language slowly transformed from village to village. Even today, we can still spot the traces of what was once a much more fluid linguistic landscape, as David Shariatmadari points out:

As the Rhine wends its way toward the North Sea, German is slowly but surely transformed into Dutch, via West Central German and Limburgish. Asking your name, the German says *wie heisst du*, the Limburger *hoe heits doe* and the Dutch speaker *hoe heet u*? From Norway to Denmark to Sweden, minute changes from one town to the next apparently add up to three different languages.[4]

The 'officialisation' of vernacular tongues made for more intrusive government and more exacting surveillance. In the age of Empire, the Jesuits were pioneers in learning and documenting the languages of those they sought to convert. Today, one of the most extensive language documentation resources, Ethnologue, is produced by a US-based Christian organisation called the Summer Institute of Linguistics, for the ultimate purpose of developing Bible translations into any tongue.

The development of the modern nation state has been marked by the standardisation and regulation of national languages. This was part of the process of Enlightenment, in which the search for linguistic purity became part of a wider process of attempting to find rational order in a chaotic world. The Académie Française, founded in 1635, began issuing dictionaries in the late seventeenth century and still plays a role in attempting to regulate the French language. Part and parcel of this process was the denigration of regional languages. National languages were often originally regional languages, raised to dominance by a mixture of deliberate efforts and natural selection. The unified Italian state that emerged in the nineteenth century turned what had previously been a prestige language of literature, based on Florentine Tuscan, into 'Italian'. The highly centralised French state that began to consolidate in the seventeenth century led to the triumph of the Île-de-France version of the Northern *Langues d'oïl*, and the eclipse of the southern *Langues d'oc.*

Standardisation usually involved disparaging 'non-standard' tongues. This process has proceeded at different rates and is tied into the wider extent of political centralisation. Compare the status of Occitan in France and Catalan in Spain. They are closely related languages, yet Catalan is a vibrant literary and administrative language spoken by millions, whereas Occitan is spoken by thousands and declining fast. Innumerable French languages have been disparaged as mere *patois* and many are on the brink of extinction.

As the old saw has it, 'a language is a dialect with an army'. That's not always strictly true; Catalonia has no army, even though independence activists might want one at some point. But a language that isn't enshrined in a state may also be highly vulnerable to those who would suppress it. During the fascist period in Spain, Catalan (together with other regional languages) was certainly not treated as a language, in part because Catalonia was a centre of armed resistance during the Civil War.

The concept of dialect assumes a standard version of a language from which it departs. In some respects that can be a self-fulfilling prophecy, as an official national language may reduce a rival variant to a small number of speakers. To classify something as a dialect can often be to collude in a process of forced centralisation and erasure.

All that said, while an official language can exacerbate regional inequalities and lead to the extinction of local cultures, its role in binding together disparate peoples into a national collective can be vital. When Indonesia declared independence from the Dutch in 1945, it had to somehow find a way to forge a nation out of inhabitants of thousands of islands, speakers of hundreds of languages and followers of disparate religions. The designation of a version of Malay spoken by a small percentage of the population as 'Indonesian' helped to ensure that no one linguistic group, such as speakers of Javanese, could dominate. As Benedict Anderson has famously argued, a nation is an 'imagined community' and the process of developing a language of administration can be a way in which disparate individuals and people can come to think of themselves as being part of the same overarching structure.[5]

The association with a nation can also ensure that a 'small' language survives. Because Latvian, Slovene and Icelandic are used in government, newspapers and universities, they are forced to develop vocabularies and registers for use in all areas of life. While most linguists will concur that any language can express 'anything' (albeit sometimes with a lot of clumsy circumlocutions) it is only by being used in a diversity of ways that a language will develop the breadth and depth to be able to confront any eventuality. When Maltese was the spoken language of the peasantry under a succession of foreign rulers, it always risked being extinguished. Now that it is an official EU language, it can speak bureaucratically. Even the more xenophobic forms of nationalism can be linguistically creative. Under Atatürk, post-Ottoman Turkish was deliberately purged of Arabic and Persian loanwords and its script was changed to Latin. The Turkish that resulted was one that was vibrant with linguistic novelty.

The Norwegian Message's twin

Ferrero did not create the modern world. They just live in it. They have little choice but to situate themselves in a world of nation states and official languages. The ever-changing Manuscript is the product of an ever-changing set of historical circumstances.[6]

Consider the Norwegian Message:

Advarsel, les og behold: Små deler kan sette seg fast i halsen eller nesen.

This is just one of two official Norwegians. And the Norwegian Message seems to have smothered its twin. The name of that twin is *Nynorsk*. The name of the murderous sibling is *Bokmål*.

Norway is a relatively young country. While a Norwegian kingdom existed in medieval times, from 1319 until 1905 Norway was in union with Sweden, then Denmark and then Sweden again, with only a brief period of independence in the early nineteenth century. While the nature of these unions was often 'personal', with a shared monarch but independent systems of government, Norwegian nationalism, as it developed in the nineteenth century, was keen to establish the separateness of the Norwegian nation.

Nationalism decrees that a nation must have a language. But what is 'Norwegian'? The language of the ruling class was a variant of Danish, a legacy of the union between the two kingdoms. The common people spoke a wide range of related tongues. As a sparsely populated country whose population centres were often inaccessible from each other for large parts of the year, there was (and still is) considerable dialectal diversity. Throughout the nineteenth century there was a long-running debate about the best approach to take in creating a distinctive Norwegian language. One was to nurture a Norwegianised version of Danish. The other, drawing on the work of the philologist Ivar Aasen in the 1840s, was to consolidate the most distinctive regional Norwegian dialects. The first approach led to the development of Bokmål, the second to Nynorsk.

While Norwegian governments did seek to encourage the unification of the two variants (known as *Samnorsk*), in the last few decades this attempt has been abandoned. Nynorsk is the minority form of Norwegian, with 10–15% of the population native speakers. Young people are exposed to both Nynorsk and Bokmål in school, although most of schooling takes place in one or the other. Municipalities can choose to adopt either standard as their official tongue (with some remaining neutral) although citizens can communicate with government in either of them. Nynorsk is more common in rural areas, although it does have a strong presence in Norwegian literature.

That the Message is in Bokmål doesn't mean that product packaging and other official texts never include Nynorsk in Norway itself. Pragmatically, though, the case for Bokmål's inclusion in the Manuscript is a strong one. It is the most popular of the two standards and Nynorsk speakers will understand it anyway. Placing both variants on the Manuscript would take away precious space and it's not as though Norwegians have fought and died for their preferred standard (although there has often been fierce debate).

Still, there's no getting away from Bokmål's similarity to Danish. This is the Danish Message:

Advarsel, læs og opbevar: Smådele kan sætte sig fast
i hals eller næse.

This is what the Message might look like in Nynorsk:

Åtvaring, les og ta vare på dette: Små delar kan setje
seg fast i halsen eller nasen.

The Nynorsk Message, while still recognisable from the
Danish Message, is a little more distinctive from it compared
to Bokmål. I consulted two academics for this translation
and they came up with broadly similar Nynorsk versions.
One of them, Dr Guy Puzey of Edinburgh University, did initially include *behald* ('keep') similar to the *behold* found in
the Bokmål version; but while he said that this is what many
Nynorsk users would do too, he also pointed out that other
users 'would avoid using too many words with a be- prefix (of
Low German origin), so they might write e.g. *ta vare på dette*
(more or less "hold on to this")'. Indeed, that is what the other
translator, Professor Lars Sigurdsson Vikør of the University of
Oslo, chose to include, although he pointed out that you might
sometimes find this phrase in Bokmål.

Even if the difference between Messages in closely-
related languages might seem slight on the page, they may
be much more distinctive when spoken. And even when the
differences come down to a few individual words, they might
take on an outsized significance to those who understand
those languages. The TV show *South Park* mercilessly ridi-
cules Canada on the basis that some Canadians pronounce
the word 'about' as 'aboot'. On such distinctions, identity itself
rests.

More siblings, more rivalry

I was reminded of the importance of minor distinctions when I received a translation of the Message into another language 'twin'. Albanian comes in many dialects, grouped into two main variants: Gheg and Tosk. Gheg dialects are historically spoken north of the Shkumbin River, which includes what is now Kosovo, and Tosk is spoken to the south. Unlike in Norway, there is only one standard version of Albanian and that is based on Tosk dialects. Even in Kosovo, written Albanian is usually Tosk Albanian. Understandably, the Albanian Message is in Tosk:

> KUJDES, LEXO DHE KUJTO: Pjesët e vogla mund të gëlltiten ose futen në rrugët e frymëmarrjes.

And this is what it would look like in Gheg:

> KUJDES, LEXO, KUJTO: Pjest e vogla mun t'gëlltiten ose futen n'rrugt e frymarrjes.[7]

When I posted the two Albanian versions on Facebook, a friend joked: 'It's hard to comprehend why they felt Gheg speakers would be able to make sense of the Tosk. That's the type of prejudice that leads to wars.' I laughed at this but I reminded him that neither of us actually knows how either version is pronounced or whether what we would consider tiny differences, Albanian-speakers would regard as of major importance. It's certainly true that some Kosovars have seen Tosk language domination as a sign of their emerging state being in thrall to Albania.[8] But if Tosk linguistic domination reflects a wider inequality between Albania and Kosovo, we cannot blame Ferrero for reinforcing it. As with Norwegian, the last thing the Scribes at Ferrero are likely to want is to have to include yet another language in the Manuscript.

The collapse of communism may have brought with it new opportunities and markets for Ferrero, but it also confronted the company with some tricky linguistic challenges. Part of that challenge was in working out how to cram more languages onto the Manuscript. Ferrero also had to navigate the tricky linguistic politics of the emerging post-communist nations. Bulgaria, Hungary, Poland and Romania posed no issues – they all had national languages and even some of their linguistic minorities helpfully spoke the language of other countries (such as Hungarians in Romania). Fortunately, according to the Codex, a warning message seems never to have been included for Czechoslovakia prior to the 'velvet divorce' into the Czech Republic and Slovakia in 1993. If so, Ferrero might have had a difficult choice to make as to whether to include both Czech and Slovak. By the second half of the 1990s, when separate Czech and Slovak Messages began to be included, the separation had been bedded in.

Here is the Czech Message once again:

UPOZORNĚNI, čtěte a uschovejte: Malé části by mohly být spolknuty nebo vdechnuty.

... and here is the Slovak Message:

UPOZORNENIE, prečítať a uchovať: Maléčasti by mohli byť prehltnuté alebo vdýchnuté.

The two languages are mutually intelligible and, while in pre-1939 Czechoslovakia, Czech tended to be the prestige language, with Slovak reduced to the status of a regional language, in the last decades of the state there was a higher degree of parity. While the standard languages are closely related, some Czech and Slovak dialects may be much tougher for speakers of the other to understand. Manuscript-wise, though, things have worked out quite harmoniously – due to the alphabetical order of the language codes CS and SK, there is one on each side of the Manuscript, meaning that Czechs and Slovaks who are too lazy to turn it over can easily find something they understand.

The Message and the collapse of Yugoslavia

I grew up ignorant of Yugoslavia. If I thought of it at all, it was as a country where people spoke something called Serbo-Croatian, although I was vaguely aware that there were other languages too. In the 1980s, my family had a Yugoslav *au pair* called Gordana. When the wars broke out in the 1990s we hadn't just lost touch, we never even knew if she was Serbian, Croatian, Bosnian or something else (she got back in touch via Facebook recently and it turns out she is Serbian).

The collapse of Yugoslavia from 1991 onwards was also a linguistic break-up. The country was never linguistically unified and a number of languages were used, officially and unofficially across its constituent republics. The 'cleanest' break was Slovenia, which achieved independence in 1991 after a ten-day war. Slovenia is over 80% Slovene, so the establishment of the state and its official language was relatively smooth. The dissolution of the rest of Yugoslavia was much messier.

What was, and sometimes still is, called Serbo-Croatian is known as a 'pluricentric' language. It is a Slavic tongue with multiple dialects consolidated into four mutually intelligible standard versions in four former-Yugoslavian republics

– Serbia, Croatia, Bosnia-Herzegovina and Montenegro. The practice of referring to these as separate languages did not start with the break-up of Yugoslavia. The four republics have their own histories and the differences are not confined to language; for example, Croatia is predominantly Catholic and Serbia predominantly Orthodox Christian. The collapse of Yugoslavia and the nationalism that fuelled the process made it desirable to emphasise the separateness of the languages.

According to the Codex, the first former-Yugoslavian language to appear on a Manuscript was Croatian in 1993 (two years after independence). Slovene made its first appearance in 1995, and 1996 saw the debut of Macedonian, the language of what is now called North Macedonia. Macedonian forms part of a 'dialect continuum' with Bulgarian and many Bulgarians see it as a dialect of the Bulgarian language.[9] Nonetheless, Macedonian and Bulgarian have remained separate on the Manuscript, although a close look shows their common features. Here is Macedonian:

ВНИМАНИЕ, ЧИТАЈ И ЗАЧУВАЈ: Ситните делови можат да бидат проголтани или вдишани.

And here is Bulgarian:

ВНИМАНИЕ, ПРОЧЕТИ И ЗАПАЗИ: Съдържа малки части, които могат да бъдат погълнати или вдишани.

1996 saw Serbian make its debut on the Manuscript. It was marked by the country code 'YU' for Yugoslavia as, at that point, the country still existed as a federal republic that included Serbia, Montenegro and Kosovo. But the Message was unmistakably Serbian as it was printed in Cyrillic. Serbian can be written in either Cyrillic or Latin whereas Croatian almost always uses Latin, with the Montenegrin and Bosnian variants of Serbo-Croatian also leaning more towards Latin. It is hard to say whether Ferrero decreed that Cyrillic be used so as not to inflame nationalist tensions, but there's certainly no mistaking this Message for Croatian:

> ПАЖЉИВО ПРОЧИТАТИ И САЧУВАТН: Играчку не давати деци млађој од 3 године да не би прогутала или удахнула ситне комадиће.

Serbian Cyrillic can be found on Manuscripts produced as late as 2004. From 2004 onwards, the Serbian Message has been printed in Latin script. Both languages coexist on the Manuscript to this day. Here they are together, first Serbian and then Croatian:

> UPOZORENJE, PROČITAJ I SAČUVAJ: Sitni delovi se mogu progutati ili udahnuti.

> UPOZORENJE, PROČITATI I SAČUVATI: Sitne dijelove moguće je slučajno progutati ili udahnuti.

There is no Bosnian or Montenegrin Message (although one Manuscript from 2008 did feature a Message, marked as Bosnian, that was in fact identical to Croatian). Despite three decades of separation, there is still no hiding from the similarities between Serbian and Croatian.

It is hard for me to know how best to relate to the apparently minor linguistic differences between Serbian and Croatian. As a language fan I celebrate nuanced difference and laud diversity. As someone who was horrified by the unspeakable suffering that accompanied the collapse of Yugoslavia, I can't help viewing the separation of Serbian and Croatian as a signifier of bloodshed. So I have some sympathy for the 'Declaration on a Common Language' issued in 2017 by a group of intellectuals from the four Serbo-Croatian republics.[10] The Declaration insists that there is a 'common standard language of the polycentric type', with four standard variants, and calls for 'freedom in dialectal and regional use' and an end to standardisation. Perhaps the recognition of dialectal diversity *within* the four languages would help to tame the stark separation of Serbian and Croatian and the rest. In other words, reconciliation in the former Yugoslavia might be best served by having *more* dialectally-variant Serbo-Croatian Messages. The current situation, where standardised versions of Serbian and Croatian stand in for the whole, may be a necessary compromise, but it is still an uncomfortable one.

The Moldovan–Romanian controversy

The most confusing relationship between Message languages is between Romanian and Moldovan. Both languages first found their way onto the Manuscript in 1996. Here is what the Romanian Message looked like then:

ATENȚIE, DE CITIT ȘI REȚINUT: Nu lăsați jucăria la indemâna copiilor sub 3 ani. Părțile mici pot fi înghițite sau inhalate.

And here is Moldovan:

ATEŃȚIE, CITIȚI ȘI PÂSTRAȚI: Jucariile nu se recomandă copiilor până la vârsta de 3 ani. Pentru sopiii mici existâa pericolul de a îrghiți jucârilile care pot nimeri în organele de mistuire sau respiratoare.

While the 'Warning, read and keep' section is quite similar, the remainder of the Moldovan Message is considerably longer than the Romanian. It translates as follows:

Attention, read and keep in mind: the toys are not recommended for children aged younger than 3 years old. For younger children there is the danger of swallowing the toys, that can then reach the digestive or respiratory organs.[11]

This seems to be a much less terse version of the Message. The overall message is the same, but the Message is not.

Romanian and Moldovan Messages coexisted on the Manuscript until 2014. From that year onwards, we have had a unified message marked as 'RO-MO':

ATENȚIE, DE CITIT ȘI REȚINUT: Părțile mici pot fi înghițite sau inhalate.

How is it that the two languages could be combined so seamlessly? The answer depends on whether you think that the Moldovan language actually exists.

The distinction between Moldova and Romania is primarily political and historical, rather than linguistic. The border between the two modern states is formed by the Prut and

Danube rivers, natural boundaries that have been highly convenient for world powers carving up territory.

In 1812, the Principality of Moldavia (which covered much of what is now Romania and Moldova and had become an Ottoman vassal state) was divided up, with the expanding Russian Empire taking the eastern half, which includes all of modern Moldova. Borders continued to change hands sporadically in the nineteenth and twentieth centuries, and part of Moldova was for a time incorporated into Romania prior to the Second World War. After the war, Moldova was a republic within the Soviet Union and declared independence in 1991 along with its other constituent republics.

Moldova has often been excluded from the development of Romanian nationalism, including the standardisation of the Romanian language, that took place in Romania proper. The Soviet years saw significant emigration into Moldova from elsewhere in the USSR, resulting in a large Russian-speaking minority. While the use of Romanian was permitted in the Soviet republic, in practice it was a low-status language, with Russian the language of social advancement, government and science. Romanian was also written in Cyrillic in the Moldovan SSR, whereas in Romania it was written in Latin script. This history did result in a Moldovan distinct from Romanian, but much of this distinctiveness had to do with its lack of use in formal contexts.[12]

Post-Soviet Moldova has been 'a country in a severe state of identity crisis, affecting both majority and minority ethnolinguistic groups'.[13] This identity crisis has taken violent form, with a brief civil war in 1992 leading predominantly Russian-speaking Transnistria, a strip of territory in the east of the country, to break away and declare independence (which is recognised only by Russia and other former Soviet Union breakaway states).

Amid this identity crisis, it is never clear whether the Moldovan language refers to Romanian as spoken in Moldova, a particular dialectal variety of Romanian, or a different language altogether. The 1991 Declaration of Independence stated that Romanian was the country's language but the 1994 constitution affirmed that 'The State language of the Republic of Moldova is the Moldovan language based on the Latin alphabet'.[14] It is ironic that the Moldovan national anthem is *Limba noastră*, which means 'our language'. The first verse explains:

> Limba noastră-i o comoară
> În adîncuri înfundată
> Un șirag de piatră rară
> Pe moșie revărsată.
>
> (Our language is a treasure
> That surges from deep shadows of the past,
> A necklace of rare gems
> That scattered all over the domain.)

Broadly speaking, to insist on the separateness of the Moldovan language today is to look towards Russia, rather than to Romania and Europe.[15] The most committed attempt to 'prove' Moldovan is a separate language was made by Vasile Stati, a Moldovan linguist, who published a Moldovan–Romanian dictionary in 2003. The project was widely met with ridicule, particularly in Romania, and not a small amount of anger. One contributor to an online symposium on the dictionary said of Stati:

'Aberration of the century' is just one of the many qualifications that the Moldovan–Romanian Dictionary received of Vasile Stati, a grotesque character, proud bearer of a flamboyant stupidity, doubled by impertinence.[16]

Over time, though, the centre of gravity of the Moldovan–Romanian controversy seems to have tilted further and further towards the consensus that there is only one language – called Romanian in Romania and Moldovan in Moldova. In 2013, Moldova's Constitutional Court declared that Romanian was the official language and that the Declaration of Independence takes precedence over the Constitution.[17] Also that same year, an Association Agreement with the EU was agreed, tying Moldova more closely into Europe and removing import duties on many goods. It doesn't seem to be a coincidence that Moldovan and Romanian were merged on the Manuscript in 2014, the year the agreement was signed.

Moldovan still haunts the Manuscript. The Message is still marked 'RO-MO' despite the fact that the International Standardisation Organisation retired the language code 'MO' for Moldovan as long ago as 2008. In October 2020, I bought a Kinder Surprise and, to my astonishment, found a separate Moldovan Message once again. This was on a separate manuscript included alongside the main Manuscript to warn of specific dangers from a particular toy.[18] Here is the Romanian message:

ATENŢIE, DE CITIT ŞI REŢINUT: Pentru motive igienice goliţi mereu jucăria după uz.

And Moldovan:

ATENȚIE, citește și păstrează: Pentru motive igienice, goliți întotdeauna jucăria după folosire.

The Codex suggests that this particular manuscript dates to no earlier than 2018, although the wording may have been used much earlier. The reason why Moldovan persists is probably just because specific warning manuscripts are updated less frequently than the principal Manuscript. Still, I yearn to see it again in Kinder Surprise Eggs. There is something about the desire to differentiate oneself linguistically in the face of overwhelming evidence to the contrary that I admire.

There is one version of Romanian that has never been included on the Manuscript, though. These days, Romanian/Moldovan written in Cyrillic is mostly found in Transnistria. Here is what it would look like:

Атенцие, де читит ши рецинут. пэрциле мичь пот фи ынгиците сауинхалате.[19]

Remember – the Message is mortal

It's easy to dismiss the ways in which human beings insist that similar languages are irreconcilably different as absurd or dangerous. There are many other examples in addition to the ones discussed in this chapter: Hindi and Urdu, differenti-ated not by their words but by script, religion and nation; the ambiguity of Flemish, sometimes just a synonym for Dutch in Belgium, sometimes a distinctive cluster of dialects spoken in Flanders. Language is never just language; it is wrapped up in religious, ethnic, national and individual identities.

English-speakers can afford the luxury of bewilderment at minor linguistic differences, because while vernacular

Englishes may differ substantially between each other, the standardised formal language is much more uniform. Even here, though, there would be problems if the Message included words that do differ. South Africans, for example, refer to a traffic light as a 'robot'. It is the English Message's good fortune that it doesn't happen to include words that are markers of cultural difference between English-speakers. I know that I go mildly berserk when I see Americans use the word 'Math'.

One of the finest satires of the absurdities of national and linguistic divides is China Miéville's novel *The City and the City*. The setting is the Eastern European twin city-states of Besźel and Ul Qoma. The two cities occupy the same space, but citizens of both are required to 'unsee' each other; if they fail or refuse to do so, they are disappeared by a mysterious power called 'Breach'. Both cities appear to have their own languages: Besź is written in Cyrillic; Illitan, the language of Ul Qoma, is written in Latin script. The practice of unseeing is facilitated by the visual differences encoded in the two alphabets and in wider stylistic differences in the look of the cities.

At one point in the book, the narrator and main protagonist, Inspector Borlú of the Besź police, is phoned by an Ul Qoman who is a 'unificationist' dedicated to merging the twin cities. The conversation includes this exchange:

> 'I'm not a political man. Listen, if you'd rather ...' I started the last sentence in Illitan, the language of Ul Qoma.
>
> 'This is fine.' He interrupted in his old-fashioned Illitan-inflected Besź. 'It's the same damn-faced language anyway.'[20]

What the reader isn't told is who is the deluded one in this conversation. The activist, who insists that the two languages are the same? Or the police officer who insists on the linguistic differences between Besź, Illitan and Illitan-inflected Besź? The answers are never given in the book. This allows the reader to simultaneously marvel at the extraordinary ability of humans to make subtle, meaningful distinctions and also the ways in which this can lead to a kind of madness.

I adore how the Manuscript enshrines minor linguistic differences as if they were insurmountable barriers to communication, even as I recognise that some of these differences are by-products of the worst human instincts. For Ferrero, deciding how much diversity to represent on the Manuscript is a difficult challenge with real consequences if they get it wrong. As they expand into new markets they are obliged to tread carefully; they cannot afford to alienate Serbians by calling their language Croatian, or Moldovans by calling their language Romanian.

Multinational corporations like Ferrero are often depicted as forces of global homogenisation. Yet they are sometimes required to bend and twist in the wind in order to adapt to the politics of particular territories. Ferrero will never be released from the obligation to pay attention to the shifting tectonic plates of language's substructure. An official language, an official nation state, an official international agreement; all of them are always provisional. We need to whisper in the ear of the Message, like the apocryphal slave did to the Roman Emperors on their day of triumph: 'Remember, you are mortal!' The dance of linguistic fragmentation and consolidation will never end.

Chapter 5

The spoken Message

When speakers of the same language cannot understand each other

In the previous chapter I showed how nationalism can turn modest linguistic differences into irreconcilable ones. One of the benefits of this process is that it forces official written language to conform more closely to the way users of the language actually speak. The effort to nurture the separate identity of Croatian compared to the rest of the Serbo-Croatian dialect continuum at least means that some of the nuances of specifically Croatian forms of the language will be respected. If Norwegians and Danes were to share an official, common language synthesised out of the multiple variants of both, it would likely end up as both useful and unloved.

The opposite also happens: speakers of mutually unintelligible languages may insist that they share a common language. That situation certainly benefits Ferrero as it reduces the number of languages they need to include on the Manuscript – and that is actually the situation they face with regard to Arabic. While there are two Messages written in Arabic script, one being Persian and the other Arabic, the single Arabic-language Message suffices for multiple countries: from Morocco to Bahrain, from Egypt to Yemen. This Message is written in what is known as 'Modern Standard Arabic', often referred to as الفصحى or *Fusha*, meaning 'eloquent':

العربية – إقرأ وإحفظ: لعبة غير مناسبة للأطفال الذين يقل سنهم عن 3 سنوات لانه يمكن إبتلاع أو إستنشاق الاجزاء الصغيرة.

Fusha, like all languages that use the Arabic script, is written from right to left. The Arabic Message does not announce itself using a language code (which would be 'AR') as do most of the rest of the Messages. Nor does it start with the word 'warning'. In fact the Message omits the word entirely. 'Read and keep' is preceded by something unique among all the Messages: the first word, العربية, Al-Arabiya, actually means 'Arabic'. It does not call it Al-Arabiya al-fusha, referring specifically to standard Arabic. Rather, the distinction between Fusha and other Arabics is elided.

The practice of eliding differences between Arabics is a major component of Arab linguistic identity and politics.[1] The *spoken* languages of Arabic-speaking countries vary to the point of mutual unintelligibility between some of them. A Moroccan Arab and a Yemeni Arab would have great difficulty in understanding each other's speech. Yet they would still share a common Arabic, at least if they were literate. Some vernacular Arabics that are closer to Fusha have a greater influence than others. Syrian, Levantine and Egyptian Arabics are often used in dubbing films and TV shows.

Most vernacular Arabics are rarely written and, when they are, it is more likely to be in informal modes of communication rather than official messages. One of the most distinct vernaculars is *Darija* or Maghrebi Arabic, spoken in North Africa. Here is what the Message would look like in the Moroccan variant of Darija (omitting the word Al-Arabiya that begins the standard Arabic Message):[2]

قرا واحفظ: اللعبة مامناسباش الدراري الصغار لي عندهم قل من ثلاثة ديال السنوات حيت ممكن يسرطوا ولا يستنشقوا الأجزاء الصغيرة.

Arabic is bound together by a common desire to remain connected to the Arabic of the Qur'an. Standard Arabic may therefore be grounded in the language of this holy text, but it has also evolved from it – as all languages do over time – and included necessary updates to its vocabulary to take into account modern developments. Muhammad himself spoke the Arabic variety of the western end of the Arabian peninsula, and even at the time there were other Arabics too, some of which became the basis of modern vernaculars. Standard Arabic tends to be influenced by the most powerful or influential Arabic society at the time. The question of which Arabic 'dialect' is closest to the standard is a contentious one that cannot be separated from regional rivalries.

One of the consequences of the coexistence of Fusha and other Arabics is that *diglossia* is normal in much of the Arab world. Diglossia refers to the situation that arises when a language community uses an everyday vernacular language alongside a 'high' variant of the language for specific situations, such as literature or official announcements. The nature of the diglossia may vary according to region, social class and other variables. For example, the distance between Fusha and the vernacular may be much greater among less-educated residents of a remote rural area when compared to a university-educated person from Damascus, Beirut or Cairo. On top of this diglossia, in some Arab countries other languages may be spoken as well, leading to 'polyglossia' or to 'code-switching' (where speakers switch constantly between languages in conversation). In Morocco, for example, French and various Berber languages exist in a complex relationship to both Fusha and Darija.

Diglossia means that it is perfectly possible that a speaker of a particular Arabic vernacular would use Fusha if they sought to warn someone formally, as the Message does. Perhaps they would even include a word for 'warning', which the Arabic Message inexplicably excludes. They might use انتبه, *Intebeh*, which features on red triangular road signs across the Arab world, warning of roadworks ahead. In fact, the Darija Message words for 'read and keep' are identical to Fusha. To switch into Fusha isn't necessarily to switch into an alienating official tongue, so much as into another register.

Arabic's 'others'

Even if diglossia means that speakers of mutually unintelligible tongues can nonetheless see themselves as part of the same language community, nationalist competition to create linguistic distinctions (that we saw in the previous chapter) is present here too. Pan-Arabism and pan-Islamism (both, ironically, subject to competition and conflict between nations, regions, ethnicities and sects as to what this unity actually means) create their own distinctions between insider and outsider. It's no coincidence that Maltese, a Semitic language related to Arabic, has always been written in Latin script, given the fervent Catholicism that has, historically, been a major component of Maltese identity. The following Maltese translation of the Message doesn't 'look' Arabic:

WISSIJA, aqra u aħżen: Ġugarelli mhux xierqa għal tfal taħt it-3 snin. Partijiet żgħar jistgħu jinbelgħu jew jingibdu bin-nifs.[3]

Hebrew is a fellow member of the Semitic language family, but its script could not be more different in its stolid blockiness (albeit, like Arabic, written right to left), as here in the official Hebrew Message:

אזהרה לקרוא ולשמור: הצעצוע לא מתאים לילדים מתחת לגיל 3 כי הם עלולים לבלוע או לשאוף את החלקים הקטנים.

After the expulsions and migrations that followed the independence of the state of Israel in 1948, the substantial Jewish communities that used to exist in the Arab world are mostly extinct (with the partial exception of much-reduced populations in Morocco and Tunisia). Jews in the Arab world often spoke or wrote in *Judeo*-Arabic. This was generally written in Hebrew script, an indication that to distinguish oneself religiously in Arab-speaking countries was also to distinguish oneself linguistically, even when one spoke Arabic. Here is a Judeo-Arabic translation of the Message:

ענדך! קראהא וחתאפّץ ביהא. אטטריפאת אצצגّאר יקדרו יצרטוהום מן לפّם וחתאאמן למנכّר.[4]

In Morocco, Algeria and some other North African countries, a number of Amazigh (Berber) languages are spoken. They are not part of the Semitic language family. While they are sometimes written in Latin scripts, there is also an ancient script called *Tifinagh*, which is visually light-years away from Arabic. This is what the Message would look like in one variant of Amazigh:

OₒO ⵜₒⵞEⴶⵜ, ⵞⵡ ⵡ Eⵔⵊ : ⵞⵥⵙⵉ ₒⵊⵊₒⵍⵍ ⵡⵡₒⵐ l 3 ⵥOⵣⵣₒOⵉ
ₒⵡ ⵔQEⵉ lⵞⵡ ₒⵡ Oⵞⵔⵞⵉ ⵜⵥⵞₒⵐOⵥⵐⵥⵉ ⵔⵞⵞⵥⵉⵥⵉ.[5]

Arabic script isn't just used to write Arabic or Semitic languages. With the spread of Islam, it became adapted to multiple other tongues unrelated to Arabic, as here in the Persian official Message:

هشدار، بخو انيد و نگهداريد: اجسام كوچك ممكن است بلعيده يا استنشاق شوند.

Part of the process of modernity in some non-Arab countries was the replacement of Arabic scripts with other scripts. Turkish, for example, switched from an Arabic script in 1928 as part of a wider set of radical language reforms. Here is the official Turkish Message:

DİKKAT, okuyun ve saklayın: Küçük parçalar yutulabilir veya nefes borusuna kaçabilir.

The Turkish switch to a Latin alphabet was motivated in part by a desire to rid the language of Persian and Arabic influences and was also a secularist statement. During the Soviet period, a host of Turkic and Persian Central Asian languages that had previously used an Arabic script were converted to Cyrillic. Following the collapse of the Soviet Union, some of them have transitioned away from Cyrillic to Latin. The Azerbaijani Message is in Latin script, but the conversion is recent enough that a Cyrillic Azerbaijani Message was used briefly in the late 1990s:

Хабәрдардарлыг, охујун вә әмел един. Ојунчаг 3 јашындан кичик ушаглар үчүн мәсләһәт көрүлмүр. Ојунчагын кичик һиссәләри нафәс вә гида органларына дүшә биләр.

So a commitment to Arabic may bind the Arab-speaking world together, but the ability of Arabic script to bind the Muslim world together is more variable. Commitment to a nation and a religion do not always go together. Arabic may connote the Qur'an, but it also connotes a particular national-ethnic group. Arabic both unites and divides.

Chinese and its others

Another Message language whose unifying characteristics may mask deeper divisions is Chinese. This is the only Message that is written in two different forms, one above the other. The first is in 'traditional' Chinese characters, as used in Hong Kong, Macau and Taiwan:

注意：請閱讀及保存 此玩具不適合三歲以下小孩，其中含細小配件，小心勿讓小孩吞食或吸入。

The other is in 'simplified' Chinese characters, in official use in the People's Republic of China and Singapore:

注意：请阅读及保存 此玩具不适合三岁以下小孩，其中含细小配件，小心勿让小孩吞食或吸入。

The Messages are identical in meaning and pronunciation, and most of the characters are identical too. If you look closer, some of them have fewer strokes: 請閱讀 (Qǐng yuèdú, or 'please read') compared to 请阅读. Simplified Chinese characters were created by the communist government in the 1950s and 60s to facilitate progress towards mass literacy. Literacy in Chinese requires knowledge of 2,000–4,000 characters and there are tens of thousands more (not all of them in current use).

Although I learned some spoken Mandarin Chinese in the early 1990s, I never learned to read or write it. At some point I internalised a commonly-told tale: that Mandarin is a version of the dialect spoken in Beijing; across China there are multiple dialects spoken, many of them mutually unintelligible; yet whether or not a Chinese person can speak or understand spoken Mandarin, they can all read it, as the characters can simply be mapped onto dialect words. This story blew my mind. Imagine a country where people spoke a plurality of tongues yet everyone could read the same language! My visits to China in the 1990s only encouraged me to believe in the story. When I spoke to someone and I didn't understand a particular word, they would often sketch out the character on their hand. Clearly, everyone in China was used to using Chinese characters as a common 'tongue'.

As I belatedly discovered, this story is a massive oversimplification, albeit not completely wrong. In fact, I could have worked that out for myself if I had thought a bit harder. For every Chinese dialect to map perfectly onto written Mandarin, it would mean that not only each word would have an exact equivalent in every dialect, the word order, syntax and grammar would also have to be the same in every dialect too. Now that would truly be astonishing! But it's not true ...

The term 'Mandarin' is used in English to describe the language that has been, since the medieval period, the language of the 'Mandarins' who ran the Chinese state. While variants of Mandarin were spoken over large swathes of China, it was the dialect of the state capitals, formerly Nanjing and then Beijing, that came to define what Mandarin was and is. It can also be called 'standard Chinese' or 普通话, *Pǔtōnghuà*, 'common speech'.

Pǔtōnghuà is different to Fusha Arabic in that many people do speak it on an everyday basis. At the same time, China is similar to Arab countries in that a great variety of Chinese languages are spoken (as well as minority languages from families unrelated to Chinese) but not necessarily written. These languages are grouped into families such as Yue (whose best-known variety is Cantonese) and Wu (of which Shanghainese is a member). While some of these do have written traditions and use the Chinese character system with some local variations, these days writing is usually confined to colloquial registers. In Hong Kong, for example, Cantonese is sometimes used in newspaper adverts but government announcements are generally in standard Chinese. So while speakers of multiple Chinese languages can generally read the same texts in standard Chinese, that isn't so much because all Chinese languages are written the same way, but because standard Chinese is the dominant written form. Depending on the context, written and spoken Chinese may have a diglossic relationship, although the mass media and the centralisation of the Chinese state means that standard Chinese is understood much more widely than ever before.

When I asked a Cantonese speaker (based in Hong Kong) to translate the Chinese Message into written Cantonese, she didn't immediately understand what I was getting at. I sent her the Message in traditional Chinese and she replied 'the text that you showed above is already in Cantonese (traditional Chinese) which is used in Hong Kong'. This is perhaps how the story that all Chinese dialects use the same characters gets around. It suggests a diglossia, at least in Hong Kong, so deep that it is difficult to distinguish what is Cantonese and what is standard Chinese. I had to make clear that what I meant was the written form of the Cantonese language itself. This is what she came up with:[6]

請注意呢個玩具唔適合三歲以下嘅幼童，裏面有細小嘅配件，小心唔好俾佢哋吞食同埋吸入。

Chinese is incredibly difficult to learn to read and write – even for native speakers – and this creates formidable challenges to speakers of unrelated languages.[7] It is the complete disconnection of Chinese characters from the sounds of the language that causes confusion to foreigners seeking to understand the interrelationships between the various Chinese languages. But it also binds Chinese people together in a way similar to Arabic. The collective decision to decouple spoken from written language helps to create a sense of commonality across vernacular language barriers.

The flip side of this sense of commonality is that it can reinforce the marginality of citizens of China who are not ethnically Chinese. Take the language of the Uyghur people, spoken by millions in China's western province of Xinjiang. Their Turkic language, written in a Persian-Arabic script, is a visual sign of their difference from the Chinese majority and their language; a reminder of the hardships they are facing under Chinese repression. To write the Message in Uyghur is to remind ourselves that Chinese is not the language of all citizens of China:

مۇنداق.ئاگاھلاندۇرۇش: ئوقۇك ۋە ساقلاپ قويۇك: بۇ ئويۇنچۇق 3 ياشتىن توۋەن بالىلارغا ماس كەلمەيدۇ. سەۋەبى، كىچىك زاپچاسلىرى يۇتۇۋېتىلىشى مۇمكىن.[8]

Mandarin and other Chinese languages can actually be written phonetically, using a Latin script. There are various systems for this, the most popular being Pinyin. For a speaker of English, it has its idiosyncrasies – 'c' represents a 'ts' sound, for example – but one of its great advantages is that it includes diacritics to mark the four tones. Transliteration is invaluable to learners of Chinese (including schoolchildren learning to write in China) and I found it easy and straightforward to read when I took Chinese classes. In Pinyin, the Message looks something like this:

Zhùyì: Qǐng yuèdú jí bǎocún cǐ wánjù bù shìhé sān suì yǐxià xiǎohái, qízhōng hán xìxiǎo pèijiàn, xiǎoxīn wù ràng xiǎohái tūnshí huò xīrù.

Pinyin and other transliteration systems turn Chinese into a set of sounds to be spoken. When adapted to regional Chinese languages, transcription also makes their difference from Mandarin visible. If all forms of Chinese were written in phonetic scripts, Mandarin would simply be one Sinitic language among others, albeit one that was the dominant language of the Chinese state and the vernacular of the majority of its population. The cultural loss, though, would be incalculable. The wonder of Chinese characters and the extraordinary effort that millions of people put in to learning them requires an acceptance of their 'cost'. Perhaps that is why the commitment to Chinese characters remains strong even at a time when modern communication methods have led to necessary compromises. Typing on a phone or computer is obviously easier in some sort of alphabet and there was a time when Chinese computing required a Latin script. These days, though, one common method by which Chinese speakers text on their phone is to use a predictive text method whereby you type in Pinyin or similar and the screen displays a list of characters to choose from.

Writing and sound

The disconnection between the languages that Arabs and Chinese people speak and the languages they read and write is only a more radical version of the situation not just in English, but in most languages. Writing rarely manages to capture the nuances of spoken languages in their entirety. That's not just true of a language like English where spelling is obviously full of inconsistencies and bizarre formulations. Even more phonetic writing systems can struggle in dealing with such things as regional accents.

Rules of spelling are a kind of collective delusion that the sounds that come out of our mouth can be pinned down. Speakers of a language that is rarely written, or where the speaker is literate in a different language, may find writing it exceptionally challenging since they are cut off from this delusion. For example, in commissioning translations of the Message, I received versions in Dari (a variant of Persian spoken in Afghanistan) and Rusyn (a Slavic language) where the translators freely admitted they had no idea how to actually write them. Transliterating writing from one script to another is fraught with difficulty and without a consensus as to how to do it, what results is a form of anarchy. Hebrew has no universally accepted system to transliterate into Latin script and I have seen the festival of חֲנֻכָּה written as Chanukah, Hanukkah, Ḥanukah and Hanoukah.

There are writing systems that transcribe what you actually hear more closely. Shorthands, for example, record the sounds the speaker makes. They are written for the benefit of the person doing the writing and are only ever read by others in certain limited circumstances (such as in law courts). This is what the Message looks like in the Gregg shorthand system:[9]

Professional linguists often resort to a specialist writing system to nail down the intricacies of representing sound accurately. The best known of these is the International Phonetic Alphabet (IPA). IPA works as a kind of 'grid', in which 107 letters, 31 diacritics, and 19 other signs can be combined to specify individual 'phonemes' (sonic units) with a high degree of precision.[10]

I don't write IPA with any confidence, although I can read it to a degree. So I used an online service to transliterate the English Message into IPA, for both the British and US pronunciations.[11] Here is the British one:

wɔːnɪŋ, riːd ænd kiːp: tɔɪ nɒt ˈsjuːtəbl fɔː ˈʧɪldrən ˈʌndə 3 jɪəz. smɔːl pɑːts maɪt biː ˈswɒləʊd ɔːr ɪnˈheɪld.

And the US version:

wɔrnɪŋ, rid ænd kip: tɔɪ nɑt ˈsutəbəl fɔr ˈtʃɪldrən ˈʌndər
3 jɪrz. smɔl pɑrts maɪt bi ˈswɑloʊd ɔr ɪnˈheɪld.

IPA manages to bring out the ways in which standard US and British English pronunciation differ (although particular British and American accents would be different again), especially the differences between the vowels in the word 'read' ('riːd' and 'rid'). It isn't perfect, though, and other systems have been proposed that identify even more minute differences between similar-sounding phonemes.[12]

In the (vanishingly unlikely) event that IPA or a shorthand system were to be used to replace all the world's writing systems, creating something like the Manuscript would be an even more challenging task than it is already. One of the advantages to the imprecision that all the Message scripts possess is that they cover up differences in accent and intonation. At the moment, the English Message could be voiced in a Scottish, Irish or London accent with no real problems.

If all of humanity used IPA, we would have the worst of all worlds: we would lose the beloved idiosyncrasies of writing systems that express who we are as people and we would also fall prey to endless claims about which minor variation in phonology is the correct one. In any case, even when a script like IPA closely approximates the sounds of spoken languages, it cannot easily represent other features of speech such as stress.

We can all become unstuck if we forget that writing is not the same as speech. Texting causes particular problems as it has the immediate, unedited quality of speech but without the ability to convey tone accurately. That's why some have suggested an emoji for sarcasm and irony. Not that I have any interest in such things ☺.

Idiolects and registers

Even those who speak standardised dialects cannot help but speak in their own *idiolect*; the bundle of vocabulary, grammar, pronunciation, tone and so on that is unique to each individual. There is a whole field of forensic science, known as forensic linguistics, that attempts to identify suspects by their written and spoken idiolects alone. The Unabomber, Ted Kaczynski, was identified when his brother tipped off law enforcement when he recognised the bomber's distinctive style in an anonymous essay.

It is difficult for us to acknowledge our own idiolects unless, like me, you spend a lot of time writing and speaking in public. I know that I overuse words like 'but', 'yet' and 'however' and that I cannot get the stress right in the word 'innovative'. Those who speak languages that are rarely written might find it easier to recognise their idiolect compared to those of us who claim to speak and write a standardised language. For example, the person who supplied me with a Swiss-German translation of the Message (which is diglossic in Switzerland with standard German) stated that the translation was in 'my own idiolect of Swiss-German'.

Diglossia might be more obvious for speakers of Arabic and Chinese, but a degree of diglossia is widespread. Even when a language community shares a common vocabulary, grammar and pronunciation, it is normal for us to speak in different 'registers' in different settings. Take swearing. I wouldn't swear in an official letter to a government department, or when I teach. I might swear in a book I am writing but only after careful consideration of whether this will compromise the unwritten rules of the language sub-community I am seeking to bloomin' well reach. I do swear like a trooper with family and friends, but *how* I do so depends on the nature of the relationship, the context in which I do it and the subject of the conversation. The nature of the register I adopt is fluid. For a number of years, I ceased swearing at home unless my kids were out of earshot. Now they are older, I have loosened my restraint.

Adopting particular registers in particular settings is inevitable in societies where we are likely to meet new people or people we know only slightly. Any kind of division of labour is likely to lead those who share in a common activity to, at the very least, develop a specialist jargon. Even societies that lack such differentiation, such as nomadic or hunter/gatherer peoples, may develop particular registers and vocabularies to use at particular times or occasions.

The Message adopts the register of official, restrained, impersonal and above all *written* communication. The Message was not designed to be spoken. At the same time, it cannot help but be heard as speech, at least in readers' minds. Written language can be re-contextualised in ways unanticipated by the authors of a message. If I were to read the Message out loud to a crowd of 30,000 people at a heavy metal festival, it would enter a very different register – that, presumably, of a bizarre attempt at humour with an uncomprehending mass audience.

How might the Message be adapted into different registers? Here is how I would speak it if I were a supermarket manager making an announcement over a tannoy to customers:

Shoppers who purchase Kinder Surprise Eggs should be aware that the toys are not suitable for children under 3 years old as they contain small parts that could be swallowed or inhaled.

If I were serving behind the counter of a small corner shop, I might say the following to a customer who had just bought a Kinder Surprise Egg:

Just so you know, those shouldn't be given to kids under 3 years old. They have little parts that they can swallow. Mind how you go.

If I saw the purchaser actually give the Egg to a kid who seemed to be under 3, I might say:

Woah! Sorry but those shouldn't be given to toddlers. They could choke on the parts.

And if I were me, and I saw a member of my family giving a Kinder Surprise Egg to a toddler, I might say:

What are you doing? I wrote an entire book on the warnings in Kinder Surprise Eggs and now you're giving one to a toddler? What's wrong with you?

The message in space

One of the most impressive abilities that we humans have is to switch between registers in the blink of an eye. The terse, official register of the Message could in principle be incorporated into conversation. While it would be odd to do this, there are other contexts in which registers can switch with great rapidity.

One of these is space flight. 'Astronaut talk' is information-rich and condensed. We are used to hearing a similar kind of talk on aeroplanes when we hear instructions to the crew such as 'cabin crew, doors to manual and cross-check'. Astronaut talk is all business. Yet astronauts also chat like everyone else and, on space flights, what results is a rapid-fire switching between astronaut talk and regular chatting.

We can see this switching in action on the following NASA transcript of the first minute and fifteen seconds of Apollo 17's mission to the Moon, at 12:33am on December 7, 1972.[13] Note that lines marked 'onboard' were heard only in the spacecraft itself:

000:00:00 Robert Overmyer (Capsule Communicator, in charge of communication with crew from mission control): ... lift-off.

000:00:01 Gene Cernan (Commander): Roger. The clock has started. We have yaw.

000:00:05 Robert Evans (Command Module Pilot) (onboard): Woo-hoo!

000:00:08 Overmyer: Clear of the tower.

000:00:10 Cernan: Roger; tower. Yaw's complete. We're into roll, Bob.

000:00:13 Overmyer: Roger, Geno. Looking great. Thrust good on all five engines.

000:00:17 Cernan: Okay, babe. It's looking good here.

000:00:21 Cernan: Roll is complete. We are pitching.

000:00:28 Jack Schmitt (Lunar Module Pilot) (onboard): Wow woozle!

000:00:29 Cernan (onboard): Okay, babe. Let's check the angles.

000:00:31 Evans: Thirty seconds. We're going up. Man, oh, man!

000:00:34 Cernan: Thirty seconds, and 17 is Go.

000:00:37 Overmyer: Roger, 17. You're Go.

000:00:45 Evans (onboard): Okay, 1 minute and 68 degrees.

000:00:47 Cernan (onboard): Okay.

000:00:48 Schmitt (onboard): Everything looks great over here, Gene.

000:00:49 Cernan (onboard): Okay. Okay, stand-by for Max – coming through Max Q. We'll be at 68 degrees.

000:00:57 Schmitt (onboard): … Okay.

000:00:59 Overmyer: 17, stand by for Mode 1 Bravo.

000:01:01 Overmyer: Mark. Mode 1 Bravo.

000:01:03 Cernan: Roger. 1 Bravo; we're Go at 1 minute.

000:01:06 Overmyer: Roger, Gene. You're looking great. Right on the line.

000:01:09 Cernan (onboard): Okay, we got the RCS command.

000:01:10 Overmyer: 17, you are feet wet – feet wet.

000:01:12 Cernan: Roger. Feet wet.

000:01:14 Evans (onboard): Man, this thing shakes like a son-of-a-gun.

000:01:15 Cernan (onboard): Yes, that's Max Q. Wait until we get out of Max Q.

This short segment of talk is a switchback of constantly-shifting registers. There are moments of truncated astronaut-speak where messages are boiled down to their essentials, such as 'We have yaw', '17 is Go' and 'Mark. Mode 1 Bravo'. There are moments where information and instructions are passed on in a slightly less abbreviated way, such as 'The clock has started' and 'Let's check the angles'. There are moments of controlled reassurance that all is well – 'You're looking great. Right on the line'. There are moments of joy and exhilaration, mixed with fear – 'Wow woozle!', 'Man, this thing shakes like a son-of-a-gun'.

There are also moments when different registers combine in peculiar ways. Cernan adds an affectionate 'Babe' to his terse 'Okay' (from the rest of the transcript it appears to be a term he uses repeatedly). Towards the end of the segment, the crew are told that they are 'feet wet' and Cernan acknowledges this with the terse astronaut-speak 'Roger. Feet wet'. This is a term borrowed from naval aviation (Cernan and Overmyer were both naval aviators), referring to flight over the sea, meaning that the craft had moved off the coast of Florida. An informal insider term is transformed here into a formal designation.

Rapid switching between registers allows us to leaven structured and formal situations with a dose of intimacy. At other times, a highly restricted register creates a kind of 'container' around it to exclude extremes of emotion and panic. On the Apollo 13 mission, when commander Jim Lovell announced 'Houston, we've had a problem', his next line is simply, 'We've had a Main B Bus Undervolt', to which mission control responds: 'Roger. Main B Undervolt.'

At times though, no linguistic container can work and our primal fears and emotions burst through. On January 27, 1967, the crew of Apollo 1, Gus Grissom, Ed White and Roger Chaffee, were conducting a pre-launch rehearsal on the launchpad prior to their intended February 21 launch date. They were locked in their capsule, which was filled with pure oxygen, when an electrical fault caused a fire to break out. There was no cool, clipped information-sharing with mission control as the crew tried and failed to escape. The recording of their words was garbled and NASA's transcription offers various alternatives, but what isn't in doubt is that their final words were screamed rather than spoken. Here is one interpretation:[14]

> Fire!
> [scuffling sounds]
> We've got a fire in the cockpit!
> [...]
> We've got a bad fire ... We're burning up!

There is a final scream or cry of pain. Then silence. With pain unbearable, with fear total, with all hope gone, language collapses into the purity of a scream.

The Message exists to prevent pain; to ensure the Egg is a source of carefully-controlled play, rather than uncontrolled panic. Official, Message-type language seeks to keep the chaos and emotion of the world under control, to ensure it is held at bay. Much of the time, that is useful and helpful. But there is also a kind of denial at work here as well; denial of the fact that language and the world which it describes is much less controllable than we would like it to be.

Onward to liberation

In the last few chapters I have attempted to show how the Message is a much more unstable thing than it first appears.

We have seen how the Message might not be quite as clear as Ferrero intended it to be. We have seen that the Manuscript does not, as it first appears, represent a series of identical translations into a series of entirely separate languages. We have seen how the standardised languages in which the Messages are written have histories that sometimes include the marginalisation or suppression of rival tongues. We have seen how some of the Messages are in languages that are rarely spoken as they are written. And finally we have seen how the Message is written in just one of the many linguistic registers that we use every day.

In the rest of this book, I intend to go much further. I want to imagine a different kind of Message. I want to test the limits of the constraining language of the Message and explore the boundaries between sense and nonsense, between control and its lack. I want to show how the Message is built on sand.

It's time to *liberate* the Message.

Part

Liberating the Message

Chapter 6

Filling in the gaps

Liberation through love

Liberating language is the job of the language fan. As the writer Lane Greene argues, there is a widespread tendency to try to 'tame' language; to enforce clear rules and set standards.[1] While Greene is optimistic that efforts at taming language will ultimately fail, I am less sanguine. If we want language to stay wild and untameable, we are going to have to work at doing so. By treating language as something to play with and subvert, the language fan preserves its wildness.

Of course, I love the Manuscript on its own terms and I celebrate its accidental beauty. This love, though, is part of the process of liberation, because the Message and the Manuscript *were not designed to be loved.* And it is this deliberate lovelessness that is part of the problem. There is something about utilitarian language, designed purely to do a job, that negates the thrilling possibilities and aesthetic delights that language affords. And when such language is confined to the page, there is little possibility of doing what the crew of Apollo 17 did and leavening its hardness by impishly interspersing informal talk. The Message is designed to be inert, lifeless. This is the death of language.

For all my love of the Manuscript's linguistic cornucopia, part of its danger lies in its plurality. The reader, searching for the Message in their own language, might be forgiven for thinking, 'Look how many languages there are in the world!' They may find all their officially-mandated presumptions reinforced – that Croatian and Serbian, Danish and Norwegian, Czech and Slovak are completely different from each other; that all Arabs speak Message Arabic, that all Chinese speak Message Chinese. The Manuscript's orderly world may not be linguistically homogeneous, but it suppresses the disorderliness of language nonetheless.

Ferrero fashioned Messages out of standardised versions of selected languages. They have no choice but to respect the official standards for the countries whose markets they are seeking to reach. There is nothing to stop anyone else from fashioning the same Message out of different languages, including nonstandard ones. In fact, I have already done this a number of times in this book. I am going to go much further, though, and present translations of the Message in many more languages, including some that would never be used for this purpose.

The website Omniglot collects translations of the sentence 'My hovercraft is full of eels'.[2] This is an allusion to Monty Python's 'Dirty Hungarian Phrasebook' sketch, in which a hapless Hungarian, played by John Cleese, attempts to use this faulty phrasebook to buy a pack of cigarettes from an English tobacconist. The Hungarian tries to ask for matches only to recite 'My hovercraft is full of eels' at the bewildered tobacconist. It is, of course, a lot of fun to read translations of that message into the Swedish Westrobothnian dialect ('Flyjgmaschijna minn jer full utå åLan') or into Lao ('ມີຍານໂຮງເຕັມ ຢູ່ໃນເຮືອພັດລົມຂອງຂ້ອຍ'). But the sentence itself, while grammatically correct, is unlikely to ever be needed in the real world. (To be even more pedantic, Cleese's accented English in the sketch is faux-Slavic, rather than Hungarian.)

The Message is a naturally occurring piece of writing and, as such, to translate it into multiple languages isn't just to have fun

– although it certainly is that – it is also to imagine a world set up in a very different way than it is at the moment. Liberating the Message means imagining a world whose linguistic politics are very different to our own. This will be a highly 'unnatural' exercise – and that's precisely the point. Translations of the Message into languages such as Ancient Sumerian or Jamaican Creole (which I will present in future chapters) can help us to question the naturalness of the Manuscript. In doing so, we might be able to look at the world with new eyes.

The liberators

The process of finding translators was social and sometimes intimate. I approached friends, friends of friends, vague acquaintances, academics and language activists. Here is an example of the kind of email I sent, in this case requesting a translation into Rumantsch (a Romance language spoken in Switzerland):

> Dear [name redacted]
> I am a sociologist and writer based in London. I am writing to ask whether you might be able to give some assistance for a book I am working on.
>
> I am contracted to write a book for Icon Books that will hopefully come out towards the end of 2021. The book will be a celebration of linguistic diversity, designed with the general reader in mind, with an outwardly gimmicky premise: For years I have been fascinated by the multilingual warning messages found in Kinder Surprise Eggs. These come in nearly 40 languages. In 2018, I recorded a podcast on the BBC Boring Talks series on the subject – https://www.bbc.co.uk/programmes/p067kw4x

I had some fun during the first lockdown this year commissioning dozens of new translations of the warning message and I have collated them here – https://medium.com/a-lockdown-miscellany/ kinder-egg-linguistics-an-update-daf98d625b37

I have found or commissioned translations in every European official language – except for Rumantsch. Might you be able to assist me by providing a translation into Rumantsch? Or perhaps refer me to someone who could? I would, of course, give full credit.

The message for translation reads as follows:

> WARNING, read and keep: Toy not suitable for children under 3 years. Small parts might be swallowed or inhaled.

I would be very grateful for any help you can give me.

Best wishes

Keith Kahn-Harris

Emails such as this were often effective. Indeed, I received many warm and enthusiastic responses. The translators often just 'got' my project. Then again, I didn't actually tell them too much about it, which perhaps helped as they could interpret my request in their own way. I like to think that they spotted that I was a language fan and maybe they were members of the same tribe or were at least fans of their own languages. Anyway, these translators were not beholden to anyone, even to me. The translations they produced are not interchangeable with each other; they do not conform to the same requirements that Ferrero are bound by. Those who produced them were mostly professional translators. Indeed, some worked with languages that are rarely even written down, let alone translated into. They are all liberated translations from liberated translators.

Filling in the European gaps

So where do we start? How about with Icelandic:

> Varúð, lesið og geymið: Leikfangið hentar ekki börnum undir þriggja ára aldri. Smáhlutir gætu lent í munni eða öndunarfærum.[3]

Viewing a translation of the Message into Icelandic might not seem like much of a liberation, but it's a first step on the road to filling in some of the 'gaps' in the Manuscript. Icelandic is excluded from the Manuscript despite Kinder Surprise Eggs being sold in the country (the Message on the foil wrapper of Icelandic Eggs appears to be printed in Norwegian and Danish).[4] It is one of the few European countries not to have a Message in at least one of its official languages, it is the only Nordic or Scandinavian country not to have its own Message, and the only country in the European Free Trade Association with no Message.

Despite the Manuscript appearing to be a monument to European linguistic diversity, there are all sorts of absences. The EU has 24 official working languages. Citizens of EU states are entitled to communicate with EU institutions in any of these languages, EU legislation is translated into all of them and members of the European Parliament can use any of them when addressing it. Two official EU languages are missing from the Manuscript: Maltese and Irish. The reasoning behind their omission may be that English is co-official in Malta and Ireland and that monoglot speakers of either language are few. Indeed, the EU has had to postpone ensuring that absolutely all legislation is translated into Irish due to a lack of qualified translators. Still, the absence must be put right. In the previous chapter I included the Maltese Message and here is the Irish Message:

Fógra, léigh agus coinnigh: Níl an bréagán seo oiriúnach do pháisti faoi bhun 3 bliain. D'fhéadfaí píosaí beaga a shlogadh nó a análú.[5]

Ferrero did not include Lëtzebuergesch, the language of the Grand Duchy of Luxembourg, the home of its corporate headquarters. The exclusion is understandable as this Germanic language is co-official with French and German in Luxembourg and residents tend to be multilingual. Luxembourg itself has only recently woken up to its native linguistic treasure. It has been co-official since 1984 and its written tradition, while modest, is growing. A Lëtzebuergesch Message strikes a modest blow for those who would wish to liberate Luxembourg from being an international 'non-place', into a distinctive country with its own specific traditions:

Opgepasst, liesen, an haalen: Des spillsaach as net geduet fir Kanner enert 3 joer. Kleng stecker kennen verschleckt oder inhaleiert gin.[6]

Outside the EU, Switzerland has a Message in three of its official languages – French, German and Italian – but not in its fourth, Rumantsch. Rumantsch is primarily spoken in the canton of Grisons, with 50,000–70,000 speakers (less than 1% of the Swiss population). It is divided into a number of dialects, together with an official standardised dialect known as Grischun. The Rumantsch Message (here provided in Grischun), demonstrates its membership of the Romance language group:

> ATTENZIUN, per leger e tegnair en salv: il termagl n'è betg adattà per uffants sut 3 onns. Las parts pitschnas pudessan vegnir traguttidas u inhaladas.[7]

Another European country with no Message in its official language is Andorra. That language is Catalan and variants of the language are also official languages in the Spanish autonomous communities of Catalonia, Valencia and the Balearic Islands. With over 4 million native speakers, Catalan is more widely spoken than some of the Message languages, including Estonian, Slovene and Latvian. It certainly has the ability to communicate 'officialese'. Teresa Labourdette, the translator of the Catalan Message, actually offered two versions, the second in an even more formal register:

> ADVERTÈNCIA, llegeix i guarda: Joguina no adequada per a nens de menys de 3 anys. Es podrien empassar o aspirar les parts petites.

> PERILL, llegir i guardar: Joguina no apta per a infants de menys de 3 anys. Peces petites que podrien empassar-se-les o inhalar-les.

Gaps in the Former Soviet Union

Looking east, there are three official languages of Soviet successor states into which, to my knowledge, the Message has never been translated.

The first is Belarusian, which is co-official with Russian in Belarus:

Увага, прачытайце і захавайце: цацка не прызначана для дзяцей ва ўзросце да 3 гадоў. Дробныя часткі могуць быць праглынутыя ці ўдыхнутыя.[8]

Despite bearing the name of the state, Belarusian's status is fragile. Although formally co-official, in practice Russian has become dominant as the state has forged close ties with its powerful neighbour. Belarusian's decline is such that some have classified it as endangered.[9]

The Tajik language is, in contrast, the sole official language of the former Soviet Republic of Tajikistan, although Russian is constitutionally 'the language of communication between the nationalities' and all nations in the Republic 'have the right to freely use their native language'.[10] Tajik is closely related to Persian, part of a dialect continuum that includes Dari, widely spoken in Afghanistan. The language is still written in Cyrillic, rather than Arabic-Persian script as it was until the 1930s:

Хушдор, хонед ва нигоҳ доред: ин бозича барои кӯдакони то 3 сола мувофиқ нест. Тафсилотхои хурдро метавонанд фурӯ баранд ё ба рохи нафас ворид кунанд.[11]

A Tajik transition back to a Persian-Arabic script might happen at some point, given that it would 'reunite' the language with its wider Persian family. For Turkmen, the language of Turkmenistan, a similar transition has already happened. The

Turkmen Cyrillic script lasted past independence until 1993, when it was replaced by a Latin script. The Turkmen Message recalls Turkish with its cedillas and umlauts:

> ÜNS BERIŇ, okaň we ýatda saklaň: Bu oýnawaç üç (3) ýaşdan kiçi çagalar üçin laýyk görülmeýär. Ýuwutmak ýa-da dem alyş ýoly bilen içine gidip biljek ownuk bölejikler bardyr.[12]

Uzbek, the language of Uzbekistan, is also a Turkic language, however it comes from a branch more distant to Turkmen and Turkish. This is reflected in its Latin-based script, to which it reverted from Cyrillic in 1992, which lacks the diacritics found in Turkish. This is from the outside of a Kinder Surprise purchased in Russia in 2020:

> Ehtiyot bo'ling: o'yinchoq 3 yoshdan kichik bolalarga mo'ljallanmagan, mayda qismlar yutib yuborilishi yoki nalas yo'llariga tiqilib qolishi mumkin. Kattalar nazorati tavsiya qilinadi.

Mongolia was not a part of the former Soviet Union, but it was a closely aligned satellite and Cyrillic came to be the main script in which the Mongolian language is written. While it faces competition today from Mongolian and Latin scripts, Cyrillic remains commonly used:

> Анхаар. Унш бас хадгал. Энэ тоглоом нь 3 нас хүрээгүй хүүхэдэд аюултai. Жижиг хэсэгүүдийг зальгах ба хоолойд тээглэх аюултай.[13]

Following the breakup of the Soviet Union, a number of regions within its constituent republics themselves declared independence from the newly independent states. One of these is Abkhazia, a slice of Georgia on the Black Sea that is only recognised as independent by Russia and a few other states. Abkhazian has been elevated to the status of a national language. The language is Caucasian but written in a modified Cyrillic script:

> Агәеантҵара! Уаҧхьаны итҩәахы: Ари ахәмарҩа хышықәса иреитҩоу ахәычҡәа иры3кым. Ахәҭа хәычҡәа иҟаоит илбаардар ма ирыхәларгалар.[14]

The challenge that Abkhazian presents to Cyrillic lies in its incredibly large inventory of consonants – somewhere between 50 and 60. In contrast, it only has two vowels. Some of the rare Cyrillic characters you can find in the message are 'ҽ' 'ҧ' and 'ҟ'. However, I was disappointed that the Abkhazian Message doesn't include the most strikingly unique character in its alphabet, the 'Ҩ', a breathy 'hoo-e' sound, a bit like the 'hui' in the French word 'huit'.

The Message goes global

In my efforts to fill in the gaps in the Manuscript by finding translations in the remaining official languages of Europe and the former Soviet Union, I started to wonder where this process might end. Was I really going to attempt to find translations of the Message into every official language? And what about the 'unofficial' ones? Ethnologue estimates that over 7,000 languages are spoken in the world today.[15] Does liberating the Message require translations into every single one of them?

At the very least we can fill in the obvious ones. In the Far East, there are official Messages in most of the national languages of the countries in this region. One country, though, with a population of over 100 million, is missing: the Philippines. This archipelagic country is, like its fellow sprawling island state Indonesia, richly diverse linguistically, with dozens of native languages and dialects. Such states require a lingua franca and two languages perform this role in the Philippines – Tagalog (a standardised version of which is sometimes called 'Filipino') and English. Here is the Message in Tagalog:

BABALA, basahin at panatilihin: Laruang hindi angkop para sa mga batang wala pang 3 taong gulang. Ang maliliit na bahagi ay maaaring lunukin o malanghap.[16]

That there isn't an official Tagalog translation is a sign of an emerging trend: if a country has at least one official language that is 'international' enough to already appear on the Message, then the 'local' official language is unlikely to be added. In this respect, the Philippines are similar to Ireland, Malta and Belarus.

The same pattern can be found in Central and South America, together with the Caribbean. Every country in this region has at least one official European language found on an existing Message: Spanish, Portuguese, French, Dutch and English. Message-wise these countries are in Europe – with one possible exception. The Codex does reveal that the Portuguese Message used in Brazil is different to the Portuguese Message found in European Kinder Surprise Eggs. Here is the European one:

ATENÇÃO, leia e guarde: As peças pequenas poderiam ser ingeridas ou inaladas.

And here is the Brazilian one:

ATENÇÃO: BRINQUEDO NÃO RECOMENDÁVEL PARA MENORES DE 3 ANOS POR CONTER PARTES PEQUENAS QUE PODEN SER ENGOLIDAS DU INALADAS.

The Brazilian Message misses out 'read and keep' and adds the 'not suitable for children under 3 years' sentence not found in the European Portuguese one. Having shared the Brazilian Message with Portuguese speakers, they could not detect any specifically Brazilian vocabulary. However, there are some subtle differences in register. The Portuguese Message uses *poderiam ser* which strictly speaking translates to 'could have been' and the Brazilian uses *poden ser* which translates less formally as 'can be'.

Colonial Messages

One might, of course, shrug and respond that Spanish, Portuguese and the rest are widely understood, even by speakers of minority languages. Yet even in the realm of official languages, South American Manuscripts are missing something important: Guarani. This language is co-official with Spanish in Paraguay and is the only official non-European indigenous language in this region (although some other indigenous languages, such as Quechua, are official regional languages or official languages for indigenous minorities in other countries). While variants of Guarani are spoken in neighbouring countries, in Paraguay it is spoken by the majority of the population, although Spanish is sometimes preferred for official purposes. A Guarani Message would be a reminder that European colonialism did not eradicate indigenous languages and that they can develop the formality of official languages too:

> ÑEMOMARANDU HAG̃UA ñemoñe'ẽ guarã ha oñangareko mba'erã: Ko ñembosarairã ndaha'éi mitã michĩ omboty'ỹva mbohapy arýpe guarã. Umi ivore'i ikatu omokõ yrõ katu ikatu oho itîme.[17]

Every sub-Saharan African country has at least one European language as official. That does not mean they are the only official languages, though. And the formal registers of European languages in government may be radically different from everyday spoken variants (if they are spoken at all). I have yet to find a Message in a language exclusive to sub-Saharan Africa. That includes South Africa. I have seen a Manuscript found in a South African Kinder Egg and it was the same as that found in East Asia. It includes English at least, which is the main language used by the South African state government. But South Africa has ten official languages in addition to English. One of them, Afrikaans, is largely mutually intelligible with Dutch, so the European Manuscript, which does include Dutch, would certainly be more appropriate than the East Asian one. Nonetheless, here is an Afrikaans Message:

> PASSOP! Lees en hou: Speelding is nie gepas vir kinders onder die ouderdom van 3 jaar nie. Klein dele van die speelding kan ingesluk word en vas sit.[18]

The lack of a South African Message in a non-European language means that Ferrero missed a chance to expand the sonic inventory of the Manuscript. Zulu is the most common language spoken at home in South Africa, with about a quarter of the population native speakers. It is not only tonal but also includes a number of 'click' consonants. While the Zulu Message might look a little plain as there are no diacritics, it includes two 'c's – pronounced with a sucking in of teeth – and an 'x' – pronounced as in a click you would make to a horse to get it to walk on (disappointingly it doesn't include a 'q', which denotes a 'popping' sound).

> ISIXWAYISO, kufunde ukugcine. Ithoyisi alilungile kubantwana abaneminyaka ngaphansi ko-3. Inxenye encane ingagwinywa noma ingahogelwa.[19]

Click consonants are found in many other languages in Southern and Eastern Africa. The facility with which native speakers drop them into words is extraordinary to listen to and embarrassing for the rest of us when we try to copy them. That Zulu doesn't mark its clicks with special diacritics reminds us that speakers of click languages are unlikely to treat them as worthy of special distinction – why should they? But another South African language, Sepedi (also known as Northern Sotho) does at least use the circumflex:

> Hlokomela; bala o kwišiše: Dibapadišwa tše; ga tša lokela bana ba mengwaga ya ka fase ga mengwaga ye meraro. Di ka ba le bokotsi.[20]

Zulu and Sepedi are both part of the Bantu group of languages, but as a cursory comparison shows, they are in different branches and not mutually intelligible.

Elsewhere in sub-Saharan Africa, I have found Kinder products (admittedly mostly Kinder Joy, but they do have a warning message in them as well) for sale via the popular African webstore Jumia. Jumia has a presence in Nigeria, Kenya, Ivory Coast, Uganda, Senegal and Ghana, as well as in several North African countries. But there is no evidence of any localised package in a non-European language, let alone a localised warning message. There is a Ferrero branch in Cameroon, but this is primarily focused on processing cocoa.

It is likely that, in some African countries, a Kinder Surprise is only affordable to a small section of the population, one likely to be westernised and educated. That might mean that Ferrero may be correct in assuming that English, French, Portuguese and Arabic translations of the Message are enough to cover the whole continent. But the difference between Ferrero's language policies in Europe – where even modest linguistic differences are acknowledged – and Africa – where hundreds of tongues and multiple language families are absent – is striking. Indeed, one could even argue that, in parts of Africa and in the 'developing' world more generally, localised Messages are even more vital than elsewhere. If an Ethiopian parent living in a rural area without an education in a European language were to buy a Kinder Surprise as a one-off, expensive gift for their 2-year-old child, might the dangers inherent in the product be less apparent than they might to a Belgian parent? It's not that Ethiopians of modest means and education are less protective of their children, but they might well be less aware that western products, for all their expensive sheen, have dangers baked into the design. A Message in at least one of the five non-English official languages of the country would be a mercy. Here is what the Message would look like in the principal official language of Ethiopia, Amharic:

ማስጠንቀቂያ፦ ካነበቡት በኋላ እባክዎ በጥንቃቄ ያኑሩት! ይህ መጫወቻ ቢውጧቸው ወይም ቢያሽቷቸው ጉዳት ሊያመጡባቸው ከሚችሉ ጥቃቅን ነገሮች የተሠራ በመሆኑ፣ ዕድሜያቸው ከሦስት ዓመት በታች ለሆኑ ሕጻናት ፈጽሞ አመቺ አይደለም፡፡[21]

Africa is also home to one of the world's most successful lingua franca: Swahili. It is an official language in Kenya, Uganda and Tanzania and is also spoken in neighbouring states. Swahili has over 100 million speakers, in cities as a first language and as a second language in rural areas, or with distinctive variants influenced by regional languages. The language was originally written in Arabic script and has a degree of Arabic influence from the long history of Arab trading with East Africa. In the colonial period it was promoted by the various European powers in the region as a useful common tongue, and this promotion continued in the post-colonial period. Swahili would therefore be a perfect Message language:

ONYO, soma na usitupe: Kitu cha kuchezea hakifai kwa watoto chini ya miaka 3. Sehemu ndogo zinaweza kumezwa au kuvutwa kama pumzi.[22]

Despite the colonial influence, the translator told me that there is no specific word for 'toy' in Swahili. Her alternative was *kitu cha kuchezea*, which literally translates as 'item to play with'.

Indian Messages

Not only is sub-Saharan Africa a Message-free zone, the Indian subcontinent appears to be as well. Kinder Surprise Eggs do not seem to be sold domestically by Ferrero in India and neighbouring countries (although they might be imported). Kinder Joys are sold in India, and Ferrero also has a factory in Baramati that manufactures them for local consumption as well as for export to other Asian countries. I have seen photos of Kinder Joys with Hindi on the wrapping, but most online shops in India only show English wrappers. The Indian Kinder website is in English exclusively, although a TV advert for Kinder Joy that I found online was in Hindi. Kinder India's YouTube channel, curiously enough, does include Hindi in its strapline, but Hindi transliterated into Latin script – *Iss mein kuch khaas hai* ('Something in it is special').

The use of English in India is not confined to an elite. While English is, along with Hindi, one of the two languages used in parliament, and its use is widespread in business and higher education, in some respects it works better as a lingua franca than Hindi does. India is a language hotspot and individual states can declare their own official language. Hindi and variants of the language are most commonly spoken as an everyday language in the 'Hindi Belt' in the northern part of the country. There has often been resistance from speakers of other languages to the dominance of Hindi, particularly speakers of Dravidian languages in the south. The use of English as a lingua franca 'solves' this problem to a degree.

Even if the choice of English makes sense on a global scale, the sheer number of speakers of Indian languages makes the lack of a Message in any one of those languages something of a missed opportunity. According to Ethnologue, there are seven languages of the Indian subcontinent in the world's top twenty most spoken languages.[23] Hindi is the world's third most spoken language, after English and Mandarin Chinese. Over half a billion people speak it as their first language and millions more as a second or third language. So a Hindi Message is long overdue:

चेतावनी, पढ़ें और रखें: खिलौना 3 साल से कम उम्र के बच्चों के लिए उपयुक्त नहीं है। छोटे भागों को निगल या साँस लिया जा सकता है।[24]

Hindi has even more speakers when one considers Urdu, to which it is closely related and mutually intelligible. Urdu is the official language and lingua franca of Pakistan and is also an official language in a number of Indian states. Hindi and Urdu are both part of the Indo-Iranian branch of the Indo-European language family. Urdu retains a stronger Persian influence on its vocabulary (but not its grammar) and is written in a variant of the Persian-Arabic alphabet:

خبردار کھلونا تین سال سے کم عمر کے بچوں کےلئے مناسب نہیں ہے۔
چھوٹے حصے کھانے یا سانس کی نالی میں پھنس سکتے ہیں۔[25]

As we have seen earlier, visual differences between scripts can be markers of ethno-religious differences. What is interesting here is that the visual distinction between Hindi and Urdu is absolute, while the linguistic distinction is more complex. The script in which Hindi is written, Devanagari, derives ultimately from the ancient Brahmic script used to write Sanskrit. Other scripts deriving from this are now used throughout India; in some cases, the family resemblance to Devanagari is clear. Bengali (also known as Bangla), spoken throughout Bangladesh and neighbouring parts of India, is one such example:

সতর্কবার্তা, পড়ুন ও সাথে রাখুন: তিন বছরের কম বয়সী শিশুদের জন্য খেলনা উপযুক্ত নয়। ছোট অংশগুলি গিলে ফেলতে পারে অথবা নাকে ঢুকিয়ে দিতে পারে।[26]

Panjabi, the most widely-spoken language in Pakistan as well as in Indian Punjab, can be written in multiple scripts. Indian Sikhs – like my translator – generally use the Gurmukhi script, which is also Brahmic:

ਚੇਤਾਵਨੀ, ਪੜ੍ਹੋ ਅਤੇ ਰੱਖੋ: ਖਿਡੌਣਾ 3 ਸਾਲ ਤੋਂ ਘੱਟ ਉਮਰ ਦੇ ਬੱਚਿਆਂ ਲਈ ਨਹੀਂ ਹੈ. ਛੋਟੇ ਹਿੱਸੇ ਨਿਗਲ ਜਾਂ ਸਾਹ ਨਾਲ ਅੰਦਰ ਜਾ ਸਕਦੇ ਹਨ.[27]

To my eyes, jaded through over-exposure to Latin scripts and diacriticless English monoculture, the many scripts used in the Indian subcontinent have a delicious beauty. Tamil, spoken in southern India as well as Sri Lanka, is all elegant curves and meticulous lines:

எச்சரிக்கை, ஞாபகத்தில் வைத்திருங்கள் : விளையாட்டுப் பொம்மைகள் 3 வயதுக்குட்பட்ட குழந்தைகளுக்கு ஏற்றது இல்லை. சிறிய பாகங்கள் விழுங்கப்படலாம் அல்லது மூக்கால் உள்ளிழுக்கப்படலாம்.[28]

Sinhala, the language of the majority ethnic group in Sri Lanka, recalls Tamil, but adds a certain knotty complexity:

අනතුර ඇඟවීමයි කියවා තබා ගන්න: මෙම සෙල්ලම් බඩුව අවුරුදු 3නෙන් පහළ දරුවන්ට සුදුසු නැත. එහි ඇති කුඩා කැබැලි ගිලගැනීමට සහ නාසයේ දමා ගැනීමට පුළුවන්කම ඇත.[29]

Malayalam, the official language of the Indian state of Kerala, offers a different kind of curvy knottiness:

മുന്നറിയിപ്പ്: വായിക്കുക, സൂക്ഷിക്കുക: 3
വയസ്സിന് താഴെയുള്ള കുട്ടികൾക്ക് കളിപ്പാട്ടം
അനുയോജ്യമല്ല. ചെറിയ ഭാഗങ്ങൾ തൊണ്ടയിലോ
മൂക്കിനകത്തോ കുടുങ്ങാൻ ഇടയുണ്ട്.[30]

Telugu, another widely-spoken southern Indian language, adds little filigrees to its curves:

హెచ్చరిక*, చదివి జాగత్తగా ఉంచండి: మూడు సంవత్సరాల
లోపు పిల్లలకు ఈ బొమ్మ సరిపడదు. దీనిలోని చిన్న
భాగాలను వారు మింగవచ్చు లేదా పీల్చవచ్చు.[31]

Receiving these translations was a joy. I was nonetheless wary of falling into the trap of 'exoticising' Indian writing; of repeating colonial tropes about the mysterious and beguiling orient. There is no doubt, though, that the diversity of Indian scripts should humble those of us who read and write European languages. Whereas in most of Europe we slogged through developing nuanced variations of Greek and Latin-derived scripts, the Indian subcontinent seems to have taken written templates in many new directions. Just think what a Manuscript in the top 20 Indian languages might look like!

Ultimately then, the gaps I most want to fill are aesthetic gaps. Filling these absences reminds us of the sensual pleasures we miss when we are confronted by a limited scriptural diet. And that's why I end this chapter with the most beautiful script I have ever seen: Tibetan script, here used to write the Message in Dzongkha, the official language of the Himalayan kingdom of Bhutan:

ཉེན་བདྷ། ཨ་ནེ་ཡི་གུ་འདི་ལེགས་ཤོམ་སྦེ། ཀླུག་ཞིནམ་ལས་ བདག་འཛིན་ཐབས་སྟེ་ བགའ་དྲིན་བསྐྱང་ གནང་། ཨ་ལུ་སྐྱེས་ལོ་གསུམ་མན་ཆད་ཀྱི་གིས་ དོན་ལུ་ལོས་འབབ་མེད་ཨིན། ག་དེམ་ཅིག་སྦེ་ ཅེདམོ་ ཅེད་བ་ཅིན་ ཅེདམོ་གིས་ཚ་ཚས་ཀྱི་ སྦོང་མར་གཏང་ནི་ ཉེན་ཁ་ཡོདཔ་ཨིན།[32]

I don't know whether Kinder Surprise Eggs are on sale in Bhutan. I do know that the world would be richer in beauty if more people were confronted with Tibetan script. To liberate the Message, therefore, is to celebrate human creation. To take three sentences created for instrumental reasons and turn them into a gallery of wonders – that is liberation indeed.

Chapter 7

Diasporas and minorities

The two Armenians

In Chapter 4 I showed how some Messages have 'twins'. While I knew that these twins existed even before I embarked on this project, there was one language on the Manuscript that I only belatedly discovered had a sibling. That language is Armenian, or should I say, *Eastern* Armenian. Because that is the variety that Ferrero chose to represent the Armenian language.

Eastern Armenian is based on the dialect spoken in Yerevan, the capital of Armenia. While it is spoken by the Armenian Diaspora in neighbouring countries, Eastern Armenian has come to stand in for 'Armenian' internationally (the Armenian constitution specifies only that the language of the country is Armenian).

Western Armenian, while it is intelligible to Eastern Armenian-speakers and vice versa, is distinctive enough to have its own literature and history. Speakers of the Western variant have attempted to assert that distinctiveness by, for example, successfully campaigning for a separate International Organisation for Standardisation (ISO) code for the language ('hyw', although the two-letter code remains the same for both: 'hy') and planning a separate version of Wikipedia.[1] So it seems only fair to add a Western Armenian Message:

ՈՒՇԱԴՐՈՒԹԻՒՆ ԿԱՐԴԱԼ ԵԻ ՊԱՀԵԼ ՓՈՔՐ
ՄԱՍՆԻԿՆԵՐԸ ԿՐՆԱՆ ԿԼՈՒԻԼ ԿԱՄ ՆԵՐՇՆՉՈՒԻԼ:[2]

There was a time when Western Armenian was the dominant Armenian, the language of the Armenians who were scattered across what is now Turkey and the rest of the Ottoman Empire. That ended in 1915, when, during the First World War, the Ottomans set in train the murder of over 800,000 Armenians. The genocide tilted the balance of Armenian towards the Eastern variant, as it became the language of a republic of the Soviet Union and then an independent state (the language was never Cyrillicised as the languages of neighbouring republics were). That Eastern Armenian was usually the language spoken by the Armenian Diaspora in Russia itself, helped to reinforce its dominance.

Even though Armenians remain a Diaspora people – the state of Armenia, with a population of approximately 3 million, is home to only about a third of the world's ethnic Armenians[3] – the existence of a state changes a people irrevocably. When a language is used in official state discourse, it takes on a greater prominence and prestige. When a corporation seeks to sell its products within a state, they are required to conform to its linguistic policies.

The Diaspora Message

All the languages into which the Message has been translated by Ferrero are the official languages of nation states, even if they are often only one of a number of official languages or, as in Norwegian, only one of a number of variants of an official language. But they are also frequently Diaspora languages too. For example, nearly one quarter of the population of Germany (over 19 million people) were either not born German citizens or have one parent who was not born a German citizen.[4] Three million of them alone have roots in Turkey. A non-German language is spoken at home by 2.5 million Germans. So, many of those Germans who buy a Kinder Surprise Egg would be able and perhaps would prefer to read the Message in languages such as Turkish, Polish and Arabic.

Of course, Diasporas do not necessarily speak any language other than that of the state in which they live. And when they do speak another language, they may not be educated in it to the point where they are literate. There are nearly 50 million people in the Chinese Diaspora, but not all of them go through the rigorous process of learning written Mandarin Chinese; Chinese minority languages such as Hakka have a disproportionate presence in some overseas Chinese populations.[5]

Diasporas often retain their language, even after generations spent in their 'host' country. There are a variety of dialects of the Romani language spoken by Roma across Europe. The survival of the language is an indicator of the strength of their separate identity, which is sometimes bolstered and sometimes weakened by persecution, racism and inequality. That said, Romani dialects are also influenced by their surrounding linguistic environment, which demonstrates how Diaspora peoples rarely live lives of complete separation from the majority culture. The variety of Romani dialects form a double-edged sword – on the one hand they reflect local distinctiveness and a kind of rootedness; on the other, it has made standardising the Romani language across national borders challenging. The following translation of the Message is in Lovari, a form of Romani that is influenced by Hungarian and West Slavic languages:

Len sama, ginaven taj ikren: Kodi igračka naj pala e čhavore kaj naj inke 3 berš. E cikne kotora šaj cerden vaj nakhaven le.[6]

Another Diaspora language, Yiddish, was once spoken by millions of Jews across Central and Eastern Europe. It was, like Romani, dialectally diverse, with its Hebrew-influenced German base infused with local influences. The Holocaust devastated the Yiddish heartlands and caused the extinction of entire linguistic communities. However, it didn't die. Its postwar fate demonstrates both the potentials and limitations of Diasporic languages.

Many of those Yiddish-speakers who survived the Holocaust emigrated to the US, Israel and to other countries. While the language continued to be spoken, it was rarely passed on to the next generation. In fact this process had started before the Holocaust. My grandparents, who were the children of Jews who had emigrated from Poland to London at the end of the nineteenth century, had a passive knowledge of the language from listening to their parents, but English was the main language spoken at home and at school. My own parents and myself have no knowledge of Yiddish other than a few words. The drive to assimilate led to the rapid decline of the language of the 'old country'. In Israel – many of whose founders were Yiddish-speakers – Hebrew grew at the expense of Jewish Diaspora languages like Yiddish.

Yiddish lived on, though. Its devotees continue to push for the language's use in writing and cultural activities. In April 2021 a Yiddish course was added to the Duolingo app. But it is strictly orthodox (known as *Haredi*) Jewish communities who have played an outsized role in ensuring the language's survival. Haredi Yiddish isn't necessarily identical to the language that their ancestors spoke. The Holocaust and emigration have meant that Yiddish has consolidated within new linguistic communities in which some of its diversity has been ironed out. Haredi Jews attempt to create communities that are insular, protected from the depredations of assimilation and the temptations of modernity. Yiddish helps to ensure that separateness, although it exists in a diglossic relationship with English, Hebrew and the other languages of the states in which Haredim live.

Given that for many Haredi children Yiddish is the first language, there is actually a strong case for a separate Yiddish Message. However, the Message would be redundant without a different kind of message: the certification of the product as kosher, known as a *hechsher*. According to the London Kashrut Board, which supervises kosher products in the UK, Kinder Surprise Eggs are indeed kosher (although not all Haredi Jews would necessarily accept the judgement of this particular body). While such a *hechsher* does not have to be included on or in the package, in countries with substantial markets for kosher foods, symbols denoting the appropriate kosher authority are sometimes included on packaging.

I received a Yiddish Message from Professor Lily Kahn of University College London. Although not herself Haredi, she was the perfect choice to translate the Message as, during the Covid-19 pandemic, she was used to writing official messages in Yiddish, having worked with London's Haredi community to produce culturally appropriate health information:

אַזהרה! לייענט און האַלט בײַ זיך. די צאַצקע איז נישט פּאַסיק פֿאַ
ר קינדער וואָס זענען ייִנגער פֿון דרײַ יאָר. זיי קענען חלילה אַראָפּ
שלינגען אָדער אײַנאָטעמען קלייינטשיקע חלקים.

The use of Hebrew script to write Yiddish emphasises its separateness. When transliterated, some of its Germanic roots become clearer, although the word for warning, *Azhore*, is of Hebrew origin:

> Azhore! Leyent un halt bay zikh. Di tsatske iz nisht pasik far kinder vos zenen yinger fun dray yor. Zey kenen kholile aropshlingen oder aynotemen kleynt-shike khalokim.

When, in pre-modern times, Jews lived in largely self-governing communities, they developed multiple ethnolects such as Yiddish. Today, other than Yiddish, most of them are faced with extinction. This is a result of assimilation as much as genocide. Ladino (Judeo-Spanish) was once spoken by the descendants of the Jews expelled from Spain and Portugal in 1492. In Salonika (Thessaloniki) in Greece, nearly half of the city were Ladino-speaking Jews until the community was destroyed by the Nazis. While Ladino today has its activists and speakers, it is mostly not being transmitted to the young. The Message in Ladino therefore takes on a wistful quality for a culture that is almost lost:

> Atension! Melda e guadra. Esti jugueti no es apropriado para chicos menos de tres anyos. Si pueden englutir pedasos chicos.[7]

The near-state experience

While the condition of Diaspora can threaten language death, a language's survival isn't automatically assured by official use within a nation state. As we saw in the case of Belarusian, official languages can also be marginalised. And even where a language's status is uncontested, that might not be enough to protect it from the dominance of English and other global tongues. A 2020 study found that the Dutch have the highest proficiency in English outside the English-speaking world (followed closely by the Nordic countries) and a 2012 report found that 90% of the population speak English.[8] Near-universal competence in English and the needs of the global economy has led to the rapid growth of Dutch university courses taught entirely in English. This has led to concerns that, without concerted action, Dutch-speaking students would be marginalised in their own country.[9] If a language is no longer routinely used in scholarly discourse, its status and prestige is at risk.

For now, though, a link to a state is still the best way to ensure that a language will survive. Some languages become *de facto* state languages by their use inside an autonomous region within a nation state. Those with the highest levels of autonomy have devolved powers so extensive they resemble independent states in many respects. One of them is Greenland, which is an autonomous territory of Denmark and has responsibility for everything but defence, foreign affairs and monetary policy. Kalaallisut – Greenlandic – is its official language, although Danish and English are also used. This is an Eskimo-Aleut language that allows for extremely long words to be created through the addition of suffixes to word roots:

Mianersoqqussut: atuaruk paariinarullu. Pinnguaq meeqqanut pingasut inorlugit ukiulinnut naleqqu-tinngilaq. Ilaminerngit iineqarsinnaapput imaluunniit najuunneqarsinnaapput.[10]

Nations may achieve *de facto* statehood before they achieve it *de jure* (if they ever do). There are somewhere between 35 and 45 million Kurds in the world, the majority split between Turkey, Iran, Iraq and Syria.[11] Kurdish nationalism therefore conflicts with four other nationalisms. While the barriers to a Kurdish state that would unify Kurdish communities in all of these countries seem insurmountable, Iraqi Kurdistan is home to more than 8 million Kurds. Following the Gulf War in 1991, the imposition of a no-fly zone by the Western Allies in part of the Kurdish region in the north of Iraq allowed for a completely autonomous region to emerge. Following the fall of Saddam Hussein in 2003, Iraqi Kurdistan has been loosely incorporated into Iraq with a high degree of regional autonomy. Kurdish is now an official language of Iraq, but not of a fully independent state. Kurdish is dialectally diverse and the variant that is mainly spoken in Iraq is known as Sorani, written in an alphabet based on Arabic script:

ئاگاداریی، بخوێنەرەوە و پابەند بە: یاری مندالّان کە گونجاو نییە بۆ
مندالّی خوار تەمەن ٣ سالّ. دەشێت پارچە بچوکەکان قوتبدرێن یاخود
هەلّبمژرێن.[12]

Sorani is not the most widely spoken version of Kurdish. That honour goes to Kurmanji (also known as Northern Kurdish) which is the predominant language of 15–20 million Turkish Kurds and is also widely spoken across other Kurdish areas (including in Iraq and Syria). The difference with Sorani is accentuated by Kurmanji's Latin alphabet:

HIŞYARÎ, bixwîne û biparêze: Lîstik bikêrî zarokên bin 3 salî nayên. Parçeyên piçûk dikarin werin daqurçandin an hêlmijandin.[13]

While nurturing a separate language is often a part of nationalist struggles, the two don't always converge seamlessly. After centuries of marginalisation, Welsh is now officially supported by the devolved Welsh government, with the language taught in schools and universities. About 30% of the Welsh population speak the language but not all Welsh-speakers want independence and Welsh nationalists do not all have fluent Welsh. The same is true for the Basque country in Spain, where Basque-speakers are a significant minority and supporting Basque independence is not necessarily synonymous with being a Basque-speaker. Regional devolution can 'split' nationalist movements between those who are content with degrees of autonomy and those who wish to be entirely independent. Either way, a minority language is likely to flourish.

However much autonomy a region may receive and however much its language may be officially supported, the use of such languages in product packaging isn't guaranteed. On visits to Spain, where Catalan/Valencian, Basque and Galician-speaking regions have considerable autonomy from the Spanish state, I have often been struck by how the use of these languages on product labels tends to be confined to Spanish products, if at all. This is a particular pity for Basque, which is famously a language 'isolate', unrelated to any other language and an invigorating conglomeration of 'z's and 'k's:

> KONTUZ, irakurri eta gorde: Jostailu desegokia 3 urtetik beherako haurrentzat. Zatitxoak irentsi edo inhalatu ahal dituzte.[14]

The same is true for Welsh in Britain. It is common to encounter it, for example, in government websites; when I submit my tax return or renew my vehicle licence there is a Welsh option. But I can't recall seeing the language on products at all.

> Rhybudd, darllenwch a chadwch: Nid yw'r tegan yma yn addas at gyfer plant o dan 3 blwydd oed. Mae yna ddarnau bach y gellir eu mewnanadlu neu lyncu.[15]

An illustrious history and literature doesn't mean a language will survive. Occitan, versions of which were once spoken throughout the south of France, was the language of the troubadour poetic tradition in medieval times. That history did not stop the inexorable progress of marginalisation by the centralising French state. To write the Message in Occitan is, perhaps, to dream of lost glories:

> ATENCION, legissètz e conservatz: Aquel joguet conven pas als mens de tres ans. Las pichòtas pèças poirián èsser engolidas o inaladas.[16]

Everyday multilingualism

The marginalisation of non-official tongues isn't inevitable in the modern state. In Germany, the consolidation of a standardised written language began with the spread of Lutheranism through printed texts in the sixteenth century and was further accelerated by the unification of the modern German state in the nineteenth century. While standard German is based on the 'high' German spoken in parts of the south and centre of the country, regional vernaculars remain widely spoken, without being extensively written. Here is the Message in Upper Bavarian, whose diacritics immediately signal it as different from standard German (this translation is from the German Message, rather than the English one):

> Lesn und aufghoidn: OBÅCHT! Ned fia Gschråzln, de kloana wia 3 Joa san. Des Zeig is oafoch zkloa fia de. Ned dass se's schlucka oda eischnaufa.[17]

Swiss-German shows that it is possible for a spoken language to exist in a harmonious relationship with a standardised one. The language that 'German'-speaking Swiss use in most situations is only intelligible with great difficulty to speakers of standard German. Yet the ability to use standard German in writing, as well as in more formal spoken situations, allows Swiss-German-speakers to access a much larger language community outside Switzerland. From this perspective, a Swiss-German Message might liberate the language into the written realm, but it would also liberate Swiss-Germans into parochiality were it not combined with continuing facility with standard German:

> WARNHIIWIIS zum Läsen und Bhalte: Spilzüg nöd für Chind under Drüü geignet. Di chliine Teili cha me veschlucke oder iischnuufe.[18]

In some countries, multilingualism can be so common that it doesn't 'threaten' a national language at all. Tagalog and English may be the national languages of the Philippines but over 100 other languages are also spoken. As an everyday first language, rather than a lingua franca, Tagalog is spoken by about a third of the population. When a standardised official language is not the language of the majority, there is a greater chance that linguistic diversity may survive. Maricar Dela Cruz, the translator of the Tagalog Message presented in the previous chapter, is one of the millions of Filipinos who work outside the country. Her friendship group has been built out of Filipinos speaking a wide range of languages. While they use Tagalog as a lingua franca, her friends helped supply me with a variety of Messages from the Philippines, such as Hiligaynon:

Paalinton, basahon kag taguon: Mga halampangan nga indi angay para sa kabataan nga ang edad manubo SA tatlo Ka tuig. Gamay nga parte pwede matulon o masimhot.[19]

Subverting the nation state

Some minority languages can be so radically different from the official national languages that they can act as a disturbing reproach to proponents of homogeneous national identities. That's all the more reason to translate the Message into them.

During the Third Reich, the existence of the Sorbian people in parts of Saxony was, at best, an embarrassment. Sorbs are ethnically and linguistically Slavic. The Nazis attempted to Germanize them and dismiss them as Germans who happened to temporarily speak a Slavic language. In the longer term, Sorbian has declined dramatically, but it still lives, a testament to the porousness of the category of 'German'. The Message in the Upper Sorbian version of the language looks, to me, more like Czech and that's all to the good:

Kedźbu: njehodźi so za dźěći pod 3 lětami. Wobsteji strach, zo so hrajka abo dźělčki spóžeraja abo zadychuja.[20]

The Sámi are the traditionally semi-nomadic peoples who move across the borders of the far north of Sweden, Finland and Norway. Their Uralic languages are entirely unrelated to Swedish and Norwegian (although they are distantly related to Finnish). North Sámi, the most common variant, is spoken by a few thousand people and a Message in that language is a reminder of the continued existence of those who were pushed to the margins by the expansionist European state:

> Várrehus! Loga ja doala. Speallu ii heive mánáide geat leat nuorabut go golbma jagi. Unna bihtážat leat hávkananvárra.[21]

The sentimental Message

Liberating the Message is a sentimental project. While, as I have argued, there is a strong case for raising the stature of minority and non-official languages – and indeed for including them on the Manuscript – I can't deny that the instrumental case for doing so is weaker than the sentimental case. It is ironic that I am pursuing this sentimental project through commissioning translations of a highly unsentimental text. Officialese is, after all, the language of the head rather than the heart.

Ferrero remains a family business, albeit one that has grown to extraordinary size. Might they not be persuaded to include at least one minority language? I have one in mind: Piedmontese, the language of the region where Pietro Ferrero was born. It is still spoken and has a degree of official regional recognition, but it isn't widely written. I don't know whether any of the Ferrero family were or are speakers, but including a Piedmontese Message in the Manuscript might signal to the world that Kinder Surprise Eggs come from somewhere; that Ferrero has room for sentiment, for place, for the fragile delights of languages outside the state:

> Les con atension: Ten la dësmora lontan dal masnà con meno ëd tre ann. Ij tòch pì cit a podrìo esse traondù o inalà.[22]

Chapter 8

Despised tongues

Creoles can do anything

Some languages are despised; dismissed as impure tongues, crossbreeds unworthy to be included on any manuscript. True liberation requires imagining what it would be like if such linguistic hierarchies were demolished, if the Manuscript featured Messages like the following:

> WAANIN, riid an kip dis: Dis toi ya a no fi pikni yongga dan chrii ier uol. It av smaal paat we di pikni kuda swala ar go op ina dem nuoz.[1]

This is Jamaican Creole, known as *Patois*. While standard English is used for most official purposes in Jamaica, Patois is the spoken language and is sometimes also written as a literary language too. While Jamaican Creole might look unfamiliar at first to an English-speaker, reading it aloud makes clear its relationship to English. The grammar, though, can be very different. The translator, Dr Clive Forrester, a Jamaican linguist now based at the University of Waterloo in Canada, explained to me how he came up with the translation:

> The translation uses the official writing system of Jamaican Creole created by Jamaican lexicographer Robert LePage back in the 1960s. It will look somewhat unfamiliar to many Jamaicans who've never seen the Dictionary of Jamaican English (compiled by LePage).

The main difference here is that unlike the English translation, the Jamaican version has clear subjects for the sentences (the subject is usually omitted in instructions which use technical English). I also used the Jamaican version for 'go up into their nose' since I think that better captures the warning that a small piece could become lodged in the nostrils rather than 'inhaled' which doesn't clearly state the danger.

Dr Forrester's choice to include the subjects of the sentences and to avoid participles actually makes the Message clearer than the official English one. The lack of a Jamaican Creole equivalent of austere, subject-less, technical English doesn't imperil an actionable Message. Nor does the closeness of the orthography to the sounds of Jamaican Creole mean that it is simple transcription; Dr Forrester drew on a clear system for writing the language. Compare this to the organised chaos of the English spelling system.

A creole can do anything that any other language can do. Creoles start off life as a solution to a problem: when speakers of different languages are suddenly brought together and have to find a way of communicating. This can happen – as in Jamaican Creole – in the forced population movements produced by Empire, colonisation and slavery. Often, creoles start life as pidgins, improvised means of communication between people who have no language in common. Speakers adapt the vocabulary of a particular language with shifts in sound, meaning and grammar to produce something that is their own.

For those of us raised to believe that there was a 'right way' of speaking a language, there is something thrillingly transgressive about a creole based on a language one knows.

Take Mauritian creole, which to me seems to thumb its nose at my school French classes:

> FER TENSYON, lir ek retenir: Sa zouzou la pas conve-
> nab pou zanfan emba trwa zan akoz zot kapav avale
> ou risse ban ti piyesse la par zot nene.[2]

The baroque fussiness of French spelling collapses here into something closer to the spoken. Yet that doesn't mean creoles cannot be written in a systematic orthography. The use of dia-critics in the Haitian Creole (known as Kreyòl) translation of the Message is an indicator of its development as a written language:

> AVÈTISMAN – pou n li epi pou n kenbe: Jwèt sa a pa
> apwopriye pou ti moun piti ki pa ko gen 3 lane. Jwèt
> sa yo gen ti pyès tou piti ki ka pase nan gòj oswa nen
> ti moun piti.[3]

Creoles are often accorded a lowly status, fit only for the masses to speak. Despite Haiti being one of the first French slave colonies to liberate itself, in 1804, standard French has remained the language of ruling and education for most of its history. While in recent years Kreyòl has begun to be used more extensively, the situation of the language is not a mat-ter for the country alone. As Michel DeGraff – the Haitian Professor of Linguistics at MIT in the US who translated the Message into Kreyòl for me – points out:

> In Haiti, for example, the vast majority of administra-
> tive, legal and educational documents are still written

exclusively in French – including documents being produced by the very organizations whose official objectives include the promotion of children's rights and education. One UNICEF site, titled 'Timoun yo! The Voice of Haiti's Children', is a perfect example: the site's home page prominently displays the UN Convention on the Rights of Child, but the site itself is in French and English and not in Kreyòl – the only language spoken by most Haitian children (and adults). In addition, publications in most Haitian state offices, including the Ministry of National Education, the State University, and human rights institutions such as the Office de la Protection du Citoyen, routinely violate Haiti's 1987 Constitution, which mandates the use of French and Kreyòl as co-official languages, with Kreyòl deemed the one single language that bonds the entire nation. In effect, such linguistic practices exclude the majority of the population.[4]

What DeGraff calls 'linguistic apartheid' is one example of the ways in which colonial inequalities persist even after formal decolonisation.[5] International bodies and corporations perpetuate these inequalities through such apparently innocuous practices as the languages chosen for translation into warning messages.

Scots is not slang (not that it would be a bad thing if it was)
It isn't just creoles that are treated as fit only for speaking. Consider Scots. Some English-speaking readers may simply see the Scots Message as a mix of Scottish slang and accented English:

> CAW CANNIE, read an haud on tae this: Toy isna fit for
> bairns unner 3 year auld. Sma pairts micht get swal-
> laed or soukit in.[6]

Ulster Scots might provoke the same reaction:

> MIND! Read an' kep. Toy's no fit for weans. Wee bits
> cud be golloped.[7]

Despite Scots and its multiple variants having an extensive
literary tradition, its use in official contexts is limited, although
increasing. The bilingual website of the Scots Language Centre
(whose Dauvit Horsbroch translated the Message) embodies
its simultaneous familiarity and unfamiliarity to English-
speakers. The organisation's Scots name, the Centre for the
Scots Leid, might feed into pejorative characterisations of Scots
as just English with a bit of slang. On the other hand, Scots is
different enough that, when street signs in Ulster Scots were
placed in a loyalist estate in Northern Ireland in 1999, vandals
tore them down, mistaking them for Irish Gaelic.[8]

The dividing lines between language, dialect, ethnolect,
slang and accent are the product of human prejudices as much
as they are linguistic categories. I was reminded of this when
I received a translation of the Message in what was described
to me as 'Potteries dialect', spoken around Stoke-on-Trent and
neighbouring towns:

> Mar mate, DUST EAR, raid dis: Dunna gi toy t' children
> under thray. Small bits mayt choke 'em.[9]

The differences between this and standard English are not
much less than the differences between Scots and standard

English. As far as I am aware, no one in Stoke has aspirations for Potteries dialect to be a language that could be used officially. Yet what Scots and Potteries dialect share is a sense that this is how a real person would warn another person of the dangers lying within a Kinder Surprise. These kinds of languages are common throughout the world, unified by their written invisibility and their protean vivacity. Here, for example, is Betawi, the dialect spoken in Jakarta, Indonesia, which infuses Malay with influences from Arabic, Dutch, Hokkien Chinese and multiple Indonesian languages:

> Awas! Dibaca sama disimpen nih: Main-mainan kagak cocok buat kanak-kanak berumur di bawah tiga tahun. Bagian-bagian cilik bisa tertelahin ataupun terhirupin lho.[10]

Translating the Message into such languages requires a degree of imagination given that they do not have standard versions and are not used for sober warning messages. This translation of the Message into Singlish, the melange of English, Malay, Tamil and various Chinese languages that is spoken (and officially discouraged) in Singapore, seems to capture a casual familiarity not found in the original:

> Better pay attention ok! Toy not for ginna under 3 hor: don't play play ... sekali kena choke![11]

For those who love languages in all their messy diversity, there is a dilemma as to how and whether one should raise the status of these kinds of languages. It is certainly true that the absence of languages like Haitian Creole from official contexts creates a dangerous gap between the population and those in power. It is certainly true that those fighting for Scots are fighting back against the disparaging of their language by the English and by some of their own rulers too. But what might get lost if the status of these and similar languages were raised? After all, Scots itself is dialectally diverse and a standardised Scots could marginalise some of its own speakers. And is there not something exciting about speaking an unwritten language that can never be imprisoned within a written script?

Writing the unwritable

I commissioned two translations of the Message into Llanito, spoken but rarely written in the British overseas territory of Gibraltar. Llanito is characterised by ceaseless code-switching between English and Spanish and is laced with words from the languages spoken by the various immigrant groups who have made Gibraltar their home, such as Maltese and Genoese. Here is the first translation, by the Gibraltarian novelist M.G. Sanchez, whose books feature extensive dialogue in Llanito:

> WARNING. Lee ehto y no lo tire. Juguete not suitable pa chavea de meno de tre anygo. Small parts might be swallowed or inhalau.[12]

The translation demonstrates how Andalucian Spanish is the principal Spanish source for Llanito. Andalucian often drops consonants, sometimes replacing them with a slight aspiration – so *esto* ('this') becomes *ehto* and *inhalado* ('inhaled') becomes *inhalau*. What intrigued me most about this translation is how Sanchez decided which bits would be in English and which in

Spanish; in other words, where one switched codes. When I spoke to him, he told me that, for example, Llanito-speakers would always use 'Warning' rather than the Spanish *Atención*. But, as he told me:

> I can't explain why. It's a way of recognising who belongs. There is a consistency for sure, the trouble is to define what generates it. Llanito for me is a language of the street. That's why capturing it is difficult – it's as elusive as quicksilver.

On reflection, though, he wondered whether it might be because 'In formal situations we almost always speak in English' – so perhaps 'Warning' and 'Small parts might be swallowed' reflects this formality.

The other Llanito Message I received was from Dale Buttigieg, a Gibraltarian linguist who has developed a standardised version of Llanito:

> WÓNING, lee êto i no lo tirê:ête huwete no'h sùtabol pa ninyô de meno de trê s'anyô. Lâ partê xikititâ podrìan tragarse o 'serse inhèiling.

In developing an orthography for Llanito, Buttigieg made frequent use of circumflexes on vowels to indicate the elided consonants. He has also altered the spelling of English words, as with *sùtabol*, to reflect Llanito pronunciation. His version of the third sentence is more Spanish than Sanchez's, using what would be in Spanish a highly informal term, *xikititâ*, for 'small' and only reverting to an English word for the final *inhèiling*.

Buttigieg's attempt to assert Llanito's distinctiveness leads him to emphasise its distance from English. While M.G. Sanchez wouldn't adopt this orthography in his own writing, as he wondered whether it might be challenging for Gibraltarians to read, he believes that Buttigieg's work is 'linguistically really important'. It refutes the pejorative view that Llanito is simply a form of 'Spanglish'. Whether it could or should be used as a formal written language remains a big question. As someone who has read and enjoyed Sanchez's work, I wondered whether part of the joy of Llanito lies in the iconoclasm of switching between Spanish, English and Something Else. An official Llanito Message, while it would represent a long-overdue recognition of Gibraltar's linguistic and cultural distinctiveness, might risk pinning the butterfly.

Is the African-American Vernacular Message a racist Message?

That such dilemmas matter was brought home to me when I commissioned a translation of the Message into what may well be the most controversial language in this book. Some linguists have argued that 'African-American Vernacular English' (sometimes referred to as 'AAVE') is a distinctive form of English that deserves to have its status raised and to be used in the US education system. In a highly controversial decision in 1996, the Oakland School Board in California decided to recognise the language their African-American students spoke as 'Ebonics' (a term that his since largely fallen out of use) and, as such, legitimate for use in education alongside dedicated classes in standard English. Some linguists affirmed the linguistic legitimacy of African-American

Vernacular English, together with the benefits of recognising the disadvantages that come from school pupils speaking an unrecognised 'second language'.[13] However, some African-American leaders pushed back strongly against the decision. Jesse Jackson, for example, saw the decision as 'teaching down' to children, and that it was an insult to claim that they do not speak English.[14]

I remembered this controversy when I published a translation of the Message into AAVE on social media by the linguist Richard E. McDorman:

> WARNING (make sho you read and keep dis): Don't be lettin yo kids use dis toy if dey unda 3 years old. Dey might could swallow da small parts or breave em in.

I received some strong responses to my post, for example:

> I have never seen AAVE written out in anything before. Any attempts to do so – and publish it as such is, to me, offensive. And even the assumption that Black Americans all or even mostly speak like this is offensive.

Another response argued that writing AAVE was, in the current context, a racist act:

> It is caricature and reeks of early sociocultural anthropology's European ethnocentrism. Yes, there have been movements in academia (including suggestions from Toni Morrison) that acceptance of vernacular leads to validation of the personage of speakers.

However, intent is not the yardstick. Authenticity is. All attempts at codifying vernacular fail because the codification cannot reflect the fluid vernacular usage. Codification of vernacular is the oppressor saying, 'I can understand this' and thus, 'I have conquered this too.' It is wrong, intellectually and morally.

The argument applies to spoken vernaculars endemic to people who have been subjugated by white supremacy for 500 years. This is not a universal argument that applies to all creoles, like Yiddish (which has established written forms, grammar, etc.). And it's not about whether a communication modality is worthy of the title 'language.' The question is whether printing something like this is right in the context of American institutional racism. I respectfully suggest that the answer is clearly no. Printing this will be called out as racist.

I was a little shaken by these responses, but the translator was aware of the pitfalls of this act of translation. He acknowledged, for example, that:

There is (obviously) no universally agreed upon orthography for AAVE. However, there are tendencies in orthographic usage among native speakers, which include a more-or-less phonetic rendering ... Since AAVE is by its nature a vernacular variety, a word-for-word translation from the literary standard into AAVE is usually not a viable translation strategy. A functional (sense-for-sense) translation is the only feasible approach.

He also warned me of the possible responses to the translation's publication:

> This is the most important issue for your purposes, I think: it's not at all clear how this will be received by the public. Some may incorrectly believe it to be a caricature of AAVE and its speakers, even though that's obviously not the intent. There is extremely little published material involving interdialectal translation in English, and even less involving translation into AAVE ... Finally, there is a risk of overtranslation, especially since I don't have much experience translating texts into AAVE, although I think it's safe to say that no one else does either.

There are major issues at stake in this debate. One of them is the extent to which recognition of an ethnolect or minority language might end up reinforcing the marginalisation of the people who speak it. Another is whether the process of writing down AAVE makes it vulnerable to ridicule and dismissal. However, some African-American criticism of written AAVE actually validates linguistic hierarchies: the notion that there are some languages that are more expressive, more suited to formal or sophisticated use. I would uphold the notion that AAVE is as capable of a wide range of expression as any other language is. The question then becomes: would African-Americans want to use it in this way? And that is not a matter for me to decide.

So while I may have started out this project with the conviction that liberating the Message means translating it into as many tongues as possible, I have become more aware of the limitations of written language to liberate 'everyone'. A spoken vernacular ethnolect can derive some of its power precisely because it is unwritten. This allows speakers to use it as a marker of group identity and solidarity; while at the same time the fact that no one 'owns' the language empowers speakers to improvise and create their own idiolects. The verbal dexterity found in hip hop derives from its closeness to unwritten ethnolects. Hip hop in standard English usually sounds forced, contrived and awkward.

The secret Message

There is power in secrecy; in evading the scrutiny that comes with writing. Throughout history, people on the margins have often created argots and cants (the two terms are interchangeable) specific to their world, sometimes designed to confuse or mislead outsiders. This is only an extension of the much wider phenomenon of jargon, the technical vocabulary found in a particular profession or field.

Should argots be treated as languages? In part, that is a question of whether it is just a matter of some extra vocabulary grafted onto an existing language or whether the argot functions like a 'full' language. But it is also a question of ethics and politics: while a linguist might feel that calling an argot a language and describing its features might 'honour' it and its speakers, it also exposes them to surveillance.

One extraordinary example of these dilemmas can be found in Martin Puchner's book *The Language of Thieves*. Puchner, who is German but now based at Harvard University in the US, remembers how his father and his uncle would occasionally teach him words from a language called Rotwelsch. Rotwelsch, which was spoken for centuries by vagrants, travellers and thieves in Central Europe, is built on German with loans and other features from multiple languages, including Yiddish, Hebrew and Romani. It also had a 'written' component, consisting of images called *zinken* that conveyed secret information to other travellers.

In trying to get to the bottom of why his family was so interested in Rotwelsch, Puchner uncovered some disturbing information. His grandfather, an archivist and expert on family names, had been a member of the Nazi Party and at one point delivered a lecture denouncing Rotwelsch for its supposed Jewish roots. This was part of a long tradition of associating the language with deviance and with Jews specifically. Indeed, one of the primary sources of knowledge for Rotwelsch has been through police reports.

Puchner's uncle also became an authority on Rotwelsch, but for a different reason to Puchner's grandfather. Perhaps as an act of atonement, he collated a vast amount of information on the language and published a book in which he translated famous texts – including from the Bible and Shakespeare – into Rotwelsch. This seemed to be similar to my own project and raised the same issues that my AAVE translation does. While the project of using translations of classic texts to demonstrate that Rotwelsch can do what a standard language can do may have been conducted with the best of intentions, it was also presumptuous: do Rotwelsch speakers (of whom very few are left) want or need this redemption? Might writing Rotwelsch and translating prestigious literature into it subvert the purposes of the language? It might be true that Rotwelsch deserves to be documented for historical purposes, but it doesn't necessarily 'need' to be de-contextualised and repurposed.

And yet, and yet ... I still come back to the ways that some languages are despised and treated as if they were 'bad' versions of a standard language. I still can't help but think that demonstrating that the Message can be written in despised tongues makes a powerful point. It also demonstrates that what unsympathetic listeners dismiss as merely slang is much more than that.

Take Anglo-Romani, the mixed language developed by Romani-speakers in the last few hundred years in the UK and other English-speaking countries. The translation of the Message into Anglo-Romani that I received from the writer Damian Le Bas brought home to me not how similar it was to English, but how different. The English-style syntax 'flatters to deceive', which is why the vocabulary's foreignness might be dismissed by some listeners but not by those who encounter it written down:

> DORDI, dihk this lil and lel it: Chavis kovva kek kushti for ticknas bittyer'n trin bershes. Bitti kovvas can be hawed or jel up the nak.

Perhaps, then, liberating the Message into creoles, argots and unwritten vernaculars is most effective when it demonstrates that they are more different than we imagined from what we assume to be their 'base' language. The AAVE translation might fail this test in part because it is a variant of English that is, in its spoken form, familiar from popular culture and, indeed, crosses over into multiple regional variants of American English.

Awareness of that risk led me to abandon attempts to produce translations of the Message into other argots that have some kind of claim to be a language. I considered Polari, a now largely-unused British argot associated most famously with gay subculture but also spoken in a wide range of marginal milieux. While a translated Message that used every possible recorded Polari word (such as *chavvie*, a Romani word, for 'child') might produce a distinctive Message, it would be a tendentious concoction that might end up demonstrating the limits of the language rather than its possibilities.

Similarly, many English-speaking Jews pepper their conversations with other Jews with Yiddish words. Indeed, some English-speaking orthodox Jews who have studied in a *Yeshiva* (an educational institution in which religious texts are studied) include so much Yiddish that their argot has been dubbed 'Yeshivish'. Yet to produce a Message in Yeshivish, or a related mix of Yiddish and English, would be to ignore the ways in which Yiddish words are only used by English-speakers at particular times and places.

While I freely admit that my project is highly contrived, there are limits – ethical and political rather than linguistic. The next chapter looks more closely at these limits.

Chapter 9

The limits of liberation

My hubris

As my project became known among friends and online contacts, I would sometimes get messages asking me whether I wanted a translation into a particular language. My answer was always 'yes'. Every translation challenge I completed would only lead me on to the next: I've got Tagalog, now what about Cantonese? I've got Catalan, now what about Basque? The further I got, the more the gaps that I had yet to fill gaped wider. I looked at lists of the world's most spoken languages and felt depressed at how many more I needed.

A collector of anything is always fated to never be completely satisfied. But this isn't just a matter of my own fragile ego. Rather, the language gaps in this book risk making a statement that I do not want to make. As I argued earlier, silence can be as eloquent as talk. To not include a translation in this book might be interpreted as being a judgement on the language's worth. Embarrassingly, the languages absent from this book tend to be clustered in certain areas of the world. However much I might have argued that it is important to include the Message in African languages, I have barely scratched the linguistic surface of the continent. Where is Yoruba or Wolof? Contrast that to Europe, where I have lingered over tongues as rare as Sorbian.

There is hubris in my aspiration to collect every language. It's not just that I am one person with limited time;

it's also that my contacts and horizons are limited. This project has reminded me that, despite the apparent limitlessness of the Internet, despite the advantages that come from my fluency in English, finding someone to translate the Message into Turkmen isn't easy. And even assuming that I can track down an expert or native speaker who could understand my English email, that doesn't mean they will reply. Why, after all, should they? It might be down to bad luck or some aspect of that nebulous thing, the 'national character', that has meant multiple requests to speakers of some languages have gone unanswered. Faroese, in particular, nags away at me. Yet the Faroese-speakers who didn't reply to my emails don't owe me anything and they aren't to know that it's the only Scandinavian language of government that I have yet to crack.

In the previous chapter, I discussed how the negative reactions to the African-American Vernacular English translation pushed me to consider what the limits of my project should be. My instincts have always told me that to liberate the Message into minority and unwritten languages would help to challenge the hegemony of official tongues. By 'proving' that the Message is translatable into 'every' tongue, I would affirm the universal dignity of linguistic diversity. Yet why should speakers of any language have to 'prove' themselves, to me or anyone else? And is there not a danger of being patronised? Although this book might have a light-hearted premise, I have no wish to treat any language or its speakers as a novelty.

Indigenous dilemmas

For these reasons, I began to question whether I should continue pursuing what had become the most challenging part of this project: translation into 'indigenous' languages. I started out with a firm conviction that, by publishing translations of the Message into some of the indigenous languages of the Americas and Australia, I would be asserting the dignity and equal value of their languages and cultures. I would be striking a blow against what one scholar called the 'language denialism' that refuses to recognise the inherent worth and expressiveness of indigenous languages.[1]

All very noble, but no indigenous language activist ever asked me to do this. I was in danger of making the mistake that I knew what the 'other' wanted better than they did themselves. Perhaps that is one of the reasons why, despite my firing off email after email to organisations for indigenous peoples, language activists and scholars, I had few positive responses – and when I did receive some interest, the trail soon went cold. One Canadian academic pointed out that many 'first nation' communities in North America were suffering disproportionately in the Covid-19 pandemic and those who might be able to provide me with a translation would be occupied on other matters. The appalling histories of persecution, genocide and discrimination of many indigenous peoples are not firmly in the past. Perhaps my request seemed like I was making light of a serious matter or holding their languages up for ridicule. And then there was the possibility that some indigenous peoples were continually being approached by well-meaning outsiders looking for some superficial element of their cultures.

My heart sank when I read the FAQ on one American 'native languages' website that explained carefully that no, they will not give you a spirit name and if you want a Native American name for your dog, you should just look up the word for 'dog' in a dictionary of a Native American language.[2]

Was I that different to those asking for a name for my dog? Better leave that as a rhetorical question ...

So, after a while, I ceased actively soliciting indigenous language translations of the Message. There were some exceptions, though. I felt that if an indigenous language had some kind of official status, it would be less in danger of being patronised. I presented a Guarani translation earlier in this book, and here is the Message in Māori (often referred to by its speakers as Te Reo – 'the language'), spoken in Aotearoa/New Zealand:

> TŪPATO! Pānui rāua me tē tūraha. Taonga kore pai mō ngā tamariki tau toru ki raro. Ētahi wāhanga iti ka taea tē kai.[3]

Māori has had official status in Aotearoa/New Zealand since the late 1980s and at least a third of the Māori population can understand the language 'fairly well'.[4] To translate the Message into Māori seems a reasonable thing to do, in part because it is often found in official contexts in Aotearoa/New Zealand itself. It isn't a patronising fantasy to imagine that, one day, it could take its place on the Manuscript. The same is true of Quechua, the language of the indigenous peoples of the central Andes, which was once the language of the Incan Empire. Even today, millions of people speak a language in the Quechuan family, particularly in Peru where it has official status in some regions:

> PAKTARAK, rikushpaka wakaychiy: 3 watayuk wawakunata yalli uchillakunapak pukllanaka mana kanchu. Hansi imakunataka lankanman, sinkanman.[5]

The dark matter of attention

One thing I was sure of, though, was that the Message was in principle translatable into the languages of indigenous peoples, or at least into those that are still regularly spoken. That doesn't mean there are necessarily words for things like 'toy', but even languages that do not have words for some things may develop ways of assimilating loanwords, or speakers handle such issues through code-switching.

While a language can cope with whatever is thrown at it one way or another, that doesn't mean that its speakers necessarily have the need, motivation or confidence to force language to bend in their direction. Official and unofficial discouragement of the use of indigenous languages also prevents the adaptation of those languages to new needs. Further, many indigenous languages are so radically different in structure to the languages of colonialism that linguistic gaps are difficult to overcome. For example, many North American indigenous languages have complex systems of 'evidentiality', in which statements are linguistically marked with the source of the information for the statement. The languages of small and/or isolated communities may develop a high degree of complexity through the limited need to communicate with strangers. It is not, therefore, a lack of linguistic sophistication that may act as a barrier to translation. Rather, as Guy Deutscher argues:

> The crucial differences between languages, in other words, are not in what each language allows its speakers to express – for in theory any language could express anything – but in what information each language obliges it speakers to express.[6]

For Deutscher, languages vary by what they draw *attention* to. While 'Eskimos' do not, as the myth has it, have 50 words for snow, Arctic peoples do indeed have vocabularies that allow close attention to be paid to the differences between types of snow, since that is a vital object of attention. Differences between languages are therefore intrinsically connected to differences in what societies and cultures see as worthy of notice.

Of course, many indigenous peoples live today within industrialised societies, albeit often marginalised and subject to discrimination, and hence have had to adapt to the forms of attention that warning messages require. But what about those peoples in the world who have limited contact with the products of modern capitalism or their linguistic paraphernalia?

The philosopher Willard Van Orman Quine famously conducted a 'thought experiment' in what he called 'radical translation' into a language entirely unrelated to that of the translator (and where there is no third language to translate through).[7] The translator may note that the word 'Gavagai' seems to be applied to 'rabbit', but what if it is actually used to apply to a fly that hovers around rabbits, or to a part of a rabbit? Quine argued that there is an 'indeterminacy' that means that a translation can never be true or false. A 'good' translation can be achieved, pragmatically at least, but not an exact one. The question, for me at least, is 'good for whom?'

A few years ago, the linguist Daniel Everett created a minor sensation in his account of one indigenous people whose language and culture present formidable obstacles to translation, the Amazonian Pirahã.[8] Some aspects of Pirahã culture and language are much simpler than colonial culture and language, including an almost complete lack of a kinship system, no number system and limited colour terms. Such apparent simplicity is known from some other peoples too. Everett argued, though, that the Pirahã language lacks a feature found in *all* other recorded languages, known as 'recursion'. Recursion allows us to 'embed' clauses within other clauses. In Pirahã a sentence like 'The toy's small parts might be swallowed' might need to be split into two sentences: 'The toy has small parts' and 'The small parts might be swallowed'. Everett argues that this lack of recursion is part of a culture that restricts communication to the needs of 'immediate experience' only. This one language constitutes, according to Everett, a challenge to Noam Chomsky's influential idea that there is a 'universal grammar' that all humans innately possess; or at the very least, it challenges the notion that if there is a universal grammar, it includes recursion.

Everett's argument has not found many supporters, and some scholars who have studied Pirahã have disputed his findings.[9] What is certainly true is that the obstacles to translation into the language remain formidable. As Everett demonstrates:

Consider the possibility of translating the following sentence into Pirahã ...: My cousin totally ran out of cash during his second year at art college in California and had to draw $10K from the Bank of Mom and Dad to pay his tuition ... There are no words in Pirahã for mother or father, only a generic word for parent, which [...] has a wider meaning than biological parent, referring also to someone one is hoping to get something from, or someone who holds power over you in a particular situation. There are no quantifier words, hence 'totally' cannot be translated. Further, Pirahã culture has no money, though they do have a vague concept of it from watching Brazilians. They have no numbers, so one dollar or ten thousand dollars would not be translatable. They have no concept or word for art. They have no word for year, per se, though they could say 'water,' referring to a high-water/low-water cycle (one year). They have no concept or word for bank. Thus this entire sentence is ineffable in Pirahã, in both form and content.[10]

Everett uses the term 'dark matter of the mind' to describe 'any knowledge that is unspoken in normal circumstances, usually unarticulated even to ourselves'.[11] This dark matter, and the barriers to understanding it creates, mean that translation isn't just a linguistic practice, it is a cultural one too. Everett therefore argues that:

> [It] is not possible in practice to translate from all languages to all languages, QED. It might be possible, though, if speakers and hearers were to come to share sufficient dark matter, via prolonged cultural contact, that they became bicultural ... Translation [is] a test for degree of dark matter overlap, of knowledge of a language, of cultural understanding, and so on.[12]

The Pirahã are beginning to share that dark matter. They do have contact with other Brazilians and, through them, are being exposed to things like money. The problem is that, as in many other colonial contexts, this 'cultural contact' is rarely a two-way process; it is an invasive one in which indigenous peoples are compelled to understand the dark matter of the other in circumstances not of their own choosing, with dangerous consequences if they fail.

In 'Darmok', a justly celebrated episode of *Star Trek: The Next Generation*, the *Enterprise* encounters a Tamarian ship orbiting the planet El-Adrel. The Tamarians are a people for whom all previous attempts at communication with the Federation have failed. While the universal translator allows individual words to be understood, they do not add up to anything meaningful. The Tamarian captain forcibly transports Captain Picard down to the planet to join him, and the Tamarian technology prevents him from being beamed back onto the *Enterprise*. He gives Picard a dagger and announces, 'Darmok and Jalad at Tanagra'. Together, Picard and the Tamarian are compelled to try to understand each other in order to fight off a dangerous monster. Eventually, Picard begins to understand that the Tamarians speak solely using allusions to mythological events in their history. It becomes clear that Darmok and Jalad were antagonists who had been forced to unite to face a beast at a place called Tanagra; the captain was attempting to recreate the conditions that led Darmok and Jalad to unite.

'Darmok' suggests that some struggles to communicate across cultural-linguistic barriers are so profound that only *shared* trauma can overcome them. The encounters between European colonialism and indigenous peoples certainly qualify as trauma, but a one-sided one in which the indigenous people are forced to do most of the work in achieving understanding. We are no longer able to create a slower, less traumatic process of mutual understanding. It is highly unlikely that there are any peoples in the world who do not have at least some knowledge of western modernity. 'Uncontacted' tribes in the Amazon are usually peoples who have actively avoided engagement with others, sometimes because of previous negative experiences of disease, murder and harassment.[13] Even they will draw selectively on technologies such as machetes where they are useful and have limited cultural impact.

The Message to the Sentinelese

One of the world's most isolated indigenous peoples, the Sentinelese who live on North Sentinel Island in the Andaman Sea, have forcibly repelled most attempts at contact and the Indian authorities prohibit approaching them. No one knows their language and they know no language but their own. They won't have heard of Kinder Surprise Eggs, but they do know that there are people who are not like them and who produce material items that are unlike anything they could produce themselves. They will certainly know that other ways of talking exist and they may have seen writing, although they are unlikely to understand its significance.

From such a limited base of understanding, what cultural knowledge would they and other uncontacted peoples need for them to understand the Message? Are there, perhaps, some 'universals' that might be a basis for understanding?

Obviously reading, writing and marking of age in counted years are not universal, but there is much else too that may be difficult to understand: the Message emanates from an unknown individual or collection of individuals. They issue instructions on the assumption that they can and should be obeyed. In a society like Sentinel Island, not only is everyone known to each other, instructions issued by individuals who are not known to oneself are unlikely to be obeyed.

The Message is also directed at an adult, or at the very least someone who is old enough to be in a position of responsibility and authority over small children. This person of responsibility acts as the gatekeeper to items the child has access to. While the responsibility of certain adults for babies is surely a universal, the stage of development where this responsibility stops varies. We can assume that no one would actively give a sharpened knife or a lighted splint to a baby without full control of his or her limbs. Beyond that, things are much less clear. Child-rearing practices differ markedly across the world and children may be given much greater licence to behave as they wish than in industrialised societies.

The complexity of the Kinder Surprise Egg as an object may also be difficult to understand. The chocolate egg may be initially unrecognisable as food by sight alone to peoples that have had no prior experience of processed chocolate (even if they know of cocoa, processed chocolate is very different). That the chocolate egg is a processed food is not, in and of itself, a sign of inedibility. Many indigenous peoples do eat food that requires extensive processing to the point where it is unrecognisable from its initial state – sago being one example.

We cannot assume that the idea that there are objects dedicated to playing – toys – and that these are particularly attractive to children, is universally intelligible. Moreover, combining an inedible toy with an edible outer layer may be difficult to comprehend. The existence of objects whose outer form is inedible but whose inner contents are edible – and vice versa – is likely to be universally familiar from eating fruits, vegetables and animals. However, eggs as an indicator of good things may not be universal. While egg-laying creatures may be present in most locations where humans have lived, that doesn't mean that the eggs of all animals are seen as edible. That isn't an insurmountable barrier to seeing the egg as tempting, given that the Kinder Surprise was created in a country where the eggs of certain birds are eaten but the eggs of snakes and lizards are not.

We can be confident about the universality of some aspects of the Message and the object it refers to: that some things are not edible, that swallowing or inhaling some objects is dangerous, and that small children may be orally-fixated. Above all, the action of warning is something that all humans do and that offers the greatest possibility of communicating the Message across cultures. We know that the Sentinelese have warned intruders through gestures and sounds of the risks they face if they come close. We know indirectly that they warned each other of one potentially catastrophic risk when they sought high ground just before the Boxing Day tsunami hit the island in 2004. In fact, one of the reasons we know this is because a Sentinelese man fired a warning arrow at a helicopter that hovered over the island to check for survivors.[14]

The red face: a universal Message?

Even if the written Message would not be recognisable as a warning to the Sentinelese, there are other features of the Manuscript that *might* signify as warning-like: the colour red highlights the word 'warning' on all the individual Messages. This is a colour that invites a very old and very deep reaction – danger!

In his essay 'The Colour Currency of Nature', Nicholas Humphrey argued that 'humans as a species find red both a uniquely impressive colour and at times a uniquely disturbing one'.[15] However, the reasons for this are not always clear:

> The reason why red should be in certain situations so disturbing is more obscure. If red was always used as a warning signal there would be no problem. But it is not, it is used as often to attract as to repel. My guess is that its potential to disturb lies in this very ambiguity as a signal colour. Red toadstools, red ladybirds, red poppies are dangerous to eat, but red tomatoes, red strawberries, red apples are good. The open red mouth of an aggressive monkey is threatening, but the red bottom of a sexually receptive female is appealing. The flushed cheeks of a man or woman may indicate anger, but they may equally indicate pleasure. Thus the colour red, of itself, can do no more than alert the viewer, preparing him to receive a potentially important message; the content of the message can be interpreted only when the context of the redness is defined. When red occurs in an unfamiliar context it becomes therefore a highly risky colour. The viewer is thrown into conflict as to what to do. All his instincts tell him to do something, but he has no means of knowing what that something ought to be.

The dual nature – vaguely threatening but sometimes alluring – of the colour red is perfectly suited to the dual nature of the Kinder Surprise Egg itself. It may be that the profusion of red on the Manuscript, while it may not communicate the specifics of the Message, might at least tell the Sentinelese that there is something strange about this object; that its allure isn't to be completely trusted.

There is one other component of the Manuscript that might have the potential to cut through layers of cultural incomprehension. Side one of the Manuscript includes a symbol of a face of an unhappy child, encased in a crossed red circle. While the '0-3' in the circle would be unintelligible to the Sentinelese, might they relate to the face? This is a stylised representation, reduced to eyes, nose, mouth and a quiff of hair. We can't assume that this would be immediately recognised as a face by all humans in all societies. That this standardised international symbol, used on many other warnings, is designed to be universally applicable is highly presumptuous. But maybe over time, and with some study, the initially uncomprehending 'reader' might at least suspect that, like the image, they too have two of one thing, with something in the middle and something below it, all encased in a finite form.

There are intimidating barriers to creating a Message for all of humanity. The universal Message will remain unwritten until such time as we can understand all humans in all their various circumstances. We should, though, pray that that time will never come. The Sentinelese, like many other uncontacted indigenous peoples, would likely be destroyed by their encounter with the rest of humanity: through diseases for which they have no immunity, through violence directed against them and through well-meaning attempts to 'improve' them. It is better, then, that the universal Message, like the Sentinelese Message, remains unwritten. To liberate the Message for them would, in fact, be to enslave them.

While the isolation of the Sentinelese protects them from us, the reverse isn't necessarily true. On the few occasions when outsiders have come to the island, the Sentinelese message has mostly been 'Warning, stay away'. There may be other messages that they could communicate to us, if conditions ever allowed. What could we learn from them? We don't know. The same linguistic and cultural barriers that prevent the Message being intelligible to them, prevents their messages being intelligible to us.

Chapter 10

What we have lost, what we have gained: The Message in time

Yuck!

If there are limits to how far we can liberate the Message today, can we liberate the Message into the past? Can we help it to break free of its time and enter the deeper stream of history?

Today's indigenous peoples are not historical fossils. We should not assume that the Sentinelese live in the same way that their ancestors did. When communication is possible with contacted tribes in the Amazon, that doesn't mean that for 'us' to speak with them is to commune with our past. Even before contact with Europeans, nomadic, semi-nomadic and hunter-gatherer peoples had their own histories, their own technological innovations and linguistic evolution.

All humans, no matter what our circumstances, are connected to each other through the need and the desire to communicate. The archaeologist Steven Mithen has speculated that one of the key drivers for the earliest proto-humans to develop advanced forms of communication was the need to convey warnings to small children. By being able to warn small children of certain dangers, mothers no longer needed to carry them for as long or as frequently as they would otherwise, thereby releasing the mothers for other work or activity. Specifically, Mithen speculates that one of the earliest warnings was of things that were disgusting:

The expression 'Yuk!', and closely related sounds such as 'eeeurrr', are found in all cultures of modern humans, accompanied by the characteristic facial expression of wrinkling the nose and pulling down the corners of the mouth. This is the expression of disgust, which since the time of Charles Darwin has been recognized as a universal human emotion. It arises when people are faced with bodily excretions, decaying food, and certain types of living creatures, notably maggots. 'Yuk!', 'eeeurr!' and related sounds are intrinsically connected to the facial expressions they accompany and are also examples of sound synaesthesia – they are slimy, sticky, smelly, oozy noises, sounding the way that vomit, faeces, spilled blood and maggots look.[1]

Of course, the Message doesn't warn of something disgusting and doesn't address the child directly. It warns the parent of the hidden dangers lurking within something good. Nonetheless, the practice of pointing out something to be avoided is common to 'Yuck!' and to the Message. At the same time, the Message's cool, distanced language also shows how far we have come; what massive edifices we have built on that foundational need to prevent harm to small children. We may have also lost something in the process. Steven Mithen argues that early communication was 'holistic', involving sounds, gestures and even music. The Message is distanced from the body, communicated solely through marks on a flat object made by people we do not know.

While we might be able to infer the basic elements of early human language, we cannot know its details, and to aspire to a full liberation of the Message back to the dawn of human history is a step too far, even for me. What we can do is to acknowledge the value of those modern forms of communication that go beyond sight and sound and use the other senses that our earliest ancestors might have also used to communicate.

The Message in our hands

In June 2020, I booked an online session with a British Sign Language (BSL) tutor and asked him to teach me how to sign the Message. I had no prior experience of sign language other than a few bits of Makaton, a sign system used with people with cognitive impairments and learning disabilities that I learned through youth work many years ago. My tutor was profoundly deaf, which meant I had to communicate through written chat; this forced me to concentrate on the signs he was demonstrating, as I could not take refuge in sound.

Before the lesson, I suspected that I would find BSL incredibly difficult. I am clumsy, uncoordinated and never feel fully in control of my body. My suspicions proved absolutely correct. Not only did I find it unbelievably hard to duplicate my tutor's signs, I seemed to forget them as soon as I had 'learned' them. The most difficult thing was discovering that sign language isn't just something that you do with your hands, it requires facial expressions too. While the 'warning' sign was just a raised finger – that was easy – it was the disapproving furrowed brow that I found challenging. I felt equally self-conscious demonstrating the risk of inhaling and swallowing by choking myself with an alarmed expression. If you want to witness my humiliation, scan the following QR code.[2]

Until my BSL lesson, I had never realised just how limited my use of language was. Trying to communicate with my whole face showed just how little I consciously use it. While I use gestures when I talk, I was never so aware of how limited my control over them was until I actively tried to control them. I began to feel awe at users of sign languages. That was only reinforced when I chaired an online panel at a literary festival that featured two authors who had written about Eastern Europe. The session was signed by the writer and translator Elvire Roberts who managed to cope with lengthy Lithuanian and Ukrainian names in a fluent blizzard of finger-spelling. When I shared my signed version of the Message with Elvire, she pointed out that my tutor hadn't really taught me standard BSL; he had adapted it to make it possible for a complete beginner to sign something that was intelligible. To learn how to sign the Message in BSL with only a few minutes' work is, for a complete beginner, an impossible task.

Still, I eventually realised that putting signers on a pedestal isn't a good idea. I'm sure that there are deaf and hard-of-hearing people who are as klutzy as I am, but that doesn't mean they can't and don't sign. It's more helpful to think of users of sign languages the same way we think of native speakers of other languages: diction, clarity and fluency may vary but the ability to communicate is common to all. Sign languages are part of the wider family of human languages, with their own grammars, regional dialects and idiolects.

To see what sign language should actually look like, I commissioned a translation into American Sign Language (ASL). BSL and ASL are not identical – they are different languages rather than versions of the same one. Scan the following QR code to see Adam Frost, a professor of ASL, signing the Message.[3]

I chose to include QR codes to link to the videos in order to make the point that, even if a mode of communication may only employ a limited range of our human capacity, humans have found ways to 'extend' ourselves. In this case, Adam Frost – who lives in the US – extended the reach of his signing so that it reached me on another continent (via email); I further extended it through uploading the video to YouTube, using a free service to create a QR code from the URL, and then pasted it into a draft document that – multiple steps later – allows you to reverse the process through scanning the code.

Another way of extending the range of sign language is to write it down. A number of sign language notation systems have been developed and, while they are not widely employed by users of sign languages, they are a boon to researchers into sign language in the same way that the International Phonetic Alphabet is a boon to linguists studying spoken languages. As with IPA, writing down sign language may allow some nuances of communication to be lost (such as facial expressions), but doing so shows how language can be transposed from one mode to another. Adam Frost provided me with the following transcription of the ASL Message into Sutton Sign Writing:

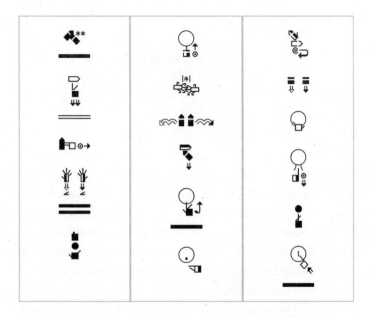

To me, Sutton Sign Writing faintly recalls Ancient Egyptian hieroglyphics or other early writing systems that were based on pictograms, such as Chinese. Over time, such writing systems often became stylised to the point that the original link to the image represented became forgotten. If Sign Writing were to be widely adopted – which is, admittedly, highly unlikely – then the pictograms could cease over time to be representations of body movements, becoming simply words, sounds and syllables. This would also be a pity. The drive to write things is part of a wider process through which humans abandoned holistic forms of communication for a narrower focus on sight and sound. As sign languages show, the capacity for other modes of communication, such as expressive movement, may usually be dormant in our species, but it can be activated when needed.

Another sense that we have allowed to wither is touch. People with visual impairments who use Braille remind us of what is possible when we train ourselves to identify subtle tactile distinctions. Braille can also be turned from a touch-based to a visual mode of communication, through transforming its raised dots into written marks on the page. While Braille can function like an alphabet – one letter is represented by a unique combination of up to eight dots – there are also 'contracted' forms that function as shorthand to speed up reading. Megan Paul, a consultant, writer and activist who is completely blind, printed out the Message for me on a machine called a 'Perkins Brailler' in the English contracted and uncontracted forms. It was an enormous pleasure for me to *feel* the Message in a way that I had not done before. To turn it into something readable for this book feels almost like a betrayal of this 3-D mode of communication. Nonetheless, here is the uncontracted English Braille Message:

⠠⠠⠺⠜⠝⠊⠝⠛⠒ ⠗⠑⠁⠙ ⠁⠝⠙ ⠅⠑⠑⠏⠲ ⠠⠞⠕⠽ ⠝⠕⠞ ⠎⠥⠊⠞⠁⠃⠇⠑ ⠋⠕⠗ ⠉⠓⠊⠇⠙⠗⠑⠝ ⠥⠝⠙⠻ ⠼⠉ ⠽⠑⠜⠎⠲ ⠠⠎⠍⠁⠇⠇ ⠏⠜⠞⠎ ⠍⠊⠛⠓⠞ ⠃⠑ ⠎⠺⠁⠇⠇⠪⠑⠙ ⠕⠗ ⠊⠝⠓⠁⠇⠑⠙⠲

And here is the contracted English Braille Message:

⠠⠠⠺⠜⠝⠬⠂ ⠗⠂⠙ ⠯ ⠅⠑⠑⠏⠒ ⠠⠞⠕⠽ ⠝ ⠎⠥⠊⠞⠁⠼
⠿ ⠡⠝ ⠐⠥ ⠼⠉ ⠽⠑⠜⠎⠲ ⠠⠎⠍⠁⠇⠇ ⠐⠏⠎ ⠍⠊⠣⠞ ⠆
⠎⠺⠁⠇⠇⠪⠫ ⠕⠗ ⠔⠓⠁⠇⠫⠲

In uncontracted Braille, 'Warning' is ⠠⠺⠁⠗⠝⠊⠝⠛, with each sign corresponding to a letter. In contracted, the same word reads as ⠠⠺⠜⠝⠬, with contractions for 'ar' and 'ing'. The contracted Message also uses single signs for some words, such as 'and' – ⠯ – and 'not' – ⠝ – as, in contracted Braille, each letter can stand for a commonly-used word.

Braille could be used by sighted people as a written language, although it is certainly visually austere and a bit bewildering to navigate at first. Yet turning modes of communication that use touch and movement into 2-D marks on the page reminds us of how sensorially limited writing is. Writing takes language away from our non-visual senses and allows the writer to be anonymous, alienated from us.

One way of making writing less alienating is to restore the link to the human body by including pictures of actual human beings. I contacted a British organisation called Easy Read, which produces adapted documents to be understandable by people with learning disabilities. They sent me the following 'translation' of the Message.[4]

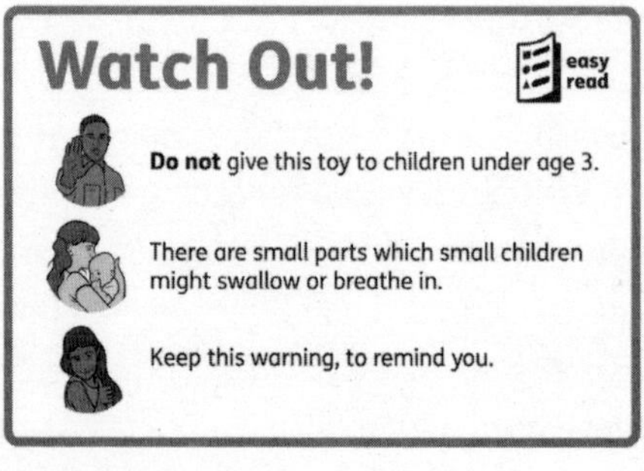

This is one of my favourite Messages in this entire book. It is brim-full of humanity and care, with affecting pictures balancing the text. The text itself warns the reader in a way that is both more direct than the original Message and yet also more intimate. It explains why you should keep the Message ('to remind you'). It does not judge. It reaches out.

And it was to *avoid* that intimacy that humans developed writing in the first place ...

The primordial dullness of the Message

The Message is closer in intelligibility to the modes of communication of the humans who first developed representational art and, later, writing, than it is to the holistic modes of communication familiar to our earliest ancestors. Indeed, the original purpose of writing is not so far removed from the reasons that the Message was written. Distancing isn't a by-product of writing – it is its purpose.

The first written script, Sumerian cuneiform, was intended to regulate and clarify the messy world of human relations, and to ensure that human behaviour conformed to laws and standards set by bureaucratic authorities. The first writing concerned the sale of a field, the tithing of a sack of barley or the bequeathing of an ox. Cuneiform developed over the course of the fourth millennium BCE in what is now southern Iraq, originally from symbols marked on clay accounting tokens. Initially pictographic, by the start of the third millennium BCE the symbols had started to take on their own phonetic value, thereby allowing them to represent components of words. Over time, pictographs were rationalised and lost their remaining symbolic value, becoming signs that represent sounds.

Written Sumerian (and, later, Akkadian) cuneiform may have started out as a tool intended to regulate and record human behaviour; it ended up becoming something greater than itself, a system that could be used to write great works of literature (as well as the Epic of Gilgamesh):

𒁹𒈣𒀸𒂍𒼋𒀸𒂍𒐋𒍦𒂍𒒕𒑉𒍑𒅅𒌝𒀀𒄡
𒉿𒑉𒌅𒄰𒀸𒂷𒄷𒍪𒀅𒄰𒀸𒂷𒅗𒊬𒁾

I was absolutely stunned that Professor Mark Geller of University College London was able to produce this Sumerian translation of the Message. Perhaps I shouldn't have been, though. Many of the cultural barriers to communicating the Message to the Sentinelese don't apply to ancient Mesopotamia. Their civilization was based around the cultivation of grain crops and transforming them into other products that were unrecognisable from their raw ingredients. They understood instructions, orders and authority. They had written law codes, manufactured trade objects and understood the concept that different sorts of humans could and should refrain from certain sorts of behaviours. While the ancient Babylonians would have found much that is incomprehensible about a Kinder Surprise Egg, there is at least enough common ground for there to be a basis on which to build a translation. Admittedly, Professor Geller did point out to me that: 'I doubt whether a Sumerian native speaker would have understood the warning because he wouldn't know the context.' But doesn't that also apply to the Message itself? Written instructions that apply to an object only make sense when we know what the object is. He also pointed out: 'nor do we have any real colloquial

Sumerian to work from'. But the official Message isn't in a colloquial register in any language.

There is something primordial about the Message. I am not talking here about the desire to warn of danger, but something we do not usually recognise as being part of our ancient inheritance – our use of writing to regulate mundane things. Sometimes, accounts of ancient writing emphasise its use to write history, religion and literature rather than the supposedly boring stuff. Accounts of the Linear B Mycenaean Greek script usually devote more time to the extraordinary quest to decipher it than they do to the tax records that were found to be written in the script once it could be read.[5] The meticulous recording of tithes of wool and grain do not appear to have the grandeur of ancient mythology. Yet it is in everyday life that we come closest to our ancestors; the otherness falls away as we encounter human beings who are as dull as we are. So it is that the Message, a text that sets no pulses racing, can help us knit together our common experience of the travails of everyday life.

This thrilling ability of the Message to let us meet with our ancestors in the writing of mundanity is counterbalanced by the evocative otherness of their scripts. Cuneiform retains its scent of the ancient. Here is another cuneiform translation of the Message, this time in Ugaritic, an early Semitic language written in symbols unrelated to Mesopotamian cuneiform:[6]

Early writing was also used to immortalise those who commissioned it, and for sacred purposes. We know of Egyptian hieroglyphics through the longevity of the stone monuments built by Pharaohs and court officials. To view the Message translated into Middle Egyptian is to imagine it carved into eternity:

Dr William Manley of Glasgow University, who produced this translation, told me:

> I did use the imperative on the basis of the English original, of course, but also on the basis of the Book of Two Ways, from about 1750 BC, which seemed to me to have an appropriate tone of barking out demands for the reader's benefit in what could be described as a hopeful but potentially hostile context (albeit the journey from death to life in the Egyptian case).

A literal translation of the Middle Egyptian hieroglyphic text would therefore be:

> Stop, you (sing. masc.). Get this message read, intended to prevent bits getting into the throat or nose. This is the little thing which is not suitable for children who do not have three years.

Dr Manley also supplied me with a translation into medieval Coptic. Coptic is a later development of Egyptian that began to be written in the Greco-Roman period. While today its use is largely confined to the Coptic Orthodox Church, it remained the principal language of Egypt until it was supplanted by Arabic in medieval times. The Coptic writing system is based on Greek:

ⲣ̅ⲉ̄ⲛⲛⲧ̄ⲛⲉⲕⲁⲁⲥⲉ̄ⲙⲡⲉⲧⲛ̄ⲣ̄ⲛ̄ⲧⲁⲩⲱⲱϣⲛ̄ⲧⲉⲓⲅⲣⲁⲫⲙⲛ̄ⲧⲉⲧⲛ̄ⲣ̄ⲁⲣⲉⲣⲉⲛⲉⲥⲛ̄ⲧⲟ
ⲗⲏⲙ̄ⲙⲱⲧⲛ̄ⲡⲉⲓⲣ̄ⲱⲃⲁⲉⲛⲱ̄ⲭⲱϫⲉⲁⲛⲉⲧⲣⲉⲩⲧⲁⲁ̄ⲩⲛ̄ⲛ̄ⲱⲏⲣⲉⲉⲧⲙ̄ⲡⲁⲧⲉⲩⲱϫⲡⲉ
ⲉⲩⲛ̄ⲧⲁⲩⲱ̄ⲟⲙ̄ⲛ̄ⲧⲛ̄ⲣⲟⲙⲡⲉⲙ̄ⲙⲟⲟ̄ⲩⲁⲗⲗⲁⲟⲩⲛ̄ⲣ̄ⲉⲛⲕⲟⲩⲓ̈ⲙ̄ⲡⲉⲓⲙⲁⲛ̄ⲑⲉⲛ̄ⲛⲁ̈ⲓ̈ⲉⲧⲣ
ⲉⲩⲥⲁ̄ⲣ̄ⲡⲟ̄ⲩⲉⲣ̄ⲟⲩⲛ̄ⲣ̄ⲓⲧⲁⲡⲣⲟⲙ̄ⲛ̄ⲛⲁ̈ⲓ̈ⲉⲧⲣⲉⲩϫⲓⲧⲟⲩⲉⲣ̄ⲟⲩⲛⲉⲃⲟⲗ̄ⲣ̄ⲓⲧⲙ̄ⲡⲓⲛⲓⲃⲉ̇

The literal translation is:

> Be ready to take thought: Read the text and note its warnings for you (plu.). This thing is not suited to be given to children who do not yet have three years. Rather there are small parts present such as may be swallowed by the mouth and such as may be taken in by the breath.

Dr Manley also clarified the relationship between the Coptic and Middle Egyptian translations:

> I had no specific reason to address the earlier text to the singular 'you' and the later text to the plural 'you'. However, each seemed more natural, perhaps because Ancient Egyptian afterlife texts are intimate and usually addressed to an individual (usually a man), whereas Coptic texts are more frequently of a type addressed to collections of people.

The time-travelling Message

The principal barrier to ancient translation is less the language itself than the size of the corpus of texts that have survived. There are many languages that we know only through fragments or which were used to write a very limited range of texts. My son, an aspiring classicist, attempted an Etruscan translation of the Message, but managed only a few words. Etruscan was the non-Indo-European language of an Italian civilization that was eventually overwhelmed by the rise of Rome. While there are thousands of inscriptions in the language and a limited number of bilingual inscriptions, these are mostly very short and do not give us enough of the language to complete a translation of the Message.

Even languages that are much better known have absences. Professor Veturliði Óskarsson, of Uppsala University, supplied the following translation into Old Norse:

Varhygð, les ok geym: Barnaleika sjá hentar eigi bǫrnum yngri en þriggja vetra. Smáir hlutir mega svelgðir verða elligar kunna í lungu fara.

Not only does Old Norse express age in a different way than we do, it has no recorded word for 'inhale'. So Professor Óskarsson worked around these issues to produce a translation that reads literally in English as:

Warning, read and keep: Children-toy this suits not children younger than three winters. Small parts may swallowed be, or can in lungs go.

Dr Lidia Wojtczak, who produced a Sanskrit translation of the Message, encountered a different problem:

सावधानं पठ्यतां सविधे च स्थाप्यतां । एतत् क्रीडनकं वर्षत्रयात्
कनीयसाम् बालानाम् कृते न योग्यम् । सूक्ष्माः भगाः ग्रस्ताः निपीताः वा
भवेयुः ।।

As she explained to me:

> Sanskrit allows for so many ways of expressing com-
> pulsion or prohibition, that it was difficult to pick. I
> ended up going for the pure Imperative in 'Warning'
> (Sanskrit: 'May there be caution') but for the much
> more polite Imperative Passive in 'read and keep' since
> this would be a direct order directed at the reader.

This profusion of choices makes sense. As a language that is
primarily known to us via its use in ancient Indian sacred
texts, it is unsurprising that the Sanskrit corpus contains a
multitude of ways of instructing and prohibiting.

Some ancient languages do not have a word for 'toy'.
Dr Alinda Damsma, the translator of the Message into Biblical
Hebrew, had to work around the lack of word for this kind of
object:[7]

הזהר וקרא ושמר הכלי הזה סכן ילדים אשר צעירים משלש שנים
כי יבלעו חלקות קטנות

This literally reads as:

> Be warned, read and keep: this thing/object endangers
> children who are younger than three years because
> they might swallow small parts.

Biblical Hebrew's terseness is perfectly suited to the sacred task of Message-writing. The language of the Hebrew Bible is so economical that it can sometimes appear highly ambiguous and at other times brutishly blunt. This comes across in English Bible translations only to a degree, but you certainly see the difference by comparing the number of words. A bilingual Hebrew–English Bible or prayer book is often challenging to typeset, as sentences and paragraph lengths do not match up. Indeed, the Biblical Hebrew Message is fifteen words long, whereas the English original is nineteen – and in a highly condensed form of English at that.

The Aramaic Message also lacks 'toy', or at least this one by Professor Daniel Boyarin does, sidestepping the problem with 'This is not suitable for' without mentioning what 'this' refers to:

אזהרתא למקרא ולמשמר: האי לאו לדרדקי דליכא להו תלת שנין. סכנתא למיבלע אי לנשופי אביזורי זוטרתי.

More precisely, this translation is into an approximation of the Aramaic in which the Jewish Talmud was written, in Palestine and Babylonia in the first few centuries CE. This Semitic language has 3,000 years of history behind it, including centuries of use as a lingua franca across the Middle East during and after the rise of the neo-Assyrian Empire from the ninth century BCE. It comes in many varieties, going under different names. Reconstructing a single Aramaic Message is difficult, given the language's history and diversity. Even Talmudic Aramaic is not just one thing, as the 'book' (actually a sprawling, multi-volume collection of Rabbinic debates) emerged over centuries in two different locations. So I was not surprised when, following an online request for help, I received a number of translations, including the one above. One competing Talmudic Aramaic translation I received used the word for 'game' rather than toy.[8] Another translation, into an earlier version of Aramaic known as 'Targumic' (into which the Hebrew Bible was translated in the centuries following the first century BCE) used the word for 'bauble-chain' or 'trinket'.[9]

Another version of Aramaic is known as Syriac. The ethnic Assyrian scholar Nicholas Al-Jeloo provided me with translations into a number of variants of the language. One of them was Western Classical Syriac, which developed in the first millennium CE in Syria and Mesopotamia and is still used as a liturgical language in the Syriac Orthodox church. Its writing system bears some superficial similarity to Arabic script, but is distinct from it:

ܐܩܘܗܕܐܟ، ܡܢܕ ܐܢܠܐܟ: ܥܕܢܢܟ ܠܟ ܢܥܓܢ ܠܥܒܓܬܟ ܐܬܠܐܝܢܠܐ ܬ 3 ܥܢܬ.
ܢܠܢܝ̈ܟ ܐܚܕܬܝ̈ܟ ܚܘܢܝ ܡܚܢܐ̇ܬܠܬܢܬ ܟ̇ܐ ܡܬܢܐ̇ܝܥܡܬܬ.

Aramaic/Syriac lost ground over the centuries to Arabic. Speakers of the descendants of these languages – contemporary Assyrians who follow Syriac Orthodox Christianity – have in recent years experienced displacement from Near Eastern countries. Assyrian still clings on though. Here is the Message in Western Assyrian – also known as *Turoyo* – as spoken in parts of southeastern Turkey and northern Syria. It is written in a version of the Syriac script known as *Serto*:

ܐܘܗܘܐ، ܡܢܢ ܡܢܝ̈: ܝܡ̇ܝܡ̇ܢܝܐ ܠܐ ܡܐ ܡܐܟܬܕ ܠܐܝ ܥܓܢܐ ܪܠܟܝ̈ܡ̇ܝܣܝ ܬ 3 ܝܡܢܐ. ܦܚܕܩܐ ܝܡܢܩܐ
ܡܐ̇ܝܝ̈ܓܘ̇ܘܢ، ܘܩܚܟܟܬܕ ܐܘ ܘܩܢܝ̈ܡ̇ܥܕ.

Some Messages make their way through time radically changed, adopting new alphabets and new guises. Others appear superficially frozen in time. A translation of the Message into Latin and Greek produces few problems. The corpus of texts we have for these languages is vast. Here is the Message in Attic Greek, the language of Ancient Athens in its golden age during the middle first millennium CE:

> τὸ νουτέθημα τοῦτο ἀναγνοὺς σῶσαι· οὐ προσῆκον
> τοῖς παιδίοις τοῖς τριέτεσιν ἢ νεωτέροις τὸ παίγνιον,
> οὗ οἷά τε ἢ κατεσθίειν ἢ ἀναπνεῖν τὰ μόρια.[10]

The Latin Message also calls out to us from the classical era:

> ADMONITUM, lege et tene: Crepundium non idoneus
> liberis minoris tres annis quam est. Parvi partes in
> spirentur et sorbeantur.[11]

Beneath the surface, though, all is different. Modern Greek is radically different from its Attic ancestor. Latin lives today in modified form as a language of the Catholic church and (occasionally) in scholarship and ceremony, but it is through its multiple Romance descendants that we come to read its Message today.

Latin transformed the languages it encountered on its journey through. We can see what the English Message would have looked like as a Germanic language, Old English, before the Norman invasion infused it with a hefty dose of Latin:

> WARNA. Rǣd ond cēp þās ġetācnunge. Ðrywintre ċild
> ne findeþ ġemǣte þisne plegan. Hit meahte forsweal-
> gan oþþe in éðian lȳtle dǣlas.[12]

We can then go forward from there and observe how Chaucer might have written the Message in Middle English:

> Manyterge, rede an kepe. þis gwgawe be nat hovable
> to sukelinges. Smale partys moȝen ben y-swolowyd.[13]

To trace the Message from ancient to modern tongues is not just to perform an act of scholarship, it is to connect with one's ancestors and assert a living connection with them. Far from simply being an activity for scholars to engage with when pestered by me, translating the Message into 'dead' languages tells us that they may not be dead at all; they are immortal.

Chapter 11

Reviving the Message

Revivalistics

A language is only immortal in one sense. As Claude Hagège puts it:

> The death of a language is only the death of speech. Thus, languages as systems of rules are not mortal, although they have no life by themselves, and live only if communities put them into speech.[1]

We can be sanguine about the death of spoken languages to the extent that linguistic evolution is what ensures that languages live. Middle English might not be spoken any more, but it forms part of the bedrock of today's English. Since it was written down, we can reconstruct its rules and understand what it was to have spoken it.

The linguist Ghil'ad Zuckermann has termed languages that are no longer spoken but that can be reconstructed 'sleeping' languages. Zuckermann is an expert in what he calls 'revivalistics', the art and science of reviving languages from their sleep.[2] Languages sleep for a variety of reasons: war and genocide that wipe out speakers, emigration, assimilation into a different language community, active suppression by those in power, the attraction and prestige of another language and the possibilities it affords. In modern times, languages have gone to sleep at an unprecedented rate, due to colonialism, mass emigration, and the power of the mass media to promote dominant languages at the expense of 'weaker' ones.

UNESCO's Atlas of the World's Languages in Danger lists 2,464 languages that are endangered to some degree (although this is not a complete list).[3] At the lowest level of risk are those defined as 'vulnerable' where 'most children speak the language, but it may be restricted to certain domains (e.g. home)'. At the penultimate level are languages that are 'critically endangered' where 'the youngest speakers are grandparents and older, and they speak the language partially and infrequently'. What's crucial is not the number of speakers but whether and how a language is being transmitted to the next generation.

While none of the official Message languages are classed as endangered, some of the translations presented so far in this book are: Māori, Welsh and Scots are 'vulnerable'; Western neo-Aramaic, Romani, Rumantsch, Sorbian, North Sámi, Piedmontese, Yiddish and Irish Gaelic are 'definitely endangered'; Occitan and Ladino are 'severely endangered'.

To bring a language back from the brink is a tough task. It can also be a highly political task, linked into liberation struggles and pushing back against the legacies of Empire and colonialism.[4] To speak and to use a language can be an affirmation of identity against those who would ignore, marginalise or destroy it. For example, the Uyghur Diaspora are drawing on their rich poetic tradition as an act of defiance against the threat of genocide and linguicide in China.[5]

For indigenous peoples, language revival can be part of a wider process of reclaiming culture and dignity after decades or centuries of attempts to erase both. After I had ceased to solicit translations of the Message into indigenous languages, I unexpectedly received one from someone I had contacted months before. Xavier Barker is an Australian linguist and activist who works at the Pama Language Centre in the Cape North Peninsula, at the far north of Queensland. He sent me his own translation of the Message into Mpakwithi, one of the languages that the Centre is working with the last few speakers to revive:

> ROWGHU, mamalithichii'ii e kwii'ii: Ndrru ghamanga yughu ndrru'a toy yana. 'ani parts-fwa kati'i unaya, njiiyii – vwinikumu.

When I searched for Mpakwithi online to find out more about the language, the little I could find suggested that it was extinct. Yet the Mpakwithi Message proves that it lives still. The insouciance with which the language incorporates the word 'toy' is a demonstration of the robust attitude to assimilating new words that language revival requires.

Normalising the Message

One thing that helps in language revival is to 'normalise' an endangered language so that encountering it is an everyday thing. The visibility of the 'linguistic landscape' is an important component in ensuring the vitality of a language.[6] That's where translations of the Message can help. When a speaker of an endangered language encounters the Manuscript, they are forced to rely on another language (if they speak one) and the message that their native tongue is inconsequential is reinforced yet again. To imagine a Manuscript covered with endangered languages is to imagine that Ferrero were committed to the struggle to support linguistic diversity. You might say it's not their job, but Ferrero expend a lot of effort on 'corporate responsibility'. Why might this not be part of that responsibility?

In early November 2020, I happened to see a tweet proclaiming that it was Võro language week. Võro is a 'definitely endangered' Finnic language spoken in south-eastern Estonia. I reached out to the Võro Institute, which promotes the language, and was able to present a translation to the world so I could contribute to the week's activities. Imagine if Ferrero had, even for just one week in Estonia alone, included Võro into the Manuscript?

> HOIATAMINÕ, loeq ja tiiq nii: Seo mängoasi kõlba-ai alla kolmõ aastagaidsilõ latsilõ. Nä võivaq mängo tsill'okõisi juppõ alla neeldäq vai hindäle kurku ajjaq.[7]

This may appear like a trivial way of supporting an endangered language. But it is often exclusion from the world of mundane public language that hurts speakers of endangered languages the most. In December 2020 I was moved by the following tweet from a fluent Scots Gaelic speaker who lives outside the area where the language is still routinely spoken:

> I would love to experience Gàidhlig spoken in the community. I want to walk into a shop or cafe and hear it spoken. So strange to have been a Gàidhlig speaker my whole life and to have only experienced this on the City link bus to Inverness.[8]

While spoken and written language are not the same, perhaps seeing the language written on more than just road signs would be at least some comfort. The Scots Gaelic Message could provide some modest consolation to this isolated speaker of a 'definitely endangered' tongue:

> RABHADH, leugh is glèidh: Dèideag nach fhreagair air clann fo 3. Pìosan beaga a ghabhas slugadh no toirt a-steach leis an anail.[9]

And perhaps seeing other Celtic languages on the Manuscript would be a source of solace too. The last redoubts of a pre-Roman branch of the Indo-European language family, pushed relentlessly to the westward fringes of the British Isles and northern France, still they endure. To Welsh, Irish and Scots Gaelic, we must add Breton, spoken in Brittany, in north-west France:

> EVEZH, da lenn ha da virout ganeoc'h: C'hoariell ha ne zere ket ouzh ar vugale dindan 3 bloaz. Lodennoù bihan a c'hallfe bezañ lonket pe enanalet.[10]

Now Manx, the indigenous language of the Isle of Man:

> BEE ER DTY HWOAIE, lhaih as freill: Cha nel y gaih shoh cooie da paitchyn ny sloo na 3 bleeaney d'eash. Oddagh ayrnyn beggey ve sluggit sheese ny tayrnit stiagh.[11]

And finally Cornish, the language of Cornwall – the last peninsular redoubt of Celtic in England:

> Gwarnyans, redyewgh ha gwithewgh: Nyns yw an wariell ma gwiw rag fleghes yn-dann 3 bloedh.

Rannow byghan a allsa bos lenkys po anellys a-bervedh.[12]

The Cornish and Manx Messages also offer consolation to speakers of languages way beyond the Celtic fringe. For these are languages that did, in fact, go to sleep. Cornish did not survive beyond the eighteenth century and the last native speaker of Manx, a fisherman named Ned Maddrell, died in 1974. Yet the languages have been subsequently revived from their slumber, through the efforts of activists and scholars. Although neither is commonly heard on the street, there are now a few hundred speakers of both, together with publishers and media. Manx and Cornish are being taught to children, although it will be some time – if it ever happens – before a young person can complete their entire education in either language. Even if both languages are classed as 'severely endangered', this is an improvement on their previous extinct status, and perhaps a beginning to a process that will end in their long-term survival.

Endangered languages in our own backyard

A few years ago, I asked a scholar of endangered North American languages how I could help to support endangered languages. He didn't really have an answer for me, but I eventually found the answer myself: start in your own backyard.

It's absolutely understandable that the languages of indigenous peoples are the focus of efforts to attract publicity to the cause of endangered languages; after all, the fate of indigenous languages is usually part of a much wider process of discrimination dating back centuries. But there are other endangered languages much closer to home that are usually ignored. I'm not talking about Celtic languages but the much less well-known languages of the Channel Islands of Jersey, Guernsey, Alderney and Sark.

Few people in the UK or elsewhere are particularly concerned about the fate of these islands. When they are thought of at all, it is as tax havens and holiday destinations. Yet however much the Channel Islands might seem to be a mixture of parochial dullness and non-specific internationalism, they have their own history and culture. The islands have been self-governing since medieval times, although as 'Crown Dependencies' the UK still has overall responsibility for them. Until the nineteenth century, the language of the islands was Norman French and some words in the language are still used in government. The four main islands developed distinctive dialects and there were even dialectal differences within the islands themselves. On Jersey and Guernsey, these dialects developed their own literary tradition.

I have long believed that one of the reasons why small territories often embrace the super-rich is that they do not have the confidence to survive as self-governing specks in a globalised world. They pay a price for this, though, in that their local culture becomes swamped in a wave of globalised blandness. So perhaps revitalising the languages of the Channel Islands can help the islanders recover some sense of what they have lost; a sense of uniqueness and cultural vitality.

While Jersey Norman French – known as Jèrriais – and Guernsey Norman French – known as Dgèrnésiais – are both classed as 'severely endangered' languages, they do at least have dedicated government officers supporting them. The languages are used occasionally on signage in the islands, and classes are available to learn them. They are spoken by only a small minority of the islands' populations and the remaining speakers are also divided by local dialects, particularly in Jersey. When I asked Colin Ireson of L'Office du Jèrriais for a translation of the Message, he consulted among speakers in an effort to achieve a consensus, eventually coming up with the following:

> Dgèrnissement. Liéthez et gardez. Jouette n'pon conv'nabl'ye pour éfants souos l'âge dé trais ans. P'tites parties peuvent êtres avalées ou heunmées.

A few weeks later I received an unsolicited translation from Clive Boutle of Francis Boutle Publishers who have brought out an anthology of Norman French literature:

> Mêfi'-ous, liêthiz et gardez: Jouette înconv'nabl'ye pouor les p'tchiots en d'ssous d'trais ans. Des p'tites parties pouôrraient êt' engaûmées ou heunmées.

Aside from some differences in word choice, there appears to be a difference in orthography, in that the second translation is festooned with circumflexes and the first only has a couple. This is a common problem with endangered languages. Even when there is a standard orthography, not all speakers will know how to use it. Nonetheless, however Jèrriais is written, there is a noticeable difference to the Dgèrnésiais translation supplied by the Guernsey Language Commission:

> DGERNISSEMENT: à llière et à gardaï: Jouaette mal à propaos pour éfànts au d'sous l'âge dé 3 àns. Des ptites parties peuvent ête avalaï ou encaombraï en respirànt.

One of the most noticeable differences is between the Jèrriais *liéthez* and the Dgèrnésiais *à llière*. Both mean 'read' but Jèrriais uses a 'th' sound which is a characteristic of the language not found in its neighbours. Such differences are to be treasured but they also mean that pan-Channel Islands linguistic cooperation – together with cooperation with mainland Norman French activists – has to be balanced with insular activism.

Sercquiais is the language of the smallest and least populous Channel Island, Sark (if you don't count Herm, where a handful of people live, and Lihou and Brecqhou which are privately owned). While, apparently, a handful of islanders still speak it, Sercquiais does not have the written tradition of Jèrriais and Dgèrnésiais, nor can the island support dedicated language activism. The Jèrriais and Dgèrnésiais language officers did put me in touch with an academic who knows the language but, alas, she never responded. The lesson here is that, when a language is on the brink of extinction, there may be no one who is fully 'responsible' for it.

The fourth Channel Island language is Alderney's Aourgnais. This is classed as 'extinct' by UNESCO and, as with Sercquiais, there is very limited literature to draw on. However, a few older island residents have memories of hearing the language as children. One of them, Royston Raymond, worked hard to wake the language from its slumber and promoted the language until his death in 2019. His collaborator, Sally Pond, with whom he compiled a 2,000-word dictionary of Aourgnais, managed to supply a translation of the Message:

Djernissement: à llière et gardâir: Jouette n'es pâr destinôï aux effàonts au d'sous l'âge dé treis aons.

Des morceaux peuvent êté avalaï ou encaombraï en respiraont.

The Aourgnais translation closely resembles the Dgèrnésiais Message. It is hard to tell whether this reflects a genuine close relationship between the languages or whether the effort to revive Aourgnais must, of necessity, graft the limited amount that is still known of the language onto the still living body of Dgèrnésiais. This brings us to the greatest barrier to language revival: a language must be documented to be revived. Human history is filled with languages for which we have no or little information. Indeed, there are untold languages that we do not know ever existed. These languages have definitely died, although some of their ancestors might still walk among us.

In my undergraduate studies in anthropology and sociology, I was taught to be suspicious of 'salvage ethnography'; the recording of the folklore, beliefs and practices of peoples on the brink of extinction. Those doing the 'salvaging', whatever their intentions, may be representatives of the same dominant peoples and institutions that are perpetrating the extinction. Further, the cultures of peoples on the brink of extinction are not necessarily the same as they have always been. There is something incredibly sad about a people's culture becoming an object in a museum, as if it were frozen in time, without its internal diversity and historical evolution.

The case for 'salvage linguistics', though, seems overwhelming, if done sensitively. By interviewing the last speakers of endangered languages and creating as full a description of the language as possible, we don't just preserve it as a memorial, but also ensure that it sleeps rather than dies. A sleeping language can always be revived.

Revived languages

The most successful example of language revival is Modern Hebrew, known as *Ivrit*. Hebrew had ceased to be a spoken language in the first or second century CE, and even before then Aramaic had become the dominant everyday language among the Middle Eastern Jewish population. Hebrew was used for sacred purposes and also continued to be written and to evolve; Hebrew prayers, sacred poetry (known as *piyyut*) and scholarly works continued to be composed. Hebrew often served as a correspondence language between dispersed Diaspora Jewish communities.

Still, as a spoken language of everyday life, Hebrew slept until the late nineteenth century, when a movement to revive the language began. This was part of the wider Zionist enterprise to create a Jewish homeland, although in its early phase some of its leaders (including Theodor Herzl) were sceptical of the possibility that Hebrew could serve as a living language in a reborn Jewish state. Yet between 1900, when only a handful of people spoke and wrote Hebrew as an everyday language, and 1948, when it became the national language of the independent Jewish state, Hebrew was revived in an incredibly short time.

Ivrit was not and is not the same as the language of the Hebrew bible. In order to turn Hebrew into a language that could be used in all situations, there was a lot of work that needed to be done. Not only did it lack many of the words needed in modern times, such as 'telephone', it also lacked the informal registers used in talk at home and on the street. So Ivrit was a creation, an invention with ancient roots. Key figures in this act of creation, such as Eliezer Ben-Yehuda – who developed the first Ivrit dictionary and whose children became the first to be raised in the language – and the poet Haim Bialik, were constantly adding to the emerging lexicon.

This process of invention continues to this day. The Academy of Hebrew Language still meets to regulate the language and to create new words. In 2009, to mark the International Year of Astronomy, the Academy held a national competition to suggest Hebrew names for the planets Neptune and Uranus (which weren't known in Biblical times).[13] The winner for Uranus was אורון (*Oron*) which combines the Hebrew word *or* for 'light' and the diminutive suffix -*on*. This planet that can barely be seen from Earth became 'little light'. For Neptune, the winner רהב (*Rahav*) is the Biblical name for a particular sea monster, which is roughly similar to the sea god Neptune. In this way, Hebrew words are not created from scratch, but from repurposed archaic words and from portmanteau constructions from existing sources.

Sometimes the Academy plays catch-up, giving their blessing (or not) to terms that are coined in writing or in speech. One day twenty years ago, when I was learning Hebrew, my tutor told me a word that had just been given approval, מיזם (*meizam*) meaning 'project' in the sense of 'initiative'. The word derives from the root of the word 'enterprise'. While the word had been coined in the 1950s, it had only been elevated to widespread use with the recent growth of the Israeli hi-tech industry. Previously, Israelis had mostly used the loanword פרויקט (*proyect*) and, indeed, sometimes they still do.

How faithfully revived languages resemble their ancestors is a question that needs to be answered on a case-by-case basis. What is beyond dispute is that revival is possible in certain circumstances. It is unclear what the future of Manx and Cornish holds, but its contemporary speakers have definitely woken the languages from their sleep. Even though Israel might be a country that is viewed with extreme suspicion in some parts of the world, the example of Ivrit should inspire anyone who wishes to revive a language. Indeed, Welsh activists have certainly learned from the Hebrew example to spread and popularise the language. Beginner's Welsh courses are sometimes known as *Wlpan*, a name derived from the Ivrit *Ulpan* ('studio') immersion method of teaching the language intensively to beginners.

Revived languages offer us something linguistically unique; the chance for archaic and contemporary linguistic forms to intermingle. The past, present and future collide in one revived language of the British Isles: Nynorn. Norn was a language brought by Norse settlers to the Orkneys, the Shetlands and the northern tip of Scotland. It was gradually replaced by Scots and became extinct at some point in the nineteenth century. The Norn corpus is limited, but that hasn't stopped a few activists from reviving it as Nynorn ('New Norn').[14] They acknowledge that Nynorn is an 'artificial creation', one motivated by curiosity to 'see what [Norn] could be like had it stayed alive until our days'. The Nynorn Message therefore represents a liberation of Norn from its slumber, and a liberation of the Message from the constraints of time itself:

ÅVARIN! Les og minst: lallið ikke makligt fyri bånn under 3ga åra aldri. Småurekar kunna vara glepter or andaðer inn.

Chapter 12

A new Message

Conlanging the Message

Language never stands still. The Message will not stay
unchanged for eternity. Like the evolution of species, though,
the evolution of languages doesn't proceed universally at the
same steady pace. Languages too go through everything from
insular stasis to mass extinction events and moments of rapid
development. Where the analogy breaks down is that, while
humans or any other creatures cannot (yet) create new species from scratch, humans *can* create new languages almost
from scratch.

'Constructed' languages – also known as 'conlangs' – are
among humanity's most audacious creations. Conlanging has
a long history. In the appendix to her entertaining book *In the
Land of Invented Languages*, Arika Okrent lists 500 conlangs
dating back to the twelfth century and finishing in the early
1970s, without claiming that it is an exhaustive list.[1]

To solicit translations of the Message into conlangs is to do
them the ultimate honour. By treating them as languages like
any other into which 'anything' can be translated, conlangs
can be assimilated into the wider human language family.
That assimilation was certainly the aim of Esperanto, the most
famous conlang of all. One of the myths about Esperanto is
that it was intended to replace all other languages. Rather,
Ludwig Zamenhof, who created it in the late nineteenth century, intended it to be an 'auxiliary' language (what is now
known as an 'auxlang'), spoken alongside others as an aid

to international understanding. While Esperanto attracted considerable enthusiasm at the time and has always had thousands of users worldwide, the language has never been anything other than marginal. Whatever potential it did have to act as a balm to the sore of global conflict was negated by the persecution of its speakers under the Nazis and the Soviets.

Esperanto has evolved into something more modest than Zamenhof intended, but just as precious: a language that is in some ways like any other, with its own community of speakers and its own literature. There are even a few hundred 'native' speakers who have been raised in Esperanto-speaking families. In 1998, the *Pakto por la Esperanta Civito* declared that 'the Esperanto community is a stateless diasporic language-collective to which people belong by free choice, or by a free confirmation, in the case of *denaskaj* [from birth] Esperantists'.[2] This 'chosenness' is one of the defining features of Esperanto and conlangs in general. As Esther Schor argues in *Bridge of Words*, her book on the *Esperantujo* (Esperanto nation):

> What strikes me, after seven years in Esperantujo, is that Esperanto bridges the dichotomy between what is 'radically given' and what is 'freely chosen.' Esperanto is not 'radically given' to anyone, not even to denasku-loj, who are free to take it or leave it. No, Esperanto is radically chosen. And to choose a language is to see the world a certain way; to question it a certain way; to assess, criticize, acclaim, or reform it within certain parameters.[3]

Conlangs are 'owned' by their speakers rather than simply given to them. Their future is open to conscious revision and change. Nonetheless, Esperanto remains wedded to the world of 'natural' languages. Zamenhof constructed it from elements of Indo-European languages, with Slavic sounds and a Romance-dominated vocabulary. It is an easy language for a native speaker of a Romance, Germanic or Slavic language to learn, but its internationalism is compromised by the narrowness of its European linguistic roots. To read the Esperanto Message is both to acknowledge a uniquely transnational linguistic community and also to recognise the limitations of our ability to transcend our own linguistic horizons:

> AVERTO, legu kaj ŝparu. La ludilo ne taŭgas por infanoj sub tri jaroj. Malgrandaj partoj eblas glutiĝi aŭ enspiriĝi.[4]

The dual nature of Esperanto – generous and open-hearted, yet unable to transcend its limitations – is shared with other conlang communities. Their idealism drives them forward and also makes them prone to rifts and disputes. Esperanto is one of a number of conlang communities that have seen schisms over different visions of the language. In 1907, a significant number of Esperantists who wished to see the language reformed along Romance lines, split off to develop the Ido language. Ido, while it saw some initial popularity, never managed to supplant its parent language. Yet it still has a few adherents. The Ido Message is a living memorial to the passion that drives a conlang community onwards and also threatens its survival.

AVERTO, lektez e konservez: Ludilo ne konvenas ad infanti sub 3 yari. Mikra parti povas esar glutata od inhalata.[5]

Artlanging the Message

The act of language creation is often viewed suspiciously or seen as a joke. That's particularly the case with the 'artlangs' constructed for use in fictional worlds. Klingon, the language spoken by the warlike race in *Star Trek*, is often treated with derision: how sad and ludicrous is it that some people love *Star Trek* so much they want to bring it to life! Yet since the 1980s, when it first began to be developed, Klingon has become a language and linguistic community as rich and multifaceted as any other. While the lexicon is, understandably, stuffed with specialist terms for particular aspects of Klingon culture, the language has sufficient breadth to produce a translation of the Message:

puqvaD mItbe' reHmeH janvam, qaSpa' DISDaj wejDIch. chaq 'ay' mach ghup qoj pur.[6]

Translations of the Message into alien artlangs may indeed look alien, yet the fact of translation also demonstrates how the act of creating a language remains human. The Message in Mando'a, the language of the Mandalorians in the *Star Wars* universe, looks mysterious in its script and comfortingly human when transliterated:

Transliteration:

> Ke'sush! Ke'miit'haa'tayl bal ke'kar'tayl! Keb'ika cuyi
> burk'yc par ik'aade. Val duur'epari kihla ne'tome bal
> abiik'amuri.[7]

One of the most beautiful aspects of artlangs is that the level of
effort required to create the language usually outstrips instances
of its use in the fictional universe. David Peterson's book *The
Art of Language Creation* offers an extraordinary glimpse into
the sheer amount of work needed to create a conlang:[8] sounds,
words, grammar, syntax, historical evolution, writing systems and so on. Peterson is best known for his creation of the
Dothraki and Valyrian languages on the TV version of *Game
Of Thrones*. The amount that these languages were used on
the show was fairly modest and he could have probably created 'just enough' to supply something that sounded credible.
Instead, he created languages that were complete enough to deal
with future needs too, such as when a writer contacted him out
of the blue to ask for a translation of the Message into Dothraki:

> ASSIKHOF, vitihiri majin vineseri: koholi vo movek-
> kho entaan. Saccheya zoli lazim che ijela che leshita.

The meticulousness of Peterson's work is such that he ensured
the translation wasn't just linguistically coherent, it also had
a degree of cultural coherence. The literal translation is as
follows:

> WARNING, observe and then remember: toy bow
> is not for babies. A small part can be swallowed or
> inhaled.

As he explained:

> There is no writing in Dothraki, so there is no read-
> ing. There is no general word for 'toy', but a toy bow
> works. Also, it needs to say specifically for babies,
> because even a child of two would be allowed to use
> a wooden weapon.

The integrity with which Peterson approaches the creation
of Dothraki and other artlangs might seem odd, given the
fictive nature of the entire enterprise. Yet all languages are
constrained to some degree in what can easily be spoken of.
Conlangs just make these constraints more visible.

Idiosyncrasy and experimentation

Some conlangs are created as a kind of thought experiment.
One example is Norþimris, the language of an imagined
kingdom situated between England and Scotland, which is 'a
sister-language to neighbouring English and Scots, and shares
many features with them, but it has had considerably less
influence from Romance over its history and retains much
more of its Germanic vocabulary'.[9] The Norþimris Message
reminds us that the nations and languages that exist in our
world today were never predestined to evolve in the way that
they did:

> WARNING, reod an behaud: Leykin ungeynand for
> barns belau 3 year. Liyl bits mout bei swalud oð andt.[10]

By far the easiest language activists to get a response from
were conlangers. I emailed Joseph Windsor, the President of

the Language Creation Society, asking for translations; he forwarded my request to their email list and within an hour or two, translations started to pour in: Arkian, Pikonyo, Tapni, Anon, Jovian, Itlani, Mila, Toenaht and more. Most of them I have never heard of, and some languages seem to have been created without any expectation that they would spread to a wider community of speakers. Yet in translating the Message they became real, joining the family of human languages striving to communicate Ferrero's immortal teachings. Here, for example, is the Message in Chlìjha, created by Puey McCleary:

> ¡PÀFHÏE: Lreîxemat xhnoë Twéret! Yhan Qròjur qui pòtyei Pènga not Qhírixiênoi vun qué ptáwa. Fhoâ notòlyë tùmlui fheil fhrùtui ma nèowë Quaîti.

There is no community of Chlìjha speakers and there may never be. But the language isn't just made up on the spot. Translating the Message involved decisions about word-choice and grammar. For example, in the extensive gloss that McCleary sent me to accompany the translation, this is how he explains the word for 'children':

> Pènga is a common word for children; Chlìjha being a bit of a poetic language also has the noun Uwétsi which can mean either 'egg' or 'child.' Since this text is a warning, it's important to be as clear and simple as possible, so Uwétsi should not be used, since the toy is already an egg of sorts.

While some conlangs are subsequently taken up and developed by a community, there is something beautiful about those that are expressions of single-minded idiosyncrasy. One of the most extraordinary conlangs is Ithkuil, created by the Californian conlanger John Quijada. The product of decades of solitary effort, Ithkuil is not intended to be an auxiliary language or an artlang. Rather, it is an experiment to pack the highest amount of nuanced detail into the smallest possible linguistic space. In a long feature by Joshua Foer in *The New Yorker*, published in 2012, Quijada outlined his aims for the language:[11]

> 'I wanted to use Ithkuil to show how you would discuss philosophy and emotional states transparently,' Quijada said. To attempt to translate a thought into Ithkuil requires investigating a spectrum of subtle variations in meaning that are not recorded in any natural language. You cannot express a thought without first considering all the neighboring thoughts that it is not. Though words in Ithkuil may sound like a hacking cough, they have an inherent and unavoidable depth. 'It's the ideal language for political and philosophical debate – any forum where people hide their intent or obfuscate behind language,' Quijada continued. 'Ithkuil makes you say what you mean and mean what you say.'

Ithkuil has nearly 100 cases, 22 verb forms and 1,800 suffixes. Words are built up laboriously from roots and, given the enormous number of permutations, it is almost impossible to learn its vocabulary in the conventional sense. Phonetically, Ithkuil deliberately draws on a wide selection of some of the most obscure phonemes found in natural languages and, when spoken, sounds like a strange collection of hard consonants, sighs, clicks and grunts.

The Ithkuil Message (provided by John Quijada himself) is an intimidating miracle of economy:

Eimzawol ústlaṭar valuktapš âmmüeṭeph iḷúihwëliňk emkàlûň opegex

To create the translation, Quijada needed to clarify the ambiguities in the Message, so the Ithkuil version re-translates into English as follows:

Be warned to remember that this toy is not suitable for young developing children due to the potential to inhale or swallow the small component parts.

The forbidding clarity of the Ithkuil Message becomes positively alien when read in its own writing system (also provided by Quijada):

Ithkuil is widely admired in conlanging circles and beyond. But its extreme difficulty means that the language tends to be studied rather than used (although Quijada has used Ithkuil to write the lyrics for his progressive rock band Kaduatán, for whom David Peterson is the lead singer). Ithkuil is unlikely to transcend its creator during his lifetime. Indeed, Quijada emphasised to me that his translation was in the version of Ithkuil published in 2011 and that in 2021 he will publish a fourth, updated version of the language. The idea of a language having an 'author' and 'versions' is foreign to natural languages and, even in the conlang world, this can lead to conflict when a conlang threatens to escape the creator's control.

Loglan, created by the author James Cooke Brown in the 1950s, was intended to be as logical as possible. The language attracted considerable interest as an attempt to prove the Sapir-Whorf Hypothesis, which suggests that one's language determines cognition; so someone brought up in Loglan would be a more logical person than someone brought up in Danish. However, the language's fate proved to be anything but logical and dispassionate. Brown insisted that, as Loglan was a work in progress, he should retain copyright over the language and he was unwilling to let it be freely developed by others. In response, the Logical Language Group split away from the Loglan community and developed Lojban, whose first version was published in 1997.

Lojbanists have rolled back from the strongest versions of the Sapir-Whorf Hypothesis (as have most linguists). As with Ithkuil, translating into the language helps to identify the hidden ambiguities in the Message. While, like Ithkuil, Lojban aims at precision, the two languages are very different to read, with the latter a cool series of lower-case letters and absolutely no diacritics:

> o'i ko tcidu gi'e ralte .i lo selkei na mapti lo verba be
> li me'a ci .i lo cmalu pagbu ka'e se tunlo gi'a se vasxu

Jorge Lambias, who supplied this translation, took issue with what he called 'the slightly bewildering "read and keep" part':

It seems that if someone is already reading it they don't need to be told to do it, and if they aren't reading it, then they won't know they had to anyway. And why do they want you to keep it? Is it so that this big effort of translating into so many languages does not end up in the trash?

This is, perhaps unfair: surely the injunction to 'read' refers to the words beyond the colon that have not yet been read? Another Lojbanist, Gleki Axokuna, didn't think that the English Message was too ambiguous, but did point out that:

> The minor challenge was when describing children 3 years old. That's somewhat tricky because before birth children exist too so their age must include 9 months more on average compared with what's written in their legal documents.

Axokuna noted that, in some cultures, age is counted from before birth, so there is nothing intrinsically logical about the phrase '3 years old' (note that the Ithkuil translation preferred 'young developing children' to 'children under 3 years old'); therefore: 'I just omitted the standard of immaturity when using the verb "verba" meaning "to be a child". Let it be left to context.':

> o'isai to ko tcidu gi'e stogau toi le keitci na ei se pilno lo verba be le nanca be li su'o ci i lo cmalu pagbu ka'e ku se citka gi'a se cokcu

The two Lojban Messages read very differently, as did a third Lojban translation I received:

> fu'e o'isai ko tcidu gi'e socygau vau ti .i lo selkei cu na mapti tu'a lo verba be lo nanca be li me'i ci .i lo pagbu poi cmalu cu ka'e se vasxu ja se tulcti fu'o

When I pointed out to the Lojbanists that the differences between the three translations were surprising for a language that aims for unambiguous logic, none of them was embarrassed. As Jorge Lambias acknowledged: 'Any idea can be expressed in many different ways in any language.' This is a reminder that, however alien some of them might first appear, conlangs can't escape being human and cannot escape the fundamental constraints of human language. No language is ever created 'out of nothing'. The conlanged Message is not fundamentally different to any other Message.

Chapter 13

The incompetently translated Message

I am really, really lazy

As I received more and more translations of the Message, I started to become envious of those who provided them. To write the Message in a new language is to write it into history. I, on the other hand, had simply been the functionary who facilitated this great work. The languages I knew well enough to translate into were already spoken for. If I wanted to create a translation of my own, I would have to learn a new language.

I knew I could do it; after all, I've learned languages to a reasonably high level before. However, I found the thought of doing so dispiriting. It's not that I don't want to learn new languages, it's just that, to get to the point of being able to translate the Message, I would have to get to a fairly advanced point. I knew from my previous experiences that a sentence like 'small parts might be swallowed or inhaled' contains exactly the sort of grammatical features, such as participles and conditionality, that learners are only exposed to after a considerable amount of groundwork. Did I really want to go through hours and hours of 'Madame Marsaud est dans la cuisine' in order to get to the heart of a language?

Maybe there was another way. Michael Erard's book *Babel No More* investigates the 'hyperglots' who can pick up dozens of new languages with little effort.[1] As Erard shows, hyperglotism is not quite as extraordinary a phenomenon as it first seems. Most hyperglots only have complete fluency in the full range of registers of a handful of languages; for the rest, their knowledge tends to be restricted to particular elements of a language, such as reading knowledge alone or casual conversation alone. One can pass as fluent simply through speaking with an impeccable accent and appearing not to have to think through what one says. Some of the language learning methods that promise fluency in as short a time as three months teach a strategic approach to learning.[2] By learning a carefully chosen basic vocabulary and grammar, it is certainly possible to get to the point of fluency in a part of a language.[3] This is how I myself learned Modern Hebrew, when at the age of 29 I was faced with the challenge of having one year in which to upgrade my knowledge of the language to the point where I could participate in academic seminars in Israel. Before the year was through, I knew words like 'authoritarian', 'volunteerism' and 'fundraising' but I didn't know the word for 'bicycle' and I was clueless about slang.

I set out to undertake an experiment in strategic language learning: what was the *least* amount of a language I could learn in order to translate the Message? Would it be possible to reach fluency in Message-speak in an hour or two? Could the rigorous toil of learning a language be reduced to a half-arsed, lazy exercise?

I decided to choose languages where it would be difficult to cheat. That ruled out any language on Google Translate or where extensive learning materials are available online. There would have to be 'just enough' material to allow me to learn the necessary features of the language, but not so much that I might accidentally learn too much.

The Munegàscu fiasco

I started with Munegàscu. This is the language of the micro-state of Monaco and I'd long been fascinated by it. As the Principality has been transformed in recent decades from a backwater to a low-tax home for the super-rich, the indigenous language has withered almost to extinction. Native-born Monégasques are now a minority in their own homeland. Their language is taught in schools, though, and there are some learning materials available. It seemed fitting to liberate the Message into Munegàscu as, in so doing, I would be striking a blow against the smothering of local cultures by an unaccountable class of billionaires. Or something like that anyway.

I drew on three resources for my translation: a grammar and a dictionary downloaded from the website of the Académie des Langues Dialectales, which is based in Monaco and promotes the language;[4] and, as a starting point, the French-language Wikipedia page on Munegàscu. In addition, as Munegàscu is a Romance language closely related to the Italic language Ligurian, I looked closely at the Italian Message.

I finished it in an hour. This is what I came up with:

ATENÇIUN, lese e cunservà: Giüghetu non adatáu per fiyœi suta 3 ane. E peçe picenine pureressu iesse avalà o inalà.

My main problem was orthography, the way in which the language is written. The grammar, dictionary and Wikipedia pages all seemed to write Munegàscu differently. The situation was not helped by the quality of the scans of the books, which was so poor that at times it was hard to tell which diacritic I should use. To err on the safe side, I took out diacritics that

I was unsure of. There were also key bits of the grammar that were missing from the sources. Child is *fiyœ* but I wasn't sure what the plural was for a noun with this type of vowel ending, so *fiyœi* is an educated guess. I also didn't know how to pluralise the participles *avalà* and *inalà* for 'swallowed' and 'inhaled' – or even if they needed to be pluralised in the first place.

I was keen to discover how accurate my translation was and so I contacted the Académie des Langues Dialectales and had a friendly conversation (in French and English) with the director. Unfortunately, he does not speak Munegàscu. He did put me in touch with a couple of speakers, one of whom had translated a Tintin book into the language. Neither of them replied; perhaps because telling them that I had tried to learn their beloved tongue in the minimum amount of time wasn't exactly a compliment. All other attempts at tracking down a Munegàscu expert came to nothing.[5] However, I did manage to get a response from Professor Fiorenzo Toso, who is an expert on Ligurian and the Genoese dialect in particular. As Munegàscu's closest relative, a Genoese translation of the Message would at least be in the same ballpark:

Attençion, da leze e conservâ: A demoa a no l'é adattâ pe-i figgeu sott'a-i trei anni. Gh'é di tocchetti piccin che peuan ëse collæ ò inalæ.[6]

My translation wasn't a million miles away and some of the differences may simply be differences in orthography: *Cunservà–conservâ*, *adatáu–adattâ*, *fiyœi–figgeu*, etc. Still, there are plenty of other differences, some of them grammatical (*lese–da leze*) and some of them lexical (*giüghetu–demoa*). And there was one thing that I was pretty sure I had got badly wrong. While I had consulted the Italian Message extensively, I had unconsciously modelled the 'toy not suitable' sentence on the English and hadn't included the definite article or the 'is'. Like the other Romance Messages, these words seemed to be essential in Genoese and almost certainly in Munegàscu too.

I am cautiously optimistic, though, that my Munegàscu Message might be recognisable to a speaker as something related to a garbled version of the language. It might even have ascended to the level of bad Munegàscu if the Académie des Langues Dialectales had learned to operate a scanner properly. Still, I had learned that depending on a brief reading of whatever stray materials are online might not be the best language-learning strategy. And so I totally ignored that lesson for my next effort, where, despite there being entire books on the language available to buy, I made myself dependent on an equally limited set of online resources.

The Tok Pisin catastrophe

Tok Pisin is an English-based creole that serves as a national language in Papua New Guinea. Unlike some other creoles, it is regularly written and there are newspapers and books in the language. As I argued earlier, creoles are no less expressive or complex than any other language, but I hoped that the way Tok Pisin emerged from spontaneously created pidgins might mean that the resulting creole could be friendly to learners. Plus, its roots in English would at least make some of the vocabulary familiar.

The Wikipedia page on the language served as a basic primer on the grammar, and with the assistance of a not-particularly-comprehensive Tok Pisin–English dictionary that I found online,[7] I was done in an hour and a half:

> Tok lukaut, ritim na holim: Toi no inap long pikinini
> yanpela yet tripela yia. Ol inap daunim o kam insait
> long maus hat liklik.

Tok Pisin words do not have complicated inflections. For example, adding the suffix *-im* to a verb simply indicates that it is transitive – so *ritim* means 'read this specific thing'. The major challenge was word order and syntax. Given that the words themselves encode limited information, word order has to do a lot of the heavy lifting. Tok Pisin reminded me a bit of Chinese, which also doesn't do declensions, but adds complexity in other areas. So I was modestly confident that I had produced something intelligible.

I checked my translation with Craig Volker, an Australian academic expert in Tok Pisin. He was amazingly swift to respond, given that he was lying in a hospital bed recovering from a heart attack. He pulled no punches, though, replying: 'I'm afraid this wouldn't be understood.' Some of the problems were to do with vocabulary; for example, the word *holim* for 'hold on to' would not be used in this context. Some of the problems were grammatical; for instance, I needed to add a verbal marker *i* between subjects and verbs (so *toi i no inap* rather than *toi no inap*). I had also not understood Tok Pisin syntax sufficiently well; for example, in Tok Pisin you 'have' not 'are' an age. And sometimes what I said just didn't make any sense, as in my bungled translation of 'inhaled'. Here is what my translation should have looked like according to Volker:

> Tok lukaut, ritim na no ken tromoi: Toi i no inap long
> pikinini i no winim tripela krismas. Ol inap daunim o
> ol inap winim na bal I pasim nek.

The discovery that Tok Pisin measures age in *krismas* made me smile and helped to sugar the pill of my embarrassment. But I did get some bits of it right, and perhaps a Tok Pisin speaker might get something from my translation.

Creoles may be among the worst languages to choose in an exercise like this. For someone like me, who is used to learning languages where the main challenge comes in learning how to decline and conjugate, a language where syntax is so vitally important doesn't come easily.

Where next, then? After the Tok Pisin debacle, I yearned for a language of a different kind; one where it didn't matter how it was spoken or even if it was spoken; one that was shorn of idioms and syntactical bear-traps. I fantasised about a practice of translation as a mechanical exercise, one where all I had to do was to ascertain the part of speech and then find a translation of that word in that part of speech. If that fantasy could be realised, then it would likely be in a conlang. And so I chose ... Volapük.

I achieve partial-semi-competency in Volapük, sort of

Volapük was the Betamax to Esperanto's VHS. Invented by a German Catholic priest called Johann Schleyer in the 1880s, it was, briefly, extremely popular before most of its adherents switched to Esperanto a few years later. The Volapük movement soon tore itself apart through internal conflict, exacerbated by Schleyer's attempts to keep control of the language. While it still has a few adherents, Volapük is remembered today mostly as an inferior predecessor to Esperanto. Part of the reason for this is that, while Esperanto is easy for speakers of European languages to learn, Volapük is much more challenging since it is an *agglutinative* language. That means that words are built up through the addition of suffixes and prefixes, which allow for a great deal of precision but can be intimidating for learners. This was a positive for me: I wanted a language that would be as clear and regular as possible, and that hadn't had a chance to evolve into a snakepit of idioms.

There is a reasonable amount of Volapük material online.[8] Indeed, the Volapük-language Wikipedia has over 100,000 articles, in part due to an enthusiast creating a bot that machine-translated articles into the language. My own translation took longer than the other two languages – about two and a half hours – but I felt more confident that my Volapük Message was reasonably accurate:

NUNED, reidsöd e kipsöd: Tupit binon nelöwedik pro ciles dis 3 yels. Dilis amlik palugonsöx u panünatemönsöx.

If the words *reidsöd e kipsöd* look familiar (and a bit silly), that's because Schleyer drew on English for many of his verb roots. The final word of the Message, though, *panünatemönsöx*, illustrates Volapük's difficulty. I spent about a third of my time trying to puzzle out the word for 'inhaled'. The final word derives from the verb *natemön*, 'to breathe', and is encrusted in suffixes and prefixes that turn it into 'might be breathed in'. I was particularly proud to have tracked down the final suffix *-öx* which denotes the potential mood. And that was my downfall …

I shared my translation with a Volapük Facebook group and was informed by a Shido Morozof that 'this translation is good, but you have mixed forms of Volapük from different periods'. The *-öx* potential mood marker was indeed in Johann Schleyer's original version of the language but it never ended up being used by Volapükists and was dropped in subsequent versions of the language. Unknowingly, I had been switching between websites that used materials from different Volapük eras, with most speakers today adopting a version that stabilised in the 1930s. I'd made other mistakes too, such as missing out the personal plural ending to *reidsöd e kipsöd*. All that said, I can't explain why one online dictionary translated 'toy' as *tupit*, which means 'spinning top' – for that one, my only fault was trusting the Internet. Here, then, is a better Volapük translation, by Shido Morozof:

> NUNED. Reidolsöd e kipedolsöd! Pledadin no binon pötöfik pro cils labü bäldot yelas läs kilas. Diladils smalik kanons paslugön u panünatemön.

As another contributor to the Facebook group put it, in my translation 'there are a few grammatical errors which will not, however, baffle a trained Volapükist'. I took that as some kind of victory.

While it's possible that a professional linguist who has worked with dozens of languages would, given the same amount of time and resources, have come up with more accurate translations, this whole experiment taught me what I already knew: a language is a system and each communicative event draws on that system. To know a language is to know much more than how a verb declines or what a word-for-word translation of a noun is. Translation requires a subtle sense of the nuances of expression; a feel for how it works. Most importantly, you cannot know in advance when a language will express something in a way that is surprising. You could learn many of the fundamentals of French grammar and never even guess that 'What's this?' translates to *Qu'est-ce que c'est?* ('What is this that this is?').

I was still drawn to the fantasy of a lazy approach to translation, though, however much I knew it to be a fantasy. If Munegàscu, Volapük and Tok Pisin would not bend to my will, then perhaps I could construct my own language that would ...

Chapter 14

ALTABAŠ! Iltigōš ōfiltatiš

A language of my very own

As we saw in Chapter 12, conlanging requires meticulous linguistic skills. My own linguistic skills are ... variable. I know more about language than most other people who are not trained linguists and I have some specialist knowledge in a few niche areas. What I don't have is '360-degree' knowledge of the multiple aspects of a language that would allow me to create a novel linguistic system; one that could express, in principle, everything that any other language could express. But then, outside of the world of conlanging, language wasn't created by human beings in a systematic process; most of them evolved over time, with speakers making up the rules as they went along. Could I not also develop a language incrementally, starting and finishing with the Message alone?

Confining my conlanging to the Message alone raised some intriguing questions. Languages as they currently exist are sprawling, open-ended systems bigger than any one message. But do they have to be? Could a language be small and complete? Could a language exist that would articulate the Message and nothing else?

I hadn't heard of a conlang that deliberately limited its potential to such a degree that it could only express one short text. In fact, I simply couldn't imagine what such a language would look like. If nothing else, this provides an ironic proof of the theory that language limits the scope of what we can think: a 'finite' language seems unthinkable.

What is possible, though, is a language of which we only know a part. Actually, that is the case with 'fluent' speakers of a language who nonetheless do not know every word or obscure grammatical feature. It's certainly the case with my French, Spanish and Hebrew: I know that it must be possible to say 'the saucepan was dissected by ravens' in all three languages, but I do not know how to do it.

My attempt to conlang the Message and the Message alone is therefore an exercise in determining how much of a language's paraphernalia it requires. Obviously, in terms of vocabulary it will be extremely restricted. Grammatically, it is less clear how much 'scaffolding' this new language might need.

I deliberately didn't plan my language in advance. Not only was my ability to do so limited, I wanted to see the language unfold as I was working. I had one rule: I would not go back and alter words and grammar to overcome challenges. Each word I created was to set a precedent.

And I only broke my rule a couple of times.

How Altabash became Altabaš

I started with a word that just jumped into my head: *Altabash*.

The word bubbled up from my subconscious at the time that I was completing my collection of Message translations into Central Asian languages. It reveals more about me than it does about those languages: some inchoate sense that this is what Central Asian countries 'sound like' that probably derives from stereotypes I am too embarrassed to address. In order to be sure that I hadn't heard the word Altabash somewhere before and forgotten the source, I Googled it. Al-Tabash is, in fact, an Arabic surname, but I have no memory of ever knowing that. Consciously at least, I don't conflate Central Asia with

Arabic as I know that their languages are derived instead from Persian and Turkic language groups.

There is also an ancient Hebrew cypher system called 'Atbash', but I don't recall knowing that before I started working on the new language (although it might have seeped into my unconscious from a long-forgotten lecture or article I have encountered in the past).

I stuck with Altabash even though I wasn't trying to model my language on Arabic, Turkic or Persian languages. It would stand for 'warning' on the English Message but that didn't mean it would translate exactly or take the form of a participle as in English.

I decided that my language would be based on a 'root' system, a common linguistic feature I am familiar with from Modern Hebrew. Modern Hebrew verbs, participles and many nouns are generated usually from a three-consonant root (although two-, four- and, very occasionally, five-letter roots are possible) and can be used to form up to six types of verb and related nouns. For example, the root כנס (k/kh-n-s) is the basis for the verbs 'to enter' and 'to insert' as well as nouns as various as 'conference', 'entrance' and 'Knesset' (the latter being the Israeli parliament). They are loosely linked together by the idea of 'entering'.

Like Hebrew, my language would have three-letter roots and all nouns and verbs would derive from them. Unlike Hebrew, the root would take the form of vowel-consonant-vowel. Why? Partly because I didn't want to be too beholden to a language I actually knew, but also because I had decided that the root in the word Altabash would be the 'aba' in the middle. I had also decided that, in my translation into this new language, every new rule I made would have no exceptions within the Message itself. That doesn't mean that the language might not have multiple irregularities and nuances, it just means that this particular text does not. For that reason, the root *aba* suggests that all roots in the new language would take the form vowel-consonant-vowel.

Obviously my language would need an alphabet. The alphabet didn't necessarily need to be a Latin one – it only had to include a and b – but I decided that my life would be simpler if I just adapted the alphabet I knew best. I also realised that, given the tight limitations of this experiment, I didn't actually need to create rules for how each letter was to be pronounced; it only had to be written.

To make my life even simpler, I decided that there would be no digraphs like 'sh' or 'th'; one letter would denote one sound, with no exceptions. That meant that either the 'sh' in Altabash would be sounded as something else entirely or I would need to change it. As the sound of Altabash was already in my head, I broke my 'no going back' rule and replaced the sh with the 'š' used to denote the sound in Czech and some other Slavic languages.

And so Altabash became *Altabaš*.

My alphabet is based on the English alphabet (as I pointed out in the previous chapter, I am lazy). I excluded 'c' and 'q' as, while I wasn't going to develop pronunciation rules, I did want to be able to roughly sound my translation out. 'C' in English can be pronounced in two ways and I have no idea what 'q' is actually supposed to be – so I left them out. However, I then immediately abandoned my desire for vague pronounceability by adding some of my favourite diacritics and decided that in this language, letters with diacritics should be counted as separate letters. I drew on old friends from Latvian, Estonian, Czech and Icelandic but stopped after that so as not to make the language any more incoherent than it already was.

Vowels:

| A | Ā | E | I | O | Õ | U |

Consonants:

B	G	J	L	P	T	Z
D	H	K	M	R	V	Ž
F	Ḥ	Ķ	N	Š	W	Đ

Building words

To create new words, I needed to understand the *morphology* of the word Altabaš; how this word had been put together from constituent morphemes (parts). Here I made another decision: my language would avoid participles as they mess with my head. So Altabaš couldn't exactly translate as 'warning'. I am a big fan of reflexive verbs – which describe an action one does to oneself – and thought that Altabaš could be made to mean something like 'Caution oneself!' This is a little odd for an English-speaker, but my language means my rules. The rest of the morphology for the word Altabaš quickly followed:

Al (marks reflexive imperative form of verb)
t (general marking for a verb)
aba (root for 'caution')
š (second person plural suffix, in a form used when addressing people who are not known to you)

'Read' and 'keep' are also verbs, and hence marked by a 't' before the root, and they are also in the second person plural, thus ending in 'š'. But they could not be reflexive verbs, so I would need to create a simple imperative prefix. To make this similar to the reflexive imperative prefix 'al', I replaced the 'a' with another vowel. I used a random number generator to choose that vowel from the six remaining ones: 'i'. So 'read' and 'keep' would both take the form 'ilt – ROOT – š'.

From that point on, I used a random number generator to generate the roots and all other suffixes and prefixes.[1] That produced the roots *igõ* and *ati* for 'read' and 'keep' respectively. I then realised that I needed a word for 'and'. This would be a prefix rather than a standalone word: *õf*. This meant that 'Warning, read and keep' would read as follows:

ALTABAŠ! Iltigõš õfiltatiš.

I capitalised the first word and added an exclamation mark as, stylistically, I liked the cut of its jib.

'Toy not suitable for children under 3 years' posed a series of new challenges. I had to work out what nouns, adjectives and prepositions would look like and pick an appropriate sentence structure. To make life easier, I decided to stick with the subject–verb–object order familiar to me from English and other languages I have studied. So the sentence starts with 'toy'. Which led to more choices: whether the language has articles and noun cases. I decided to say yes to both.

The root I generated for toy was *õbi*. With nouns and verbs derived from the same root, the concept that links both in this case is 'play'. So a toy is a 'plaything' or 'that which is played with'. As the basic form of a verb is marked by adding the prefix 't' to the root, I generated a consonant to mark the basic form of a noun: 'n'. A noun of this kind – indicating the object of the action referred to in the verbal form of the root – would need to be marked with a further prefix. As I had used a vowel–consonant prefix to further specify the verb form, I generated a similar prefix here: *zā*. So toy became *zānōbi*. I then decided to add a suffix that combined marking the nominative case – which identifies the subject of a sentence – and the definite article 'this'. The former was a consonant, the latter a vowel: *zo*. So in this sentence, 'this toy' translates to *zānōbizo*.

The root for 'suitable' is *iba*. Adjectives are marked with the consonant prefix 'd' and they do not agree with the noun, which is highly convenient for me. Negativity is marked by a three-letter suffix at the end of a word: 'ðen'.

So 'this toy is not suitable' translates to *zānōbizo dibaðen*.

Compounding my incompetence

'For children under 3 years' presented more challenges. According to my shaky knowledge of grammar, it is a combination of two prepositional phrases. Drawing on my even shakier knowledge of compound nouns, noun cases and agglutination, I thought it would be fun to turn this part of the sentence into a single word; compounding 'children under 3 years' and marking the 'for' with a case ending. I don't know what this case is actually called and I am too lazy to investigate further, but the consonant ending 'ð' marks it.

In order to create a compound noun for 'for children under 3 years' I first of all decided that age would be expressed in my language in a similar way to English. I initially wanted to use the following formula:

Noun prefixes – 'child' root – preposition suffix – 'under' root – '3' root – 'year' root – case ending

The reason for the lack of noun prefixes for '3' and 'year' was to avoid cluttering up the lengthy compound with more components. The meanings of these particular roots should be clear from the context. However, combining roots together would lead to some potentially awkward vowel clusters. As a quick and dirty solution, I chose an as-yet-unused letter, 's', that would be used as a separator in instances like this.

I had some unfinished business with nouns. While the 'n' prefix marks a noun, a further vowel–consonant prefix specifies the type of noun. Whereas 'toy' is generated from the root as the object of the action implied by the verbal form of the root, the relation of 'child' to its root is more complicated. Obviously, my language required a complex system to derive nouns and verbs from roots, but fortunately all I needed to do here was create another two-letter prefix that would imply the person who embodies the root. Or something like that. There's probably a linguistic term for this sort of thing but I don't know it.

So with some letter-generation, child became *tenako* and that was the end of the matter. Except it wasn't. I still needed to find a way to pluralise. I decided that the plural form of a noun would be formed by doubling the final consonant–vowel combination. That makes children *tenakoko*, which sounded quite sweet to me. I then generated a prepositional prefix – 'ķ' – together with the other word roots and I was ready to go. Here is the translation of 'for children under 3 years': *tenakokoķonisehisapuð*.

Yes, it's long, but there are plenty of languages, such as Hawaiian, where long compound words are commonplace.

Oh God, there's still another sentence to go

Here is the Message so far:

> ALTABAŠ! Iltigõš õfiltatiš. Zānõbizo dibaðen tenakokoᶄonisehisapuð.

The final sentence – 'Small parts might be swallowed or inhaled' – contains an adjective and a noun, which I already knew how to construct. However, even though I wanted to avoid participles, the sentence ends with two of them. Plus the 'might' added an extra dose of complication.

Moving grimly forwards, I decided that to avoid participles I would use the following word order: 'They might swallow or inhale the small parts.' I further adjusted the start of the sentence to express 'they might swallow' as 'they are able to swallow or to inhale', which is how it would be expressed in Hebrew.

'They are able' requires the present tense of the verb. I constructed this as follows:

El (present tense prefix)
t (verb prefix)
ājo (root)
ḥ (third person plural suffix)

So: 'they are able' is *eltājoḥ*.

The infinitive form of the verb was created by omitting the first verbal prefix from the root and adding the suffix 'ž'. So: 'to swallow' is *tuvaž*. 'To inhale' was generated the same way, with the addition of the prefix 'or' to mark the prefix 'or'. Why not, right? So: 'or to inhale' is *ortahež*.

'The small parts' presented a problem, as everything I knew of this language made me feel that this would be a compound word, and yet 'toy not suitable' had used two separate words. Fortunately, this apparent inconsistency is explained by a grammatical feature of the language, although I don't actually know what it is. I did retain the same noun–adjective word order so it read 'the parts small'. I also needed to create the definite article 'the' and a suffix for the accusative case as 'small parts' is the object of the sentence. So, after generating two more roots – *ebō* and *idu* – as well as an accusative case suffix 'm' and a definite article suffix 'e', 'the small parts' translated to *tenebōbōtidume*.

Here it is, then, the full Message in my unnamed language:

ALTABAŠ! Iltigõš õfiltatiš. Zānõbizo dibaðen tenakokoķonisehisapuð. Eltājoḥ tuvaž ortahež tenebōbōtidume.

What on earth have I done?

I suppose the great strength of this Message is that it doesn't look like any other Message, or any other language. By generating most of the letters randomly and ensuring that the alphabet includes elements from multiple languages, I created something that's decidedly odd. There are limitations to this oddness, of course, since my alphabet doesn't encode every sound from every language. My get-out clause is that my refusal to state how letters are to be pronounced – or even if spelling is phonetic – means that the language could include anyone's preferred sounds if they want to pronounce it that way.

Of course, that only dodges the issue. A spoken language has all sorts of elements that contribute to speakability, such as prosody, intonation and stress, and I haven't considered them at all. A language is a system in which the component parts interact with each other. In creating my version of the Message, I reduced language down to a matter of vocabulary, grammar and alphabet. Even in those terms alone, the way I structured the Message raises all sorts of questions of how viable the entire language could be. If I wanted to use this as a starting point to create an entire conlang – which, rest assured, I do not – the problems and inconsistencies in my nascent language might end up being disabling.

One of the most glaring problems with the language concerns the roots. The text of this book was almost finalised when I woke up with a start one morning to a sudden realisation of something that I should have spotted much earlier: the vowel–consonant–vowel pattern of the roots does not produce enough unique permutations to meet the requirements of an entire language. Are 1,029 possible root combinations really enough?

I had another root-related concern. Could a speaker of the language identify them amid the swarm of prefixes and suffixes? How would speakers pick roots out of a compound word such as *tenebōbōtidume*? I also didn't clarify the order in which suffixes and prefixes are appended to each other and how they might avoid being 'mistaken' for roots. So why would a speaker of my language not hear the start of the word *tenebōbōtidume* as a root *ene* prefixed by a 't' and its suffix as the root *ume*? The issues that I deliberately avoided would have to be confronted in a real language.

My language lacks any kind of context. I know nothing of its speakers, what sort of society they inhabit and what their history might be. Can a language without any sociocultural context really be said to be a language at all? Artlangs such as Klingon or Dothraki were created to fit into a particular fictional universe. Auxlangs like Esperanto are designed to facilitate a particular type of communication and, if they are successful, create their own linguistic communities. Even those conlangs that are designed to test out a particular linguistic theory, such as Lojban, are indelibly marked by the nature of the overall project. I am not sure whether my purpose – to create a language solely for the purpose of translating the Message, without drawing on systematic linguistic knowledge and cutting corners where possible – is enough.

But here's the incredible thing: the nature of language itself means that none of these limitations would prevent my language coming to life as a complete system, if there was the will to do so. Take the root issue. If the vowel–consonant–vowel pattern is too limited to produce enough unique words, then perhaps three-letter combinations are only one kind of root. Four-letter roots might also exist (maybe vowel–consonant–vowel–consonant) and all the three-letter roots generated for the Message happen to fall, by coincidence, into the three-letter category. Alternatively, it may be that by increasing the number of ways in which roots can be turned into nouns and verbs, the language could make do with a relatively small number of combinations.

Moreover, even if I might be accused of making mistakes in my account of this language due to my spotty knowledge of linguistics and grammar, it may be that I have only *described* features of the language incorrectly, not that they are 'wrong' in the first place. A language cannot be wrong. It is irrelevant what the correct name is for the case ending for the compound word 'for children under 3 years'; all that matters is that the case exists. I may have had difficulty in describing the type of noun generated from a root, but what matters is that the noun was created; someone else can decide on its classification.

If I have been inconsistent in places or misunderstood my own rules, that also doesn't have to be a problem. Although conlangs are sometimes designed to be entirely regular, natural languages rarely are. Ironically, in its improvised incoherence, my language resembles natural language more than some conlangs do.

Perhaps my language contains idioms and forms that have been retained from an earlier phase in the language's history. When David Peterson created the High Valyrian language for *Game of Thrones*, his starting point was a handful of words and two short phrases from George R.R. Martin's original books: *Valar morghulis* ('all men must die') and *Valar dohaeris* ('all men must serve').[2] In the process of developing the grammar, the verbal declensions started to depart from the forms used in the original phrases. It wasn't a problem: Peterson incorporated them into the language as remnants from an earlier phase in the language's history, thereby adding to the conlang's richness.

The wonderful thing about linguistics is that it knits together the sprawling, ever-shifting mess that is a language into a semi-coherent whole. No constructed language, however poorly constructed, can ever lose! I was reminded again here of the practice of Midrash, discussed earlier in the book: by refusing to identify mistakes as such, a text or a language can become even richer than it originally was by adding new layers of meaning to it.

Liberating my Message

My language could truly become a language if it were liberated from my own hands. That could be done through other conlangers taking it on as a project (which is unlikely). But to a degree, my language can liberate itself. While I was entirely focused on creating a language for one very specific purpose, I also realised that even the tiny amount of the language that I had created allows for new messages to be made. The English Message allows one to say, '3 small children might keep toy', which isn't very elegant but does produce a meaning different to that found in the Message itself. I was hopeful that I might be able to do something similar with my Message. My choice to use a root-based system allowed me to succeed beyond my wildest dreams ...

Take the method I used to create the word 'toy' from the root for play. 'Food' could be 'that which is swallowed' – *zānuva* – and 'air' could be 'that which is inhaled' – *zānahe*. That method also allows me to create a word that translates approximately to 'that which is read', which could very well be a book – *zānigõ*.

Perhaps you have concluded by now that 'this book is unreadable' – *zānigõzo digoðen*. You might even want to shout from the rooftops, 'Warning! Don't read this book' – *Altabaš! Iltigõšðen zānigõmo!* But if you simply think that this particular chapter of the book was a mistake, you could say that 'this chapter (i.e. small part of the book) is unreadable' – *zānigõstenebõtiduzo digoðen*. Or, more damningly, if you feel that 'this chapter is unreadable and childish', you could say: *zānigõstenebõtiduzo digoðen õfdako*.

Maybe, to forestall such criticism, my editor will tell me 'don't keep this chapter' – *iltatišðen zānigõstenebõtidumo*.

If you are feeling more charitable, you might want to write a review on Amazon that tells everyone: 'Read this book!' – *Iltigõš zānigõmo*! You can help me make some serious money from the toddler market by reassuring buyers that 'this book is suitable for children under 3' – *zānigõzo diba tenakokoḳonisehisapuð*.

While there is a huge amount I do not know about my language, even this tiny sliver implies a much bigger system. And any system can be repurposed, developed and refined so that all traces of the persons who created it are lost. The Message, therefore, can be a starting point for a whole language and that language will eventually submerge the Message itself.

The ultimate success of my own Message would be if it were liberated to the point of nonexistence. Why not start this process off? I invite the reader to come up with a name for this language using the principles I have set out during this chapter. It could translate to 'the language' or 'the Message language' or 'the lazy language' or 'the incompetent language' – you have all the ingredients to generate these words from randomly generated roots. You might want to take my creation further by working out what proper nouns look like in it, or how it can assimilate loanwords (how would you adapt the English word 'Message', for example?). Send me your creations and I will post them online. If there are enough of them, then maybe my creation will be liberated out of existence and this sorry episode in my life will be forgotten.

Part 4

The Babel Message

Chapter 15

One world, one Message?

Will English conquer the Manuscript?

A spectre is haunting the Manuscript – the spectre of English.

Today, the English Message is just one of 34 Messages. It is located where it is on the Manuscript by virtue of the position of 'EN' in the alphabet. We have no reason to think that the English Message is the 'original' version. The only thing that distinguishes the English language on the Manuscript is that fragments of it also appear in the producer and importer information sections.

English is a global tongue, spoken in a great many countries as a first language and also as an auxiliary language throughout the world. According to Ethnologue, there are 370 million first-language speakers of English and 894 million second-language speakers. While other languages have more first-language speakers (Mandarin Chinese has nearly a billion), no other language comes close to the number of second-language speakers.

At the very least, the Manuscript could take off some northern European languages, such as Dutch and Swedish, and English would serve for a healthy majority of speakers of these languages. Certainly Ferrero seems to trust, maybe correctly, that the English Message, together with a few other global tongues such as French, Spanish, Arabic and Chinese, will do the job just fine in some parts of the world.

The remorseless rise of English as a global language has its advantages, and not just for native English-speakers. In 2011 Chandra Bhan Prasad, an Indian activist from the *Dalit* (untouchable) caste, organised the erection of a temple to the 'Goddess of English'.[1] Prasad argued that wider knowledge of English among Dalits would help lift them out of poverty, since so many new jobs in India now require English. For Prasad, English could be the 'symbol of Dalit renaissance' while Indian languages are the language of the caste system that has oppressed them. Wherever you are in the world, to speak English is to be part of a globalised culture, and 'the global' can be a source of hope to those who feel stuck within limited horizons.

The global dominance of English can have a negative impact on native speakers of English. The standard of language teaching and learning is declining fast in the UK, US and other countries where English is the first language for the majority. In the UK, for instance, between 2013 and 2019 there was a fall in the number of students taking GCSE foreign language options of 30–50% depending on region.[2] While the common perception that 'everyone speaks English so why do you need other languages?' isn't wholly incorrect, it is based on an overestimation of the level of English that second-language speakers may have, and it ignores the difficulty of understanding other cultures without having access to their languages.

Ideally, a global auxiliary language is a second language for all its speakers, owned by no one and used by everyone. Esperanto and other conlangs have never managed this and it's doubtful that any such language ever could. English may be a global auxiliary language but it is also the first language of hundreds of millions, the majority residing in wealthy and powerful countries. The global rise of English cannot be divorced from English-speaking countries and their imperial histories.

Some have argued that the problems inherent in English's use as an auxiliary language can be addressed through simplified versions of the language that will be easily accessible to non-native speakers. Companies and international bodies could, in principle, use these codified versions of English to ensure clarity when communicating. One of the first attempts at simplifying English was created in the 1930s by Charles Kay Ogden and is known as Basic English. It still has its enthusiasts but neither it nor its rivals have ever taken off. When I attempted to translate the Message into Basic English myself, its problems became evident:

> Attention! For reading and keeping: The plaything is not right for boys or girls under 3 years. They may put the small parts down the throat or take them in through the nose.[3]

This is certainly a comprehensible Message. The simplified grammar forced me to use a less condensed, more active construction. The main problem was the vocabulary. Ogden's basic word list contains only 850 words. It doesn't include words for 'toy', 'suitable', 'warning', 'swallow' or 'inhale'. It does include 'reading' and 'keeping' as participles but I couldn't work out whether the rules of the language allowed me to turn them into verbs. Basic English allows you to use the basic word list to construct compounds in order to expand the vocabulary, and Ogden created an expanded word list based on this: 'plaything' and 'down the throat' are taken from it. And this is where the problem lies with Basic English. Unless the text you want to translate uses only the 850 basic words – a tall order – then you will need to use standardised circumlocutions that will sound odd to a native speaker and are themselves linguistic codes. Simplification can therefore allow complexity to surreptitiously re-enter language through other means.

The minimal Message

The project of simplifying English or any other language also assumes that the primary barrier to comprehension is simply that of understanding enough vocabulary and grammar. But the differences between languages may be more profound than that; in which case simplification doesn't solve the problem.

In her book *Imprisoned in English*, Anna Wierzbicka, a Polish linguist now based in Australia, argues that:

> English is a language of global significance, it is not a neutral instrument or one that, unlike other languages, carves nature at its joints; and [...] if this is not recognized, English can at times become a conceptual prison.[4]

Wierzbicka points to the 'conceptual categories' encoded in English and how they do not necessarily translate as universally as English-speakers might think. Here she summarises the dangers of leaving these issues unacknowledged:

> First, there is a wall between ourselves and other people: we cannot put ourselves, conceptually, in the shoes of someone whose conceptual categories are

different from ours and who doesn't think in terms of categories like 'color,' 'river,' 'brother,' 'depression,' 'cooperation,' 'fairness,' 'story,' 'mind' or 'right' and 'wrong.' ... Second, one gets a slanted picture of what it is to be human: one may not see that the givens of human life, recognized, evidence suggests, in all languages, include being born, living for some time, and dying; having a body, and being able to think, feel, want, and know; and at the same time, we may imagine that they include certain things that in fact are conceptual artifacts of the English language and Anglo culture, such as, for example, 'having a mind,' being 'male' or 'female,' and 'having a sense of right and wrong.' Third, one cannot understand oneself: one takes one's own conceptual categories and cultural scripts for granted, one doesn't appreciate their distinct character, shaped by a unique history and culture, and consequently, one cannot get an insight into what it is to be an 'Anglo' – a bearer of a particular culture and an inhabitant of a particular conceptual and cultural universe.[5]

Wierzbicka exhorts English-speakers to recognise the ways in which the apparent universality of English disguises an insidious cultural blindness. I am unsure, though, how this argument might apply to the Message. While in Chapter 9 I discussed the cultural assumptions behind the Message, they are only incomprehensible to the shrinking number of people who have little or no contact with industrialised society and its products. Although the nature of warnings may be understood differently across cultures, even limited engagement with the modern nation state will demonstrate that written warnings by unmanned collectives are things that exist in the world.

Anna Wierzbicka is one of the main linguistic theorists behind the development of 'Natural Semantic Metalanguage' (NSM). This is an attempt to identify the core universal semantic features that apply across languages and cultures; these are known as 'semantic primes' and can be translated universally. Out of NSM has grown 'Minimal English', a core lexicon for the language that can form the basis of universal translations. The vocabulary of Minimal English is tiny – about 250 words – and is accompanied by an injunction to not 'assume that you can use a semantic prime in a certain way just because it is allowable in English'.[6] What would the Message look like in Minimal English? Perhaps like this:

Children can eat hard object and be killed.

Actually, even this minimal Message includes one noun that is not a semantic prime – 'object'. I find it difficult to believe that there is a language that doesn't have a way of identifying an unnameable thing. That's the point, though – I don't know it for sure. In addition, I am unsure whether 'can' is universal either. And the passive-voiced 'be killed' may make no sense in some languages for all I know.

Attempting to translate the Message in a minimal version of English or any other language is a humbling exercise. What it shows is that a truly universal Message could not be achieved by translation. Rather, the Message would need to be *rewritten* to be tailored to the specific characteristics of every linguistic community. An auxiliary language like English, however widely understood, cannot do this, as it assumes that it can be 'translated' by each speaker into their own native language. Ferrero has recognised the need to rewrite the Message in a few cases. As we saw earlier, the German Message, for example, is unique.

Liberating the Message – from me

As I wrote this last paragraph, a cold shiver went down my spine. I could no longer avoid the nagging doubt that I have tried to suppress:

What if I hadn't liberated the Message at all?

While I had explicitly rejected the search for an 'original' Message as irrelevant and unknowable, I had also treated one particular Message as 'my' original. In doing so, while I had taken ownership of the Message, had I not also bound it more tightly to the English language? Maybe all the new translations I had commissioned were still tethered to the world's most dominant language? Perhaps a deeper liberation might have involved translating every official Message into every other language, thereby creating a mass of Messages so overwhelming that they would definitively smash any notion of an original.

This is a book that could only have been written by an English-speaker. Despite my knowledge of translation theory and the sociology of language, despite my awareness of cultural and linguistic difference, despite my knowledge of other languages, I can still not entirely shake the presumption that my native language can somehow give me access to all other languages. That is the privilege, the delusion, of someone whose life experience has taught that I can find a speaker of any language who also speaks my own language.

On further reflection I realised that all was not lost. All the translators had to cope with the constraints of English by adapting the Message in ways that I rarely understood. They are *rewritten* Messages. Of course, some translators supplied me with commentaries on how they had rewritten the Message (particularly in ancient tongues and conlangs) but most were content to leave me to my delusions. They were indeed liberating the Message – from me and my sticky English-speaking fingers.

Auxiliary languages like English that also have their own native speakers contain the seeds of their own liberation. Languages such as English may have sometimes been a tool of domination, but their subjugated speakers turn them into something new that resists control. That is why creoles are so significant and why their status needs raising. The world is today filled with 'Englishes' that offer new possibilities to the language. With the number of second-language speakers many times more than the number of native speakers, English might be on the way to being wrested from the grasp of English-speakers. With standard English increasingly undermined by a proliferation of new diglossia and dialects, some writers, such as David Crystal, have welcomed the diversification of 'English'.[7] The time is approaching when, if Ferrero were to decide that the Message should be reduced to English alone, the question would surely follow: 'What sort of English?' If the Message were only in one form of English, that would erase not just a diversity of other languages, but the diversity of English itself.

Nonetheless, we cannot assume that English – in whatever form – will remain the world's preferred auxiliary language indefinitely. As Nicholas Ostler shows in his book *The Last*

Lingua Franca, throughout history multiple languages have been used to linguistically knit together whole swathes of the world.[8] While English is the first to have a truly global scope, at certain points in history it would have been hard to imagine that Latin, Persian or Akkadian would be dethroned from their pre-eminence. While English has a long future ahead of it by virtue of its huge number of native speakers, its future as a global lingua franca depends on the continuing economic, social and cultural dominance of English-speaking countries, which is less assured. As Ostler asks, noting the rise of China and other economically powerful states: 'Will use of English be acceptable in a world economically dominated by powers who feel proud to have achieved parity, and more, with English speakers?'[9] That doesn't mean that another language will necessarily supplant English; in fact Ostler suggests that it's possible the future world will be more multilingual, albeit containing a smaller number of languages.

Some people will not wait for the historical tide to turn. In 1996, Diego Marani, the Italian novelist and translator, created 'Europanto', a 'system for the creation of a new language of the future'.[10] Europanto is as much a satirical protest as it is a language. As Marani explained: 'It is intended to give voice to the frustrations of the vast majority of people who are forced to use English even though their command of the language is not very good.' Instead of competing with English, Europanto attempts to speed up its internationalisation and to cut it off from Anglo-American culture. The aim is 'to cause the language to implode, to destroy it from within'. By enriching English with words from their own languages, speakers of Europanto will, over time, create a new language. Whether Europanto will be a creole, a form of code-switching or a 'macaronic' language (one that uses a mixture of languages) isn't clear. Marani himself, who used to write regular newspaper columns in Europanto, is no longer developing it. Perhaps it works best as permission to play with English. And while Europanto is not intended for native English-speakers like me, it did inspire me to create a new Message along its lines, drawing on French, Spanish and German:

> WARNING, read y keep: Spielzeug no suitable para Kinder under 3 years. Small pièces might be verschluckt or inhaled.

When my friend Nick Gendler read the Europanto translation, he reminded me of 'Franglais'. The English humorist Miles Kington used this 'language' in books and magazine columns both as a way of satirising English infelicities with foreign languages and also just because it was funny. As a tribute to Kington, Nick offered the following Franglais Message:

> Attention: lire et keep. Toy ne suitable pas pour enfants sous l'age de trois. C'est possible que petit parts might be mangered ou inhaled.

Nick's gloss on the translation was as follows:

> You'll see that I have deliberately substituted the French word 'manger' for swallow, because no Franglais-speaker will know the word for swallow and eat is pretty much the same thing. I've also mangled the translation more generally, with the superfluous phrase 'c'est possible' in order to demonstrate that a

linguistic half-wit like me would stumble about trying to express myself if I were trying to convey the message to a French-speaker. I would introduce as many words as I know in the other person's language even if I didn't need them, in order to hopefully land one word or phrase that correctly expressed my intention, and to kid myself that I was a competent speaker.

For Nick, as for Miles Kington, a 'good' Franglais translation is one that reproduces a *lack* of knowledge of French by an English-speaker. But here's the thing: this Franglais Message is understandable and follows a certain logic. The same is true of real code-switching languages already presented in this book, such as Singlish and Llanito. They can work as well as any other language. They are often denigrated or, like Franglais, treated as a joke, but there is genuine subversive potential in their ability to tunnel under linguistic citadels.

At this point I am apparently obliged to mention the 'Babel Fish' from *The Hitchhiker's Guide to the Galaxy*. I have now done so.

There is another spectre haunting the Message – the spectre of Google Translate.

If global English threatens to reduce the Message to one, Google Translate seems to point in the opposite direction: to a world in which no one needs to learn another language.

While other translation apps are available, I'm not ashamed to admit that I *love* Google Translate. There are few things more addictive than idly wondering how you say 'squirrel' in Mongolian and satisfying your curiosity with a click (it's *Хэрэм*, by the way). I also use the app on a daily basis to do serious work. One of my jobs is running The European Jewish Research Archive, an online repository of social research on European Jewish populations.[11] Part of my work involves tracking down relevant publications in any available language. The archive now includes items in 27 languages, from Bulgarian to Yiddish. I do not speak 27 languages and I couldn't do my job without Google Translate. That doesn't mean it is a flawless system. The degree to which the app produces translations of a publication's title or abstract in a grammatical form of standard English varies. But it almost always gives me enough of a gist of the meaning to ascertain whether or not a particular publication is relevant to the archive's interests.

I used Google Translate extensively in researching this book. While I made an iron rule not to use the app as a substitute for commissioning translations of the Message from actual human beings, it did come in handy for other things. When I transcribed Messages in non-Latin scripts, I pasted them into the app in order to check I hadn't made a mistake. Google Translate helped me to confirm suspicions that some versions of the official Message were not identical in their wording.

Over time, though, I started to use Google Translate the other way round, using the Message as a way of exploring the app's limitations and capabilities. I conducted an experiment to compare how the official Messages in three different languages – Spanish, Swedish and English – translate into each other on Google Translate. Here is a reminder of the versions of the Message as they appear on the Manuscript:

WARNING, read and keep: Toy not suitable for children under 3 years. Small parts might be swallowed or inhaled.

ATENCIÓN, lea y guarde: Juguete no apto para meno-res de 3 años. Las partes pequeñas podrían ser ingeridas o inhaladas.

VARNING, läs och behåll: Leksak ej lämplig för barn under 3 år. Små delar kan fastna i halsen eller näsan.

Here is the English Message translated into Spanish and Swedish:

ADVERTENCIA, lea y guarde: Juguete no apto para menores de 3 años. Las piezas pequeñas pueden tra-garse o inhalarse.

VARNING, läs och förvara: Leksaken är inte lämplig för barn under 3 år. Små delar kan sväljas eller inandas.

Here is the Spanish Message translated into Swedish and English:

OBSERVERA, läs och spara: Leksak är inte lämplig för barn under 3 år. Små delar kan sväljas eller inandas.

ATTENTION, read and save: Toy not suitable for chil-dren under 3 years. Small parts could be swallowed or inhaled.

Finally, here is the Swedish Message translated into English and Spanish:

WARNING, read and keep: Toy not suitable for chil-dren under 3 years. Small parts can get stuck in the throat or nose.

ADVERTENCIA, lea y guarde: Juguete no apto para menores de 3 años. Las partes pequeñas pueden atascarse en la garganta o la nariz.

Not one of these Messages is identical. The differences seem fairly minor and, at least in the Spanish and English versions, the Messages remain coherent and grammatical. As I already knew, there is never only one way of saying something in any particular language. Viewed more broadly, the implications of this experiment are far from banal. Language and meaning involve subtle distinctions and nuances; if we trust Google Translate to navigate these complexities, we cannot know the consequences.

In my project to liberate the Message into dozens of new languages, I trusted strangers and their knowledge of particular languages, but at least I could ask them questions and they could gain some background information from me that explained what the Message was. With Google Translate, I had to trust a 'black box' that neither knew nor cared about the Message.

As with many other online apps, the exact nature of the system that powers Google Translate is unknown to us. Since 2016 it has used a 'neural' form of machine translation that learns and improves as it goes, rather than applying fixed grammatical rules and dictionary-based translations. At the core of the system are extensive text corpuses in multiple languages with existing translations between these corpuses used to model new translations. At the time of writing there are 109 languages available, with many more in development. These include all the official Message languages plus lesser-known tongues such as West Frisian and Galician.

Every Google Translate language can be translated into every other language, which is both the wondrous marvel of the system and its greatest limitation. As one might imagine, not every language pair has an extensive range of translations. I checked UNESCO's *Index Translationum*, which catalogues translated books, to see if anything had been translated from Icelandic to Tajik, or vice versa.[12] The answer was no. Even if there were examples of translations between this language pair, it could well have been done via a third language, most likely English, which is a common practice when translating between lesser-spoken languages. This is, in fact, how Google Translate manages it. It is never clear when the app is translating directly and when it is translating through English or another widely-spoken language.

Even given this limitation, Google Translate is impressive. I put the system to the test by translating the Message successively through all the Manuscript languages. I started with English, then went through Azeri, Bulgarian and the rest until I reached Chinese, before translating back into English again. This is the outcome:

> Use later, read and write. This game is not suitable for children under 3 years old. Small parts can be used or absorbed.

Okay, this isn't entirely accurate – 'use later' and 'absorbed' are clearly errors – but it remains intelligible and more or less conveys the correct message. It may be that starting with English helps, since the Message is pinging back and forth between English and other languages. So I tried the experiment again, starting and finishing with a lesser-spoken language,

Macedonian. Here is the Macedonian original:

ВНИМАНИЕ, ЧИТАЈ И ЗАЧУВАЈ: Ситните делови можат да бидат проголтани или вдишани.

And here it is after the translation sequence:

погледни изглед изгледа. Мали парчиња може да се проголтаат или вдишат.

In English this translates to:

look look looks. Small pieces can be swallowed or inhaled.

It is astonishing to see that the second sentence is pretty much as it should be. The first sentence, though, is much further away from the original than the English sample, both in its repetitive syntax and its loss of capitalisation.

Nonsensical Messages

When we use Google Translate, or another form of machine translation, we are looking for sense and intelligibility. I received a translation of the Message into a language called Karamanli Turkish. This is a dialect of Turkish spoken by Orthodox Christians, whose descendants now live in Greece following the post-First World War expulsions. It is written in the Greek alphabet:

ΟΥΓΙΑΡΕ, οκού βε τουτ σουνού: Μπουό ουντζάκ ούτς γιασιντάν κουτσούκ τζοτσουκλάς ίτσιν ιουγκούν ντείλντις. Κουτσούκ πααρτζαλεριν γιουλτούμα για ντα νεφές μπορουσουνά κάτσμα ρίσκι βάρντις.[13]

After I posted the Karamanli Turkish Message on Facebook, a friend alerted me to the automatic translation that appeared on his feed:

> Good morning, let's go to the world: we are going to have a good time for you. We are looking forward to the future of the world.

I presume that Facebook's translation algorithm not only mistook this for Greek, but in its drive for intelligibility 'corrected' it into something that made sense but was completely unrelated to the original. Google Translate fared better. Like Facebook it judged the Message to be Greek but contented itself with a transliteration into Latin script. When I told the app that the transliteration was Turkish, it had a go at translating it, coming up with:

> UGYARE, okou tout presentation: Buo onjak uts yasidan koutsuk jotsuklas itchin yugun evidenced. There was a risk that the holy paratzalers could cause breath injury in the form of swallowing.

The fact that most of this is unreadable is a good thing. It tells the reader that this is unlikely to be any kind of translation. In other cases, Google Translate's incorrect language recognition can be dangerous as it is *almost* correct. The app recognises Faroese as Icelandic, for example, and it does so fairly coherently, leading to who knows what misapprehensions. Humans are pattern-recognising creatures and machine translation can satiate our lust to recognise by producing translations that are linguistically 'correct' but not translations at all.

Still, at least when you use Google Translate to translate something into your own language, you can tell sense from nonsense. Using it to translate into a language you do not know is a much riskier proposition. An image from 2008 still circulates virally of a bilingual English-Welsh road sign whose original reads 'No entry for heavy goods vehicles. Residential site only'. The Welsh version translates to 'I am not in the office at the moment. Send any work to be translated'.[14] You can understand how it happened – a local council worker emailed the text to a translator and mistook his auto-respond for the translation.

With Google Translate, all we have are auto-responses. In 2020 an organisation was formed in Japan to campaign against the over-reliance on machine translation into English in constructing official signs.[15] Sometimes the resulting errors can be subtle but devastating, such as the Kyoto department store's slogan 'Rising Again, Save the World from Kyoto JAPAN', and at other times they can cause hilarity, such as the sign: 'Please do not move while driving'. Machine translation errors that find their way onto tattoos are often funny too, but I doubt the victims are laughing, such as the owner of the Hebrew tattoo which reads: 'Babylon is the world's leading dictionary and translation software'.[16]

Maybe such misunderstandings will be ironed out in the future as Google Translate continues its remorseless development and people become more aware of how (not) to use it. And machine translation helps to counteract some of the global drive towards linguistic uniformity. A world where machine translation is ubiquitous and near-perfect would be – theoretically at least – a world in which it would be possible to be a monoglot speaker of Munegàscu and still take a full part in a globalised world.

However well machine translation might end up working, and whatever its considerable advantages are, the technology contains much deeper dangers. When we input nonsense and instantly receive sense, we are in danger of falling into some dangerous delusions about what language is. The magnificent diversity of languages is erased and the beautiful differences between them are flattened. The casual use of machine translation risks cutting ourselves off from what makes language so delightful; its messiness, its confusion, its liberating possibilities.

Most of all, I worry that Google Translate risks taking away the form of linguistic pleasure that I have celebrated in this book – the pleasure of *not* understanding. As we draw to a close, I want to extol the utopian possibilities of not understanding a language, the end of which would be a dystopia.

Chapter 16

Babel as utopia

וַיְהִי כָל־הָאָרֶץ שָׂפָה אֶחָת וּדְבָרִים אֲחָדִים:

וַיְהִי בְּנָסְעָם מִקֶּדֶם וַיִּמְצְאוּ בִקְעָה בְּאֶרֶץ שִׁנְעָר וַיֵּשְׁבוּ שָׁם:

וַיֹּאמְרוּ אִישׁ אֶל־רֵעֵהוּ הָבָה נִלְבְּנָה לְבֵנִים וְנִשְׂרְפָה לִשְׂרֵפָה וַתְּהִי לָהֶם הַלְּבֵנָה לְאָבֶן וְהַחֵמָר הָיָה לָהֶם לַחֹמֶר:

וַיֹּאמְרוּ הָבָה נִבְנֶה־לָּנוּ עִיר וּמִגְדָּל וְרֹאשׁוֹ בַשָּׁמַיִם וְנַעֲשֶׂה־לָּנוּ שֵׁם פֶּן־נָפוּץ עַל־פְּנֵי כָל־הָאָרֶץ:

וַיֵּרֶד יְהוָה לִרְאֹת אֶת־הָעִיר וְאֶת־הַמִּגְדָּל אֲשֶׁר בָּנוּ בְּנֵי הָאָדָם:

וַיֹּאמֶר יְהוָה הֵן עַם אֶחָד וְשָׂפָה אַחַת לְכֻלָּם וְזֶה הַחִלָּם לַעֲשׂוֹת וְעַתָּה לֹא־יִבָּצֵר מֵהֶם כֹּל אֲשֶׁר יָזְמוּ לַעֲשׂוֹת:

הָבָה נֵרְדָה וְנָבְלָה שָׁם שְׂפָתָם אֲשֶׁר לֹא יִשְׁמְעוּ אִישׁ שְׂפַת רֵעֵהוּ:

וַיָּפֶץ יְהוָה אֹתָם מִשָּׁם עַל־פְּנֵי כָל־הָאָרֶץ וַיַּחְדְּלוּ לִבְנֹת הָעִיר:

עַל־כֵּן קָרָא שְׁמָהּ בָּבֶל כִּי־שָׁם בָּלַל יְהוָה שְׂפַת כָּל־הָאָרֶץ וּמִשָּׁם הֱפִיצָם יְהוָה עַל־פְּנֵי כָל־הָאָרֶץ:

And the whole earth was of one language and of one speech.

And it came to pass, as they journeyed east, that they found a plain in the land of Shinar; and they dwelt there.

And they said one to another: 'Come, let us make brick, and burn them thoroughly.' And they had brick for stone, and slime had they for mortar.

And they said: 'Come, let us build us a city, and a tower, with its top in heaven, and let us make us a name; lest we be scattered abroad upon the face of the whole earth.'

And the LORD came down to see the city and the
tower, which the children of men builded.

And the LORD said: 'Behold, they are one people, and
they have all one language; and this is what they
begin to do; and now nothing will be withholden
from them, which they purpose to do.

Come, let us go down, and there confound their language, that they may not understand one another's
speech.'

So the LORD scattered them abroad from thence upon
the face of all the earth; and they left off to build
the city.

Therefore was the name of it called Babel; because
the LORD did there confound the language of all the
earth ...[1]

The Babel myth is of great antiquity, with similar stories found
in Sumerian and Assyrian literature. Its themes still resonate
today: human hubris, human conflict, and the confounding
diversity of the languages humans speak. Jewish tradition
states that the ruins of the tower still exist, making Babel stand
as a crumbling monument to the confusion of tongues.

Why should a profusion of tongues lead to confusion? For
the medieval Jewish commentator Rashi, drawing on earlier
traditions, the problem was that a confusion of tongues made
cooperation impossible. The inability to cooperate in building
led to conflict and violence, as he says: 'One asks for a brick
and the other brings him lime: the former therefore attacks
him and splits open his brains.'

In his great work *If This Is A Man*, Primo Levi describes
another nightmare version of Babel, the Buna synthetic rubber

works at Auschwitz-Birkenau where he was enslaved by the Nazis:

> The confusion of languages is a fundamental compo-
> nent of the manner of living here: one is surrounded
> by a perpetual Babel, in which everyone shouts orders
> and threats in languages never heard before, and woe
> betide whoever fails to grasp the meaning. No one has
> time here, no one has patience, no one listens to you.[2]
>
> [...]
>
> The Carbide Tower, which rises in the middle of
> Buna and whose top is rarely visible in the fog, was
> built by us. Its bricks were called Ziegel, briques, teg-
> ula, cegli, kammeny, mattoni, teglak, and they were
> cemented by hate; hate and discord, like the Tower
> of Babel, and it is this that we call it: – Babelturm,
> Bobelturm; and in it we hate the insane dream of gran-
> deur of our masters, their contempt for God and men,
> for us men.
>
> And today just as in the old fable, we all feel,
> and the Germans themselves feel, that a curse – not
> transcendent and divine, but inherent and historical
> – hangs over the insolent building based on the confu-
> sion of languages and erected in defiance of heaven
> like a stone oath.[3]

It is as though the builders of the Tower of Babel had continued building after God had confused their tongues; through
violence and brutality they push through their sacrilegious
project. Yet the fate of Buna was ultimately the same as the
Tower – neither was ever finished.

What Levi communicates so viscerally is how terrifying it can be to be assailed by orders given in languages one cannot fully understand. The biblical Babel story also shows how lack of understanding can be so unnerving that it can destroy cooperation and cause human beings to put as much distance as possible between each other, or even to kill them.

Jorge Luis Borges' famous short story 'The Library of Babel' also constructs Babel as a maddening dystopia. Borges' library is the universe itself; a universe of identical rooms containing books of identical length in an identical script.[4] There is a book in the library for every possible combination of letters, meaning that most are unintelligible but also that every possible intelligible book also exists. The librarians are driven to despair and irrational behaviour by the search for meaningful books and, above all, the index to all the other books within the library.

In Babels real, fictional and mythical, the human desire for intelligible order is so strong that, when it can't be found, humanity risks collapse. Does this have to be true, though? Does lack of understanding necessarily lead to discord? One way to approach this question is to reverse it: does understanding each other necessarily lead to concord?

Language and conflict

Senlin Ascends, the first volume in Josiah Bancroft's fantasy novel sequence *The Books of Babel*, takes place in a completed Tower that is full of both wonders and horrors.[5] The Tower is divided into 'ringdoms' that are in a constant state of conflict with each other and among themselves. The Tower is a piteous place, where slavery, torture and violence are common. The bewildered protagonist, a schoolteacher called Thomas

Senlin, comes to the Tower on honeymoon, is immediately separated from his wife and is forced to navigate a new world whose rules are never explained to him. Yet however much the Tower in the story might be a place of discord, the inhabitants appear to speak the same language.[6] In the world that Bancroft describes, God never interceded to prevent Babel being built, but the outcome wasn't actually that different: human beings who cannot trust or cooperate with each other.

To explain conflict as a result of 'misunderstanding' – linguistic or otherwise – is too simple. Some of the worst conflicts in human history have been between people who speak the same language and understand the motivations and desires of the other side; the American Civil War, for example, was fought between people who understood each other, but wanted different things. In other conflicts, different sides may have spoken different languages, but this was not the source of the conflict; the Second World War was not a struggle between the German language and the languages of the Allies, it was a struggle between the Germans and the Allies.

We can certainly point to conflicts where language has been an exacerbating factor, as in the former Yugoslavia. We can also point to cases where the attempt to suppress languages may trigger violent resistance, as in the 1976 Soweto uprising in apartheid South Africa, which was sparked by an attempt to introduce Afrikaans to the medium of instruction in its schools. In such cases, linguistic struggles were also manifestations of much deeper divisions. Scratch the surface of a linguistic dispute and there is often much more to it. While Belgians don't slaughter each other because of it, the constant friction between Dutch- and French-speakers cannot be separated from economic divisions (the mostly French-speaking south was once much wealthier than the Dutch-speaking north, and the situation has now reversed).

Babel as Utopia

While the Tower of Babel story may still resonate, there is a counter-narrative in which Babel is celebrated by those who promote linguistic diversity. For example, Babel's Blessing is a London-based 'grassroots language school', which promotes cultural exchange and community building.[7] My bookshelf contains works such as Gaston Dorren's *Babel: Around the World in Twenty Languages*, John McWhorter's *The Power of Babel: A Natural History of Language*, and an edited collection, *Babel: Adventures in Translation*. Such works evoke a Babel of chaotic, exciting, and invigorating linguistic diversity.

This book has certainly celebrated our post-Babel inheritance. I want to go further, though. The marvels of linguistic diversity are not 'the other side of the coin' of the more negative aspects of human diversity. They are not some kind of consolation for human conflict. Rather, not understanding each other's languages can be an aid to *resolving* conflict and maybe even preventing conflict emerging in the first place.

A common language flatters to deceive. It can make us lazy. We may assume we understand each other and avoid doing the hard work of achieving a deeper understanding. Indeed, *not* understanding the language of the other can actually help us get on with them. Over the last few years we have seen how previously just-about-manageable social and political conflicts have started to rage out of control. One of the key drivers of this is social media, which relentlessly confronts us with inconvenient and disenchanting knowledge about other people. I'm sure that I am not the only one to see people I thought I knew and respected reveal sides of themselves online that I wish I had never seen. As the sociologist Richard Sennett has argued, living together in complex societies requires that we do not reveal all of ourselves to others all the time.[8] There are times when it would be helpful not to know the languages of others; to be insulated from their thoughts and beliefs.

Not understanding can allow for a deeper and more robust form of getting to know the other. In finding a way to communicate, slowly, over time, we can learn how to communicate more carefully. I'm afraid that, at this point, I'm going to have to mention another *Star Trek: The Next Generation* episode, despite not being a diehard fan of the franchise. In 'Loud as a Whisper', first aired in 1989, the *Enterprise* is tasked to accompany a negotiator called Riva to resolve a conflict on the planet Solais V. Riva is deaf and mute but travels with a 'chorus' with whom he is in telepathic communication and who communicate on his behalf. When one delegate of the rival parties in the conflict kills the chorus, Riva almost abandons the peace process. In the end, he is persuaded by the crew of the *Enterprise* to return to the planet and use their assistance in communicating. Riva resolves to restart the negotiations but dismisses the help of the crew. Instead, he will teach the warring parties his sign language. This will be a slow process but one that will ultimately build a deeper kind of connection.

So even though I have insisted on the value of a superficial approach to language, it doesn't have to end there. To appreciate a language you do not understand for its surface characteristics is to insist on the absolute beauty of its words, regardless of what they are used for. This can be a starting point for something more. I know that I fell in love with Finnish as much for its sound as anything else. Over time, this has led me to learn the language, to delight in its grammar and also to appreciate Finnish people and the society they have built. I know, though, that I am a promiscuous language-lover. Perhaps the delicate Cyrillic modifications of Abkhazian might inspire me to learn more about the people who speak the language. Perhaps the gorgeous Indian scripts will lead me to delve deeper into the diversity of the subcontinent. And perhaps you, the reader, might fall in love with one of the Messages you have read in this book and this might lead you to take your own journeys.

I fear silence rather than the cacophony of tongues. Silence can speak as aggressively as any insult. While the silence of some of the indigenous activists I approached might also be the silence of resistance rather than threat, I still long to hear the sounds and trace the shapes of the letters in their languages. Where there is the babble of unknown tongues, there can be aesthetics, wonder and the possibility of connection.

Babel, or at least a version of Babel, is my utopia; a towering edifice of gloriously confused tongues; a monument to the pleasures and possibilities of not understanding. Can the Message take us to that utopia? It can certainly set us on a journey towards it. By liberating the Message we can liberate ourselves from the shackles of linguistic uniformity and enter a strange new world of wondrously confused tongues.

Chapter 17

Ending at the beginning

We all need origin stories; after all, everything comes from something. Whether it was the Big Bang, God, or gods that began it all, the lure of tracing everything back to an ultimate cause is strong. That is why the Babel myth is so alluring; it incorporates language into a story of absolute beginnings and absolute endings. Just like the human species, so the emergence of language and linguistic diversity took place over an enormous span of time. Languages evolve, they diverge, they become incomprehensible to others. This is an open-ended story.

It's easy to acknowledge this point in theory, but in our guts it can be hard to accept. The language one speaks seems like a colossal monolith, handed down intact to us; a system bigger than us all. While we may on occasion experience those jarring moments when an older generation uses a term in a different way to ourselves – the furious reaction of my sister when my mother called her a 'slut' for having a messy bedroom springs to mind – the larger edifice seems sturdy. It is not easy to accept that we would have difficulty understanding a speaker of our own language even a few centuries back (or even that what we think of as our language didn't exist back then).

The Message was composed and translated during a tiny fraction of human time. The warning sheet is a snapshot of what official versions of multiple languages looked like at one moment on their unstoppable journeys towards transformation and eventual oblivion. The multiple other translations I have presented in this book also emerged from a particular time and place (even the translations into ancient languages depend on the current scholarly state of the art).

I know all this, yet I am still consumed by the urge to trace the Message back to its origins, to the dawn of language itself.

We cannot go on a journey back to that time; we cannot hear their language and they cannot hear ours. But perhaps we can content ourselves with a more modest journey, back to a time when many of the languages of the Message were just one language.

Languages, like humans, have family trees. Twenty-seven of the languages on the European Message sheet are part of the same language family – Indo-European.[1] That includes everything from Albanian to English to Farsi. Many more languages not included on the sheet are also Indo-European, including Hindi to the east and Irish in the west.

We know these languages are part of the same family tree because of a sustained scholarly effort since the eighteenth century. Polyglots had long noted the striking similarities between languages spread over the globe. In 1789 the Anglo-Welsh judge William Jones argued for a common ancestor to Sanskrit, Latin and Greek. In the early nineteenth century, scholars such as Rasmus Rask, Jacob Grimm and Franz Bopp extended these commonalities to German, Persian and other languages. They looked for 'cognates' in multiple languages: so 'mother' is *mater* in Latin, *matr* in Sanskrit and *madar* in Persian; 'seven' is *sibun* in Gothic, *sedmi* in old Slavic and *shtatë* in Albanian; 'mouse' is *mus* in Ancient Greek and *mukn* in Armenian.

In one of the most extraordinary scholarly projects in human history, researchers have worked backwards from these languages, back to a single common ancestor, known as Proto-Indo-European, the first outlines of which were published in the mid-nineteenth century. Key to this project was the discovery that while all languages change over time, they do so in predictable ways. This means that even if there isn't a written record of a particular word in a particular language at a particular point in its history, you can work backwards from the records that you do have to infer what the word would have been.

Proto-Indo-European was never written down. It was probably spoken sometime between 3000 and 2000 BCE and while there are multiple hypotheses as to where it was spoken, the most popular is that it emerged in the Pontic-Caspian steppes, in what is now southern Russia and Ukraine.[2] The people who spoke it were likely to have been pastoralists, herding horses and cattle across the grasslands. Through a mixture of migration, conquest and cultural influence, their language spread and spawned languages everywhere from the Indian subcontinent to the western edges of Europe and (eventually, via English and other languages of Empire) across the entire world.

Proto-Indo-European is neither a living nor a sleeping nor a dead language; it is a partially reconstructed language. Over 1,500 word roots have been identified, together with some of the grammar. Short texts have even been translated into it. There are many gaps in our knowledge and much will never be known. In any case, rather than a single language it is more likely to have been a cluster of dialects.

From the very start of this project I wanted a translation of the Message into Proto-Indo-European. Realistically, though, given the fragmentary state of the reconstructed language, such a translation would have been very difficult to achieve. However, some Proto-Indo-Europeanists have gone further than partial reconstruction to produce a fully-fledged language: Modern Indo-European, the creation of the organisation Academia Prisca. They have not only created a grammar and a language course, they have much grander ambitions, including 'The adoption of Modern Indo-European by the European Union as its main official language'.[3] Given this ambition, a translation of the Message presented a very modest challenge to them. Academia Prisca's co-founder, Fernando López-Menchero, responded to my email request within a day, supplying me with the translation with which I will end this book.

If Academia Prisca's vision is realised, then 27 languages on the Manuscript would be reduced to one. The 5,000-year circle will be closed, complete. Despite my admiration for the audacity of Academia Prisca, I regard the possibility of the loss of such linguistic diversity with horror. Yet even if Modern Indo-European were to supplant many or all of the other Messages, I console myself that it too would change. Any language will slip through our fingers over time. No Message will endure into eternity.

The inevitable transformation of tongues presents a particular challenge for warning messages. Since 1945, scientists have been grappling with the task of marking locations where radioactive waste has been buried. These locations will be unsafe for tens of thousands of years, much longer than the history of writing so far. We cannot assume our descendants will still be able to read our words. Pictures and icons may or may not prove more enduring. Some have even suggested that warnings to our descendants would need to be encased in a religion or myth in order to survive.[4]

The Message too will only endure as long as there is a Ferrero to carry out the endless task of rewriting.

In Ted Chiang's short story 'Tower of Babylon', a miner called Hillalum joins the centuries-old project of building Babel, just before the moment of completion.[5] He joins the crew that reaches the vault of heaven and, with enormous difficulty, tunnels through it – only to find that he is back at the base of the Tower.

So it is that the Message cycles endlessly back and forth between tongues, between incomprehensibility and clarity. Its failure to ever achieve perfect meaning is a noble one, a human one. Amid that failure, is there not also a dream of communication, of reaching out to care for our children who will come after us?

This world, this egg: filled with gestating possibility, fragile when mistreated, it comes with no warning message. We must create our own. Let us celebrate the difficulties of doing so; for it matters less that we deliver the message, than that we raise our voices and exult in the task.

Probhoudhos: lege segheqe. Ənəptom pútlomos upo trisú wétessi rebhṛ. Paulās áitejes en qémōntor ánōntorwe.

Oh God, I forgot to include Morse code! It's—

Is your lust to read translations of
the Message still unsatiated?

Could you translate the Message into a language
that doesn't appear in this book?

Can you solve or add to the mysteries of the Manuscript?

Then take the next step on your journey by exploring
the additional content for this book on my website:

[Or: https://kahn-harris.org/babeladditional/]

Warning! For true Manuscript fans only

If, like me, you find the Manuscript tantalising, why not take a trip with me across it?

First of all, we have to orient ourselves.

There are many versions of the Manuscript, and new ones are continually being produced. For the last few years, the changes between versions have been very minor, so the chances are that your Manuscript will resemble the one printed in this book fairly closely. The one I am working from has the code number 79013029 on the bottom right-hand corner of the second side. If yours is different, do not be alarmed, I will ensure you do not lose your way.

Now caress the Manuscript. Most versions are printed on glossy paper, but if you are fortunate you might find one printed on matt. Your fingers will likely trace four vertical creases from where the paper was folded to fit into the capsule, although I have found horizontal creases in some, and the Manuscripts found in jumbo-sized Eggs are unfolded and unblemished. The Manuscript might be attached to another piece of paper of similar size that gives a visual guide to the toy. It detaches easily from the Manuscript; make sure you do so, as you would not want anything to distract your attention.

Side one, column one
The Manuscript is printed on both sides. Side one is the side with the red warning image on it. We will begin our journey in the red-outlined box on the upper left region. The box is filled

with almost unreadably dense bold capitals, some of which are also underlined in red.

The text starts with the words 'IMPORTED BY'. The next two words, *ИЗГОТОВИТЕЛЬ/ВИРОБНИК*, are in Russian and Ukrainian. They translate as 'manufacturer', rather than 'importer' as we might have expected. This is followed by the name and address of the Ferrero Group's corporate headquarters in Luxembourg. The word 'address' is also translated into Russian and Ukrainian.

How do we account for the fact that this one address is treated as an importer in English and a manufacturer in Russian and Ukrainian? This is an early reminder that we should not assume that every word on the Manuscript is necessarily a translation. In this case, the extreme lack of space may mean that the creators of the Manuscript decided they would condense importer and manufacturer into one abbreviated sentence. We are reminded here of the scale of the Ferrero enterprise, the size of the spear of which the Manuscript is the point. That the same company contains separate divisions that produce and import, shows how far it is a world of its own making.

The second paragraph gives an address for Ferrero in Argentina and Mexico. This paragraph is not underlined in red as is the first paragraph. This is likely to be a way of distinguishing the importance of Ferrero's HQ from its satellite offices.

The Manuscript is not just about safety, then. Ferrero have chosen to squeeze information about the company onto its faces too.

Below the upper left-hand box we come to one of the few expanses of space on the entire piece of paper. It contains two symbols. The one on the left we met in Chapter 9. The one on the right is less instantly understandable and seems to consist of a large-type C followed by a large-type E:

The two symbols are, in fact, connected. The warning image is mandated in the *EU Directive on the Safety of Toys*, which states:

> Toys which might be dangerous for children under 36 months of age shall bear a warning such as 'Not suitable for children under 36 months' or 'Not suitable for children under three years' or a warning in the form of the following graphic.[1]

It also says:

> These warnings shall be accompanied by a brief indication, which may appear in the instructions for use, of the specific hazard calling for this precaution.

The guidelines state that the symbol must be at least 10mm in diameter – and I can confirm that it is, just.

The 'CE' mark indicates that a product conforms to the relevant EU standard and can be sold anywhere in the EU. While it does not imply a certification of quality, it does proclaim to the world that the Manuscript, at least, follows EU standards. The marking must be taller than 5mm (which it is).

With the reader now reassured that the Manuscript message is legal (at least in the EU, EFTA, the UK for now and some states that aspire to EU membership), we move on to the first actual Message – only to find that it is not actually a Message at all.

This is Armenian, written in sentence case (which, as in English, means a capital letter at the start of a sentence, with lower case for the rest). The text is prefixed by the code 'AR' in white letters within a small black rectangle. This presumably stands for 'Armenian' or 'Armenia'. The International Organisation for Standardisation (ISO) has a set of agreed codes for language (ISO 639) and for countries (ISO 3166). The correct ISO code for the Armenian language is 'HY'. The correct ISO code for Armenia is 'AM'. Why 'AR' is used here is unclear, as it denotes the language of Arabic and the country of Argentina in the ISO codes.

This Armenian message is not, as I said, a Message. Rather, it explains that this is a Kinder toy, and its authorised importer is Ferrero Russia. The address and phone number of Ferrero Russia follow. The message ends by explaining that the toy is made in Italy and supplies the month and year of production.

Side one, columns two to four

Going up to the top of the next column, the Messages at last begin. All of them are prefixed by the ISO two-letter code denoting the language rather than the country. While the Messages may look the same at a casual glance, there are differences in content and presentation. In particular, not all Messages include specific mention of the 3-year age minimum.

Here is a summary of the principal differences:

Messages: Side one, column two					
Language code	Language	Mentions 3-year limit?	'Warning' capitalised?	'Read and keep' capitalised?	Other noteworthy details?
AZ	Azerbaijani	No	No	No	Message is encased in inverted commas
BG	Bulgarian	No	Yes	Yes	
CS	Czech	No	Yes	No	
DA	Danish	No	No	No	
DE	German	Yes	Yes	No	'Warning' (*Warnhinweis*) appears after 'read and keep' and followed by exclamation mark
EL	Greek	No	Yes	No	

Messages: Side one, column three					
Language code	Language	Mentions 3-year limit?	'Warning' capitalised?	'Read and keep' capitalised?	Other noteworthy details?
EN	English	Yes	Yes	No	
ES	Spanish	Yes	Yes	No	
ET	Estonian	No	Yes	Yes	'Warning' (*TÄHELEPANU!*) followed by exclamation mark
FI	Finnish	No	Yes	No	
FR	French	No	Yes	No	
HR	Croatian	No	Yes	Yes	

Messages: Side one, column four					
Language code	Language	Mentions 3-year limit?	'Warning' capitalised?	'Read and keep' capitalised?	Other noteworthy details
HU	Hungarian	No	Yes	No	'Warning, read and keep' followed by exclamation mark
HY	Armenian	No	Yes	Yes	Entire Message capitalised. Note contrast with first Armenian message. Correct language code is used here
IT	Italian	No	Yes	No	
KA	Georgian	No	NA	NA	Georgian does not have separate capital and lower-case letters

At the bottom of column four we have another non-Message message, preceded by the language code 'KY' for Kyrgyz, the language of Kyrgyzstan. The contents of this message are virtually identical to the first Armenian message.

We have now reached the end of side one, but our journey still has a long way to go. Follow me into the land of side two ...

Side two

The first column on side two is relatively straightforward. It is after that that things start to get more complicated.

Messages: Side two, column one					
Language code	Language	Mentions 3-year limit?	'Warning' capitalised?	'Read and keep' capitalised?	Other noteworthy details
LT	Lithuanian	No	Yes	Yes	'Warning' (*DĖMESIO!*) followed by exclamation mark
LV	Latvian	No	Yes	Yes	
MK	Macedonian	No	Yes	Yes	
NL	Dutch	No	Yes	No	
NO	Norwegian	No	No	No	
PL	Polish	No	Yes	No	

Side two, column two only contains two actual Messages. I will summarise them before explaining the middle non-Message message:

Messages: Side two, column two					
Language code	Language	Mentions 3-year limit?	'Warning' capitalised?	'Read and keep' capitalised?	Other noteworthy details
PT	Portuguese	No	Yes	No	
RO-MO	Romanian-Moldovan	No	Yes	Yes	This Message is unique as it covers two languages. I discuss it in detail in Chapter 4

The bottom two thirds of column two is prefixed by the codes 'RU-KZ-BY'. These are ISO country codes for Russia, Kazakhstan and Belarus. We know they cannot be language codes as, while the Russian language is also 'RU', 'KZ' and 'BY' do not exist under ISO 639.

It's not clear why these three country codes are printed together. The first half of this message is written in Russian and the second half in Kazakh (which also uses the Cyrillic script). The wording of the messages in both languages is more or less identical to the ones for Armenia and Kyrgyzstan. The major difference is that in this case, the place of manufacture is listed as China rather than Italy.

Below this message we find the tall capital letters 'EAC'. This is the Eurasian Conformity mark and is similar to the CE mark on side one. It denotes conformity to the standards of the Eurasian Customs Union, which covers Armenia, Belarus, Kazakhstan, Kyrgyzstan and Russia. The relevant standard here is TR CU 008/2011 which covers the safety of toys.

After the excitement of side two, column two, column three is more straightforward:

Messages: Side two, column three					
Language code	Language	Mentions 3-year limit?	'Warning' capitalised?	'Read and keep' capitalised?	Other noteworthy details
SK	Slovak	No	Yes	No	
SL	Slovene	No	Yes	Yes	
SQ	Albanian	No	Yes	Yes	
SR	Serbian	No	Yes	Yes	
SV	Swedish	Yes	Yes	No	
TR	Turkish	No	Yes	No	

Column four begins with a non-Message message prefixed by the code 'UA', which is the country code for Ukraine. This message is in Ukrainian and reads:

> Kinder toy collections. The batch number coincides with the date of manufacture. Date of production: 03.2020. Importer, address: see information on the package. Shelf life is unlimited.

The rest of the column contains four Messages. None of them is preceded by language codes and none of them is written in scripts that have separate capital letters, so I have amended the table accordingly:

Messages: Side two, column four		
Language	Mentions 3-year limit?	Other noteworthy details
Persian	No	
Arabic	Yes	First word of the Message is 'Arabic'
Chinese (traditional characters)	Yes	Wording of both is identical. Traditional Chinese characters are used in Taiwan, Hong Kong and Macao. Simplified Chinese characters are used in China and Singapore
Chinese (simplified characters)	Yes	

We are not done yet. Below the Chinese Messages are some further tiny characters and alphanumeric codes which translate as: 'This toy complies with GB6675·2003 and GB5296.5-2006'. These are the Chinese codes for, respectively, the safety of toys and for the marking of safety warnings on toys.

We finish our journey with two further codes, 'LEC 008' and '79013029'. Your Manuscript may contain slightly different versions of these codes. They are codes used by Ferrero itself. The eight-letter number code marks the version number of the Manuscript. I have as yet been unable to discover what the alphanumeric code refers to. Maybe readers would like to attempt to solve this mystery?

Notes

WARNING, read and keep

1. Kahn-Harris, Keith. *Strange Hate: Antisemitism, Racism and the Limits of Diversity*. Repeater, 2019.

Introduction: A surprising obsession

1. Padovani, Gigi. *Nutella World: 50 Years of Innovation*. Rizzoli International Publications, Incorporated, 2015: 192.

Chapter 1: The Message

1. Benelli, B., C. Donati, N. Consonni, and B. Morra. 'Food Products Containing Inedibles: Children Recognition of Their "Double Nature" and Manipulation-Play Behaviour'. *International Congress Series*, Advances in Pediatric ORL. Proceedings of the 8th International Congress of Pediatric Otorhinolaryngology, 1254 (1 November 2003): 497–500.
2. Eldred, John S., and Stuart M. Pape. 'Toys and Confectionery – A Legally Hazardous Combination?' *Food and Drug Law Journal* 53, No. 1 (1998): 1–8.
3. Michigan Lawsuit Abuse Watch. 'Wacky Warning Label Contest'. Accessed 10 January 2021. https://www.lawsuitfairness.org/wacky-warning-label-contest
4. Hackner, Stacy. 'That Margaret Mead Quote'. *Stacy Hackner*, 21 April 2020. https://stacyhackner.wordpress.com/2020/04/21/that-margaret-mead-quote/
5. Robinson, Patricia A. *Writing and Designing Manuals and Warnings, Fifth Edition*. CRC Press, 2019; Wogalter, Michael S. *Handbook of Warnings*. CRC Press, 2006; Wogalter, Michael S., Dave DeJoy, and Kenneth R. Laughery. *Warnings and Risk Communication*. CRC Press, 1999.
6. It turns out that I am not the only person to have paid attention to the warning messages. After the hardback version of this book was published, I stumbled on a discussion on a linguistics message board from 2011 that featured translations of the Message. At the time of writing it is still online, although no one has added to the thread since 2016: https://cbbforum.com/viewtopic.php?t=1529
7. Perec, Georges. 'Approaches to What?' In *Species of Spaces and Other Pieces*, 205–7. Penguin Books, 1997.
8. Ibid.: 205.
9. Potter, Jonathan, and Margaret Wetherell. *Discourse and Social Psychology: Beyond Attitudes and Behaviour*. London: Sage Publications, 1987.
10. Sacks, Harvey. 'On the Analysability of Stories by Children'. In *Directions in Sociolinguistics: The Ethnography of Communication*, edited by John J. Gumperz and Dell Hymes, 329–45. Holt, Rinehart and Winston, 1972.
11. Barthes, Roland. *S/Z: An Essay*. Farrar, Straus and Giroux, 1974.

12. Benjamin, Walter. *Illuminations: Essays and Reflections*. Houghton Mifflin Harcourt, 2019: 25.
13. Bellos, David. *Is That a Fish in Your Ear?: Translation and the Meaning of Everything*. Penguin UK, 2011.
14. Steiner, George. *After Babel: Aspects of Language and Translation*. Oxford University Press, 1998.

Chapter 2: The Manuscript

1. This is a rough estimate, compiled from ethnologue.com and various other sources.
2. Padovani, Gigi. *Nutella World: 50 Years of Innovation*. Rizzoli International Publications, 2015.
3. Ibid.: 146.
4. ALUMINIUMFOLIEN-KATALOG DEUTSCHLAND. 'Kinder Überraschung Organigramm – Ferrero', 2017. https://aluminiumfolien-katalog.jimdofree. com/wichtiges-zum-afk-vorneweg/3-%C3%BC-ei-organigramm/
5. 'Helmut's Sammlerseiten'. http://www.euro-kat.de/
6. German, Dutch, Swedish, Danish, Finnish, Italian, French, English, Spanish and Portuguese.
7. Barenblat, Rachel. 'Fan Fiction and Midrash: Making Meaning'. *Transformative Works and Cultures* 17 (15 September 2014). https://doi. org/10.3983/twc.2014.0596
8. Sikoryak, R. *Terms and Conditions*. Drawn & Quarterly Publications, 2017.

Chapter 3: Learning to be superficial

1. https://wikitongues.org/
2. Schafer, R. Murray. *The Tuning of the World*. Knopf, 1977.
3. Backhaus, Peter. *Linguistic landscapes: A comparative study of urban multilingualism in Tokyo*. Clevedon, UK: Multilingual Matters, 2008.
4. This Japanese Message comes from a Codex Manuscript dated to no later than 2007.
5. The Thai Message is taken from a Manuscript found in Brunei in 2018.
6. I have used the Lexilogos online keyboard in this project: https://www. lexilogos.com/keyboard/index.htm
7. See, for example: https://www.youtube.com/watch?v=V9LQDTiDcrA
8. The Korean and Vietnamese Messages are taken from a Manuscript found in Korea in 2018.
9. Bulgarian, Danish, German, Greek, English, Spanish, French, Hungarian, Armenian, Italian, Macedonian, Dutch, Norwegian, Portuguese, Romanian, Albanian, Swedish, Turkish, Arabic.
10. Note that a colon at the end of an Armenian sentence serves as a full stop.
11. Watson, Cecelia. *Semicolon: How a Misunderstood Punctuation Mark Can Improve Your Writing, Enrich Your Reading and Even Change Your Life*. HarperCollins, 2020.
12. Garfield, Simon. *Just My Type: A Book About Fonts*. Profile Books, 2010.

Chapter 4: The official version

1. CEN members include the following countries whose languages appear on the Manuscript: Austria, Belgium, Bulgaria, Croatia, Cyprus,

Czech Republic, Denmark, Estonia, Finland, North Macedonia, France, Germany, Greece, Hungary, Ireland, Italy, Latvia, Lithuania, Luxembourg, Netherlands, Norway, Poland, Portugal, Romania, Slovakia, Slovenia, Spain, Sweden, Switzerland, Turkey and the United Kingdom. There are a number of separate EN71 documents referring to different aspects of toys.

2. I am working off the 2015 version of this document. Another was published in 2020 after I had completed the research for this book.

3. Ibid.: 5.

4. Shariatmadari, David. *Don't Believe A Word: The Surprising Truth About Language*. Hachette UK, 2019: Kindle edition.

5. Anderson, Benedict. *Imagined Communities*. 2nd edn. London: Verso, 1991.

6. At the time of writing, they are currently being forced to deal with the consequences of war in Ukraine and sanctions on Russia; which will inevitably lead to changes in where their products are manufactured; which will inevitably lead to changes in how the Manuscript will be written in future.

7. Translation by Mirkena Palluqi.

8. Lefebvre, Jean-Sébastien. 'Gheg or Tosk: Dialect Still Divides Kosovo'. *Cafébabel*, 18 March 2008. https://cafebabel.com/en/article/gheg-or-tosk-dialect-still-divides-kosovo-5ae006aff723b35a145e1031/

9. Radio Bulgaria. 'Bulgarian Academy of Sciences Is Firm That "Macedonian Language" Is Bulgarian Dialect', 12 November 2019. https://bnr.bg/en/post/101203235/bulgarian-academy-of-sciences-is-firm-that-macedonian-language-is-bulgarian-dialect

10. http://jezicinacionalizmi.com/deklaracija/

11. Translation courtesy of Lina Vdovîi.

12. Ciscel, M.H. (2007). *The Language of the Moldovans: Romania, Russia, and Identity in an Ex-Soviet Republic*. Lanham, MD: Lexington Books: 12.

13. Ibid.: 3.

14. http://www.presedinte.md/titlul1

15. Ciscel, *The Language of the Moldovans*: 81.

16. 'Un Monument al Minciunii Şi al Urii – "Dicţionarul Moldovenesc-Românesc" al Lui Vasile Stati'. *Contrafort*, no. 7–8 (2003): 105–06. http://www.contrafort.md/old/2003/105-106/570.html

17. Radio Free Europe/Radio Liberty. 'Chisinau Recognizes Romanian As Official Language', 5 December 2013. https://www.rferl.org/a/moldova-romanian-official-language/25191455.html

18. The English message read: 'WARNING, read and keep: For hygienic reasons always empty the toy after use'. I'd thrown away the toy before I read the message so I can't tell you what it was or why you should empty it.

19. Transliterated by Oana Uta.

20. Miéville, C. (2010). *The City and the City*. Pan Macmillan: 42.

Chapter 5: The spoken Message

1. In the discussion that follows, I am grateful for the assistance of Alex Bellem of Durham University.

2. I used a professional translator for this one, commissioned via the website Fivver.com

3.   Translation by Malcolm Callus.
4.   Translation by Jonas Sibony.
5.   Translation by Meryam Dermati.
6.   Translation by Stella Sai-Chun.
7.   See the well-known essay by David Moser, 'Why Chinese is so damn hard', originally published in 1991: http://pinyin.info/readings/texts/moser.html
8.   Translation by Rahima Mahmut.
9.   Transcription by Gabriel Kanter-Webber.
10. International Phonetic Association. 'IPA Charts and Sub-Charts in Four Fonts'. Accessed 11 January 2021. https://www.internationalphonetic association.org/IPAcharts/IPA_chart_orig/IPA_charts_E.html
11. https://tophonetics.com/
12. https://navlipi.org/
13. Apollo Flight Journal. 'Apollo 17. Day 1: Launch and Ascent to Earth Orbit'. 2017. https://history.nasa.gov/afj/ap17fj/01_day01_launch.htm
14. 'Report of Apollo 204 Review Board', 5 April 1967. https://history.nasa.gov/ Apollo204/summary.pdf: 5-8 to 5-9.

Chapter 6: Filling in the gaps

1.   Greene, Lane. *Talk on the Wild Side: Why Language Won't Do As It's Told*. Profile Books, 2018.
2.   Omniglot. 'My Hovercraft Is Full of Eels in Many Languages'. Accessed 11 January 2021. https://omniglot.com/language/phrases/hovercraft.htm.
3.   Translation by Veturliði Óskarsson.
4.   See the following 'unwrapping' video of a Kinder Surprise bought in Iceland: https://www.youtube.com/watch?v=sXVGA6UUKBE
5.   Translation by Liam Ó Cuinneagáin.
6.   Translation by Henry de Nassau.
7.   Translation by the organisation Lia Rumantscha.
8.   Translation by Alena Markova.
9.   Smolicz, Jerzy J., and Ryszard Radzik. 'Belarusian as an Endangered Language: Can the Mother Tongue of an Independent State Be Made to Die?' *International Journal of Educational Development*, Education in Transitional States, 24, no. 5 (1 September 2004): 511–28. https://doi. org/10.1016/S0738-0593(03)00072-5
10. 'Tajikistan's Constitution of 1994 with Amendments through 2003'. Constitute. https://www.constituteproject.org/constitution/Tajikistan_2003. pdf?lang=en
11. Translation by Kamila Akhmedjanova.
12. Translation by Merjen Arazova via Elliott Hoey.
13. Translation by Khulgana Daz.
14. Translation by George Hewitt.
15. Ethnologue. 'How Many Languages Are There in the World?', 3 May 2016. https://www.ethnologue.com/guides/how-many-languages
16. Translation by Maricar Dela Cruz.
17. Translation compiled by Bruno Estigarribia from online contacts.
18. Translation by Danelle Vermuelen.
19. Translation by Cariola Mostert.
20. Translation by Norah Makhubela.

21. Translation by Yoseph Mengitsu.
22. Translation by Ida Hadjivaynis.
23. Ethnologue. 'What Are the Top 200 Most Spoken Languages?', 3 October 2018. https://www.ethnologue.com/guides/ethnologue200
24. Translation by Rashad Ali.
25. Translation by Rashad Ali.
26. Translation by Rashad Ali.
27. Translation by Param Singh.
28. Translation by Tamil Studies UK.
29. Translation by Carmen Arlando.
30. Translation by Anupama Mundollikkalam.
31. Translation by Anupama Mundollikkalam.
32. Translation by Tsheten Lhamo.

Chapter 7: Diasporas and minorities

1. 'Requests for New Languages/Wikipedia Western Armenian'. https://meta.wikimedia.org/wiki/Requests_for_new_languages/Wikipedia_Western_Armenian
2. Translation by Krikor Moskofian.
3. World Population Review. 'Armenia Population 2020'. https://worldpopulationreview.com/countries/armenia-population
4. Deutsche Welle (English). 'German Population with Immigrant Background Reaches New Peak in 2017'. 1 August 2018. https://www.dw.com/en/german-population-with-immigrant-background-reaches-new-peak-in-2017/a-44906046
5. Academy for Cultural Diplomacy. 'Chinese Diaspora Across the World: A General Overview'. http://www.culturaldiplomacy.org/academy/index.php?chinese-diaspora
6. Translation by Yaron Matras.
7. Translation by Vivienne Capelouto.
8. EF EPI 2020 – EF English Proficiency Index. 'The World's Largest Ranking of Countries and Regions by English Skills', 2020. https://www.ef.co.uk/epi/; 'Special Eurobarometer 386. Europeans and Their Languages'. European Commission, 2012. https://ec.europa.eu/commfrontoffice/publicopinion/archives/ebs/ebs_386_en.pdf
9. Licheva, Veronika. 'Court Rules That English Classes Will Continue Being Taught in Dutch Universities'. *Dutch Review*, 6 July 2018. https://dutchreview.com/dutch-news/court-rules-that-english-classes-will-continue-being-taught-in-dutch-universities/
10. Translation by Naja Motzfeldt.
11. Institut Kurde de Paris. 'The Kurdish population', 12 January 2017. https://www.institutkurde.org/en/info/the-kurdish-population-1232551004
12. Translation by Yaron Matras.
13. Translation by Yaron Matras.
14. Translation by Gorka Mercero Altzugarai.
15. Translation by Owen Shiers.
16. Translation by James Thomas.
17. Translation by Erich Schmidt.
18. Translation by Christian Thalmann (which he calls 'my own idiolect of Swiss-German').

19. Translation by Zareth Angela Vergara.
20. Translation by Julian Nyča. Thanks also to Jan Havliš.
21. Translation by Lily Kahn and Riitta Valijärvi.
22. Translation by Andrea Cavaglia.

Chapter 8: Despised tongues

1. Translation by Clive Forrester.
2. Translation by Richie Ruchpaul.
3. Translation by Michel DeGraff.
4. DeGraff, Michel. 'Haiti's "Linguistic Apartheid" Violates Children's Rights and Hampers Development'. Open Global Rights, 31 January 2017. https://www.openglobalrights.org/haiti-s-linguistic-apartheid-violates-children-s-rights-and-hampers-/
5. DeGraff, Michel. 'Against Apartheid in Education and in Linguistics: The Case of Haitian Creole in Neo-Colonial Haiti'. In *Decolonizing Foreign Language Education: The Misteaching of English and Other Colonial Languages*, edited by Donald Macedo, ix–xxxii. Routledge, 2019.
6. Translation by Dauvit Horsbroch.
7. Translation by Jenny Bailie.
8. BBC News. 'Vandals in Language Blunder', 18 October 1999. http://news.bbc.co.uk/1/hi/northern_ireland/478513.stm
9. Translation by Gavin Bailey.
10. Translation by Jeremy Wallach.
11. Translation by Thomas Kim.
12. Translation courtesy of M.G. Sanchez.
13. Linguistic Society of America. 'LSA Resolution on the Oakland "Ebonics" Issue', 1997. https://web.archive.org/web/20070808162212/http://www.lsadc.org/info/lsa-res-ebonics.cfm
14. Lewis, Neil A. 'Black English Is Not a Second Language, Jackson Says (Published 1996)'. *The New York Times*, 23 December 1996. https://www.nytimes.com/1996/12/23/us/black-english-is-not-a-second-language-jackson-says.html

Chapter 9: The limits of liberation

1. Roche, Gerald. 'Indigenous Language Denialism in Australia'. Language on the Move, 11 November 2020. https://www.languageonthemove.com/indigenous-language-denialism-in-australia/?s=09
2. Native Languages of the Americas: Preserving and promoting American Indian languages. 'Native Languages of the Americas: Contacts and FAQ'. http://www.native-languages.org/faq.htm
3. Translation by Jack Walker.
4. Stats NZ. 'More than 1 in 6 Māori People Speak Te Reo Māori', 8 November 2020. https://www.stats.govt.nz/news/more-than-1-in-6-maori-people-speak-te-reo-maori
5. Translation by Arawi Ruiz of the Quechua Academy of Humanities.
6. Deutscher, Guy. *Through the Language Glass: Why The World Looks Different In Other Languages*. Random House, 2016: 151.
7. Quine, Willard Van Orman. *Word and Object*. Technology Press of the Massachusetts Institute of Technology, 1960.

8. Everett, Daniel. *Don't Sleep, There Are Snakes: Life and Language in the Amazonian Jungle*. Profile, 2008.

9. Nevins, Andrew, David Pesetsky, and Cilene Rodrigues. 'Pirahã Exceptionality: A Reassessment'. *Language* 85, no. 2 (2009): 355–404.

10. Everett, Daniel L. *Dark Matter of the Mind: The Culturally Articulated Unconscious*. University of Chicago Press, 2016: 270–71.

11. Ibid.: 1.

12. Ibid.: 271.

13. Wallace, Scott. *The Unconquered: In Search of the Amazon's Last Uncontacted Tribes*. Crown, 2011.

14. Misra, Neelesh. 'Stone Age Cultures Survive Tsunami Waves'. NBC News, 4 January 2005. https://www.nbcnews.com/id/wbna6786476

15. Humphrey, Nicholas (1976). 'The Colour Currency of Nature'. In: Porter, T. and Mikellides, B., eds., *Colour for Architecture*. London: Studio Vista London, pp. 95–8. I discovered this essay via Guy Deutscher's book *Through the Language Glass*, cited previously.

Chapter 10: What we have lost, what we have gained: The Message in time

1. Steven J. Mithen. *The Singing Neanderthals: The Origins of Music, Language, Mind, and Body*. Cambridge, MA: Harvard University Press, 2006: 203.

2. https://youtu.be/Rn9DrUB41os

3. https://youtu.be/IHI78_Dgv5E

4. Translation by Kelvin Dobson. https://easy-read-online.co.uk/

5. Fox, Margalit. *Riddle of the Labyrinth: The Quest to Crack an Ancient Code and the Uncovering of a Lost Civilisation*. Profile Books, 2013.

6. Translation by Lily Kahn and Ben Whittle.

7. Readers who are familiar with Biblical Hebrew might note that some of the words and constructions in this translation do not appear in the Bible itself in the same exact form. As with other translations into ancient languages, both the limitations of the corpus and the anachronism of the translated text mean that a degree of creativity is necessary. In this case, the translation clearly owes something to Rabbinic and later versions of Hebrew.

8. Translation by Nir Nadav: אזהרתא, קרייה ונטריה: הדא אטלולא לאו מכוון לינוקא לבר מתלת שני. חלקי זוטי בר איפגומי הוו

9. Translation by Peter Miller: אזהרה: קרא ונטר. פתכייתא איסורנתי לטפלכון. אינהו ליבלעון אתבזוקניון

10. Translation by Jeremy Swist with the assistance of Joseph Langseth.

11. Translation by Kobi Kahn-Harris.

12. Translation by 'Dr St Ridley Santos'. Simon Roper also supplied an alternative Old English translation.

13. Translation by 'Dr St Ridley Santos'.

Chapter 11: Reviving the Message

1. Hagège, Claude. *On the Death and Life of Languages*. Yale University Press, 2009: 30.

2. Zuckermann, Ghil'ad. *Revivalistics: From the Genesis of Israeli to Language Reclamation in Australia and Beyond.* Oxford University Press, 2020.

3. Moseley, Christopher (ed.). 2010. *Atlas of the World's Languages in Danger*, 3rd edn. Paris, UNESCO Publishing. Online version: http://www.unesco.org/culture/en/endangeredlanguages/atlas

4. Roche, Gerald. 'Language Revitalization and Radical Politics'. *Language on the Move*, 13 January 2020. https://www.languageonthemove.com/language-revitalization-and-radical-politics/

5. *The Observer.* '"Do You Know That I Am with You?": Uighur Poetry Preserves Culture under Attack', 6 December 2020. https://www.theguardian.com/world/2020/dec/06/do-you-know-that-i-am-with-you-uighur-poetry-captures-fading-memories-of-home

6. Landry, Rodrigue, and Richard Y. Bourhis. 'Linguistic Landscape and Ethnolinguistic Vitality: An Empirical Study'. *Journal of Language and Social Psychology* 16, no. 1 (1 March 1997): 23–49. https://doi.org/10.1177/0261927X970161002.

7. Translation by Sulev Iva.

8. https://twitter.com/arranlouise/status/1333913957107716097?s=20

9. Translation by Christine Stewart of Bòrd na Gàidhlig.

10. Translation by Ofis Publik ar Brezhoneg.

11. Translation by Culture Vannin.

12. Translation by Tony Hak.

13. Philologos. 'Shedding a Little Light on Sea Monsters and Planets'. *The Forward*, 6 January 2010. https://forward.com/culture/122761/shedding-a-little-light-on-sea-monsters-and-planet/

14. Norn. 'Philosophy of Nynorn'. https://nornlanguage.x10.mx/index.php?nynorn_phil

Chapter 12: A new Message

1. Okrent, Arika. *In the Land of Invented Languages: A Celebration of Linguistic Creativity, Madness, and Genius.* Spiegel & Grau Trade Paperbacks, 2010.

2. Schor, Esther. *Bridge of Words: Esperanto and the Dream of a Universal Language.* Henry Holt and Company, 2016: 270.

3. Ibid.: 322.

4. Translation by Simon Varwell.

5. Translation by Loïc Landais.

6. Translation by Jackson Bradley.

7. Translation by Tom Ruddle.

8. Peterson, David J. *The Art of Language Invention: From Horse-Lords to Dark Elves, the Words Behind World-Building.* Penguin, 2015.

9. Norþimris. 'An Introduction to Norþimris'. https://northimris.wordpress.com/

10. Translation by Neil Walley.

11. Foer, Joshua. 'Utopian for Beginners'. *The New Yorker.* 17 December 2012. https://www.newyorker.com/magazine/2012/12/24/utopian-for-beginners

Chapter 13: The incompetently translated Message

1. Erard, Michael. *Babel No More: The Search for the World's Most Extraordinary Language Learners*. Simon & Schuster, 2012.
2. See, for example, the website Fluent in Three Months: https://www.fluentin3months.com/
3. Foer, Joshua. 'How I Learned a Language in 22 Hours'. *The Guardian*, 9 November 2012. https://www.theguardian.com/education/2012/nov/09/learn-language-in-three-months
4. http://www.ald-monaco.org/
5. After the hardback edition of this book was published, I finally managed to obtain a Munegàscu translation. You can find it on my website.
6. Translation by Fiorenzo Toso.
7. https://www.tokpisin.info/
8. For example: http://www.xn--volapk-7ya.còm/

Chapter 14: ALTABAŠ! Iltigõš õfiltatiš

1. If the generator came up with a pre-existing combination or letter, I would move each letter one place down in the alphabet until I found one that was unused.
2. Peterson, David J. *The Art of Language Invention: From Horse-Lords to Dark Elves, the Words Behind World-Building*. Penguin, 2015: 199–207.

Chapter 15: One world, one Message?

1. Pandey, Geeta. 'An "English Goddess" for India's down-trodden'. *BBC News*, 15 February 2011. https://www.bbc.co.uk/news/world-south-asia-12355740
2. Jeffreys, Branwen. 'Language Learning: German and French Drop by Half in UK Schools'. *BBC News*, 27 February 2019. https://www.bbc.co.uk/news/education-47334374
3. I used the resources from the following website for my translation: http://ogden.basic-english.org/
4. Wierzbicka, Anna. *Imprisoned in English: The Hazards of English as a Default Language*. OUP USA, 2014: 4. I discovered this important book via David Shariatmadari's book *Don't Believe A Word* (Hachette UK, 2019).
5. Ibid.: 193.
6. Natural Semantic Metalanguage. 'Vocabulary and Grammar of Minimal English'. https://intranet.secure.griffith.edu.au/schools-departments/natural-semantic-metalanguage/minimal-english/what-is-minimal-english/vocabulary-and-grammar-of-minimal-english
7. Crystal, David. *The Stories of English*. Penguin UK, 2005.
8. Ostler, Nicholas. *The Last Lingua Franca: The Rise and Fall of World Languages*. Penguin UK, 2010.
9. Ibid.: 268.
10. Marani, Diego. 'EUROPANTO. From Productive Process to Language. Or How to Cause International English to Implode'. Europanto. http://www.europanto.be/gram.en.html
11. https://www.jpr.org.uk/archive

12. UNESCO. 'Index Translationum – World Bibliography of Translation'. http://portal.unesco.org/culture/en/ev.php-URL_ID=7810&URL_DO=DO_ TOPIC&URL_SECTION=201.html
13. Translation by Costas Avramidis.
14. Dewey, Philip. 'Meet the Man Responsible for the Most Infamously Bad Welsh Road Sign'. *Wales Online*, 28 September 2018. https://www.walesonline.co.uk/news/wales-news/ man-responsible-welsh-translation-gaffe-15214716
15. McCurry, Justin. '"Hello Work" or Job Centre? Language Experts Spell Trouble for Japan's Mangled English'. *The Guardian*, 18 November 2020. https://www.theguardian.com/world/2020/nov/18/ hello-work-or-job-centre-language-experts-japan-english
16. Bad Hebrew Tattoos. 'When A Dictionary Leaves Its Mark on You'. https:// www.badhebrew.com/2013/04/when-dictionary-leaves-its-mark-on-you.html

Chapter 16: Babel as utopia

1. Genesis 11:1–8. JPS 1917 translation.
2. Levi, Primo. *Survival In Auschwitz*. Simon & Schuster, 1996: 38.
3. Ibid.: 72–3.
4. Borges, Jorge Luis. 'The Library of Babel'. In *Labyrinths: Selected Stories & Other Writings*. Penguin, 1970: 78–86.
5. Bancroft, Josiah. *Senlin Ascends*. Hachette UK, 2017.
6. Full disclosure: I've only read the first book in the series. Perhaps future volumes mention different languages.
7. https://babelsblessing.org/info/
8. Sennett, Richard. *Together: The Rituals, Pleasures and Politics of Cooperation*. London: Penguin, 2012.

Chapter 17: Ending at the beginning

1. Bulgarian, Czech, Danish, German, Greek, English, Spanish, French, Croatian, Armenian, Latvian, Lithuanian, Macedonian, Dutch, Norwegian, Polish, Portuguese, Romanian, Russian, Slovak, Slovene, Albanian, Serbian, Swedish, Ukrainian, Farsi.
2. Anthony, David W. *The Horse, the Wheel, and Language: How Bronze-Age Riders from the Eurasian Steppes Shaped the Modern World*. Princeton University Press, 2010.
3. Academia Prisca. 'Modern Indo-European'. https://academiaprisca.org/en/ indoeuropean/
4. Duncan, Dennis. 'Languages Lost in Time'. In *Babel: Adventures in Translation*, edited by Dennis Duncan, Stephen Harrison, Katrin Maria Kohl, and Matthew Reynolds. Oxford: Bodleian Library, 2019: 152–65.
5. Chiang, Ted. 'Tower of Babylon'. In *Stories of Your Life and Others*. Pan Macmillan, 2014: 1–34.

Appendix

1. Official Journal of the European Union. 'Directive 2009/28/EC of the European Parliament and of the Council of 18 June 2009 on the Safety of Toys'. 20 June 2009. https://eur-lex.europa.eu/legal-content/EN/TXT/HTML/ ?uri=CELEX:32009L0048&from=EN#d1e32-30-1

Index of languages

The following is an index of languages into which the Message is translated in this book. 'Official' translations that appear on actual Manuscripts in use today or in the past are highlighted in bold.

Abkhazian 114
African-American
   Vernacular English 150
Afrikaans 117
Albanian (Tosk) 68
Albanian (Gheg) 68
Amazigh 85
American Sign Language
   (Link to video) 177
American Sign Language
   (Sutton Sign Writing
   transcription) 178
Amharic 120
Anglo-Romani 155
Aourgnais 201–2
Arabic 39, 82
Aramaic (Talmudic) 188
Armenian (Eastern) 53
Armenian (Western) 127
Azerbaijani 53
**Azerbaijani (Cyrillic
   characters)** 86

Basic English 249
Basque 135
Belarusian 112

Bengali 122
Betawi 146
Bulgarian 46, 71
Braille (English, Contracted)
   180
Braille (English,
   Uncontracted) 179
Breton 197
British Sign Language (Link
   to video) 176

Cantonese 90
Catalan 111
Chlìjha 213
**Chinese (Traditional
   characters)** 38, 87
**Chinese (Simplified
   characters)** 87
Chinese (Pinyin
   transliteration) 91
Coptic (Medieval) 185
Cornish 197–8
Croatian 72
Czech 42, 69

Danish 67